The Consultant's Guide to Proposal Writing
Second Edition

The Consultant's Guide to Proposal Writing

How to Satisfy Your Client and Double Your Income

Second Edition

Herman Holtz

WILEY

John Wiley & Sons, Inc.
New York • Chichester • Brisbane • Toronto • Singapore

Library of Congress Cataloging-in-Publication Data

Holtz, Herman.
    The consultant's guide to proposal writing / by Herman Holtz.—
2nd ed.
      p.   cm.
    Includes bibliographical references.
    ISBN 0-471-51569-8
    1. Proposal writing in business. 2. Business consultants.
  I. Title.
HF5718.5.H63   1990
808'.066658 — dc 20

89-22663
CIP

Printed in the United States of America

90 91 10 9 8 7 6 5 4 3 2 1

Preface

The basic premise on which the original edition of this book was based was that many consultants recognized the importance of proposals in their marketing and needed a guide to help them produce more effective ones. The success of that book substantiated the premise and inspired the writing of a second edition.

In introducing the second edition of *The Consultant's Guide to Proposal Writing*, I can remark on some new developments that you and others interested in improving your proposal skills ought to know about. The federal government, for example, is a greater market than ever for your services, and the Department of Defense, the largest government market by far, is in the process of revamping their procurement systems to increase efficiency and control. The still increasing popularity and population of desktop computers everywhere is also more significant than ever in its effects on marketing consulting services generally and writing proposals especially.

Despite new developments and changes, the opening statements of the preface to the original edition of this book are as valid and timely today as they were when I first wrote them:

> If there is one skill that I have found to be utmost in importance to the success of the typical independent consultant, it is skill in marketing: the ability to win clients and contracts. And if there is one ability that I have found to be utmost in importance to achieving that skill in marketing the consultant's services effectively, it is the ability to develop winning proposals—the task that we all so often refer to erroneously as "proposal writing."
>
> However, even the, development (writing) of effective proposals is only one element of proposal-related ability. Another element is probably of equal

importance and perhaps of even greater importance. It is the ability to *use* proposals effectively. Many consultants who do write adequate proposals fail to utilize them effectively, and so do not draw full benefits from their proposal-writing skills. Helping you become fully aware of and fully dedicated to maximizing your success through wise and faithful practice in both areas is therefore a major objective of this book.

Unfortunately, many consultants *still* groan at the mere thought of writing a proposal (of writing anything, for that matter), as observed in the preface to that first edition. For those who find writing a painful process, there is now a great deal of relief in the continuing evolution of desktop computers and the software available to ease the agonies of writing.

Even in my own case (and I enjoy writing and rewriting), this evolution has made writing a much easier and more pleasant task. I wrote the first edition of this book on a CP/M computer, using an early version of WordStar (3.0), which those familiar with early desktop computers will recognize as primitive by today's standards. Here, a mere handful of years and two computers later, I am using one of the latest and fastest desktop computers available, and I now regard that old computer as only a slight improvement on the typewriter!

Many of the techniques and tactics I explain and recommend have become infinitely easier to use because of the greatly enhanced capabilities of modern computers. To be accurate, the enhancements and enlarged capabilities are really the result of enormously improved software, but the new software is possible only because of greater hardware capabilities— increases in memory, speed, and storage.

I therefore urge you to learn to work directly at the computer keyboard if you do not already do so. You cannot enjoy the full benefits of computer capabilities otherwise. Learn to use all the relevant software. Build your disk-based computer libraries carefully and thoroughly; they will soon become your most powerful tool for creating effective proposals. In fact, writing proposals will become far easier, after a time, not only because of your developing experience and skill, but even more because of your expanding resources in your computer files.

If you have not yet acquired a computer or if you are contemplating buying a new computer, be sure it is as up to date and of as large a capacity as you can afford. For example, computers with an 80386SX chip are available today for almost the same price as those with the older 80286 chip, but the 80386 computers are far more powerful machines. A 40-, 50-, or 60-megabyte hard disk is today only slightly more than a 20- or 30-megabyte hard disk, and the greater capacity of the larger disk will mean a great deal to you eventually, as you build the resources of software and data you need.

Learning to use the various types of software is also most important. It was only after I had been tapping away at a keyboard for a long time, using little but word processing software, that I began to realize that word processing software is not the only kind of software a writer needs and can use gainfully. In addition to the word processors, there are spelling checkers, thesauruses, grammar-checkers, outliners, database managers, memory spoolers, file managers, spreadsheet programs, communications software, readability-measurement and -enhancement programs, and even others to help you. In fact, whereas most of these were separate programs a few years ago, most of the modern word processors include many of these programs. It was once necessary to learn each type of software through long and often painful experience. Today, most of the major programs have special tutorials and pull-down menu systems that make the learning process much easier and, perhaps even more significantly, provide so much on-the-spot guidance that they reduce the need to learn the program.

The computer makes life easier for everyone, and that includes authors of successful—winning—proposals.

HERMAN HOLTZ

Silver Spring, Maryland

Contents

List of Figures

The Consultant's Guide to Proposal Writing
Second Edition

CHAPTER 1

An Orientation in Proposals

A proposal request is an invitation to make a sales presentation, and that is a marketing opportunity, in some respects a unique marketing opportunity if you take full advantage of it.

WHY SHOULD CLIENTS WANT PROPOSALS?

As with most things, retaining a consultant offers both risks and benefits to clients. The client who learns to request and use proposals wisely when finding and retaining consultants can reduce the material risks and can gain important benefits available in only this way. However, even clients who have used proposals do not always know how to gain the maximum benefits from them. In your proposals, you must help clients learn how to benefit maximally from using proposals.

Not all executives and staff specialists know immediately when they ought to get outside help, much less when they should ask for proposals to help identify and choose the right help. Some clients always request proposals when seeking to retain a consultant, but some request proposals only when they plan a large project. Also some clients rarely or never request proposals, even though they seek the same thing as those who do— that is, they seek information with which to decide where, how, and from whom to purchase professional services.

This much is fundamental: The proposal is one way, and an increasingly popular way, for a client to obtain information with which to evaluate and select a consultant. Once clients become familiar with the proposal approach to their quest for consulting services and understand fully its usefulness, most clients embrace it.

The chief difference between the client who regularly asks for proposals and the one who does not is usually that the latter lacks both experience with proposals and familiarity with the advantages of this method of purchasing services. Being unfamiliar with proposals, for whatever reason, such clients are usually not fully aware of the benefits—or even the necessity—of the proposal request as a key to finding the right consultant, even for small projects and transient needs.

Properly implemented, the request for proposals (RFP) is by far the most efficient and most effective tool the client can use for the task. The response to the RFP provides all the information necessary for the client's final decision—if the client has provided an adequate "bid package" (all information necessary for response to the RFP) and the consultants have responded effectively. (If you or any other consultant fails to respond effectively, that fact is itself useful information for the client in reaching a decision.)

There are a number of obvious reasons for the proposal request, and there are some less obvious ones. This chapter looks at the obvious ones first.

Technical/Professional Capabilities

The client seeking a consultant has two critical concerns. The primary concern is the relative importance of the outcome that the client wants the consultant to facilitate or to achieve. Quite often, the desired outcome bears directly on the welfare, and perhaps even the survival, of the client's organization. For example, an ailing organization urgently in need of adding some vigor to its marketing may be gambling its very existence on the effectiveness of the help provided by the consultant.

Further, even the healthy organization cannot always withstand disaster and must steer clear of undue risks. Thus, in many, if not most, cases, the client is gambling more than money in retaining you or any other consultant. Quite frequently, the client's direct welfare—its business welfare, that is—is very much at stake. Based on the results of your work and on your recommendations, the client may very well undertake major projects and spend large sums of money in marketing campaigns, reorganization, purchase of capital items, or any of many possible costly and perhaps risky undertakings. If the advice is the result of gross misjudgment or is based on capabilities you claim but do not truly have, it is quite possible that the client may meet with total disaster. (This has happened, especially in the days of the so-called efficiency experts of a number of years ago; unfortunately there are also more recent examples of disasters resulting from bad advice.)

The second concern of the client's search for a consultant is the personal welfare of the individual who retains the consultant. This individual may be the proprietor or chief executive of the client organization, and his or her personal position with the organization or even his or her career generally is also at stake. An unfortunate decision can destroy a position and a career.

So quite often, the client has both general and personal business concerns—risks, as well as benefits—involved in requesting proposals and evaluating them to reach a decision. Ergo, the client must identify and assess each of your—and every other proposer's—capabilities.

What Are "Capabilities"?

In light of these concerns, it should cause no wonder that the alert client seeking a consultant is looking for hard evidence of each consultant's capabilities. If a client in the cosmetics field perceives a need for a marketing consultant, he or she is going to want some clear and convincing evidence that you offer not only general marketing capabilities, but also capabilities in marketing cosmetics. Whether marketing capability is or is not easily transferable from one industry to another, many clients do not believe that it is. Instead, they firmly believe that their own marketing problems are unique and require correspondingly unique marketing experience. Further, the cosmetics-industries client will certainly want some clear and convincing evidence that those cosmetics-marketing capabilities are genuine and not merely claimed. (The client who learns to use proposals in choosing consultants soon learns to seek evidence and not accept mere claims of the capabilities required.)

The Question of Perception. The client is not necessarily correct in assuming that the marketing consultant—you—must have specific background in marketing cosmetics to handle the assignment effectively. The fact that you have not marketed cosmetics before does not preclude your producing a highly effective marketing plan. But that is not the point. The point is that this client *perceives* cosmetics-marketing experience as a needed qualification and will therefore scan proposals for evidence of that specific experience. Whether the client's premise is valid is another matter (which is discussed later, when the focus is on proposals from the proposer's viewpoint).

Experience, both in general (e.g., marketing) and in specific fields (e.g., cosmetics), represents some rather general capabilities. Other items must also be listed, such as the applications you can provide in the field of expertise. In marketing, some of the applications—what you can do for the client—might be these:

Develop general marketing strategies

Write advertising copy

Devise packaging alternatives and recommendations

Conceive special promotional campaigns and plans

Conduct market surveys

Scout and analyze competition

Make presentations to the top officials of the client organization

Train staff people in the client organization

Design and recommend distribution systems

Segment the market, and plan strategies and promotions for each segment

Devise and conduct research

The Question of Competence.   In addition to an enumeration of kinds of capabilities, the client must consider another aspect of capabilities: technical/professional competence. That is, given your specific experience in the many tasks and disciplines in the field of interest, the client wants to know how competently you practice your profession and use your technical expertise. Evidence of experience per se is not enough; even inept practitioners can often point to a great deal of experience in the field. The client will want to see evidence that the consultant has an acceptably high degree of competence and is good enough at the tasks required by the client. Several items of information help the client to judge the competence and the capability of the consultant:

Formal education and academic record

Understanding of client's problem/need, as evidenced in proposal

Proposed solution/approach to solution

Track record: verifiable history of success at the tasks

Outstanding accomplishments: remarkable successes, innovations

Other noteworthy and relevant achievements

Career history: former employers, positions, clients

Honors and awards

Testimonials from former employers and/or clients

Other Benefits to the Client

Not all clients realize it at first, but they can derive another substantial benefit from requesting and reviewing proposals. This benefit makes it worthwhile for the client to encourage the greatest number of responses despite the time and energy required to review a large number of proposals. The client benefits from the presentation of multiple analyses of his or her problem (in a sense, all client needs are problems and may be so characterized) from a variety of specialists, reflecting a wide variety of views and approaches. This wealth of analyses becomes a valuable databank.

Obviously, you and other consultants who submit proposals are not going to carry out a complete and detailed analysis of the problem in your proposals, but you must do at least some preliminary analysis and propose at least a general approach to solving the problem. If the client has done a good job of writing the statement that explains the problem, the proposals submitted usually provide the thoughtful client a wealth of insight and expert preliminary advice. Even if many of the proposals are of little or no direct benefit in this regard, many will contain valuable information. In fact, it rarely occurs that the proposals submitted, individually and collectively, do not represent a greater knowledge of and insight into the client's problem than the client already has. This benefit alone is worth the cost of preparing the request and reading the proposals, aside from the enormously improved vantage point (the much-expanded base of knowledge, that is) it gives the client for selecting a consultant.

This is not to say that the client is actively seeking free consulting services, although this is what the client gets, in effect. That is inevitable; many business people find it necessary to furnish free samples to prospective buyers ("prospects"). You cannot prove your abilities satisfactorily without demonstrating them somehow in your proposals and other presentations. Nonetheless, the cynical use of this means to get free analyses is not entirely unknown, unfortunately, and you must use judgment in deciding how much to reveal in your proposals and presentations. (Mercifully, the practice of deliberately "picking your brains" to euchre you into giving away your services is fairly rare, and most prospects are sincere in requesting proposals and asking for specific information.)

HOW MUCH DO YOU HAVE TO GIVE AWAY?

Aside from the possible hazard of giving prospects too much information in your proposals, you must consider the cost to you of proposal writing. It is a time-consuming and—therefore—costly marketing process. Time is not only the most costly resource you have, but it is also the chief commodity you sell. From that viewpoint alone, you must judge how much you should reveal in a proposal—that is, how much is necessary to win the contract? That amount is all that you ought to give away.

There is no precise formula for measuring how much you must give away. Your objective is to provide the prospect with enough information to prove your case and win the contract, but no more. That's a circular argument, of course, but deciding how much is enough is purely subjective, and you must estimate it yourself. Perhaps the best guideline to help you judge this is a list and brief description of at least five elements that the effective proposal must always include:

1. Evidence of your clear *understanding* of the client's problem
2. An approach and *program plan or design* that appears to the client to be both well-suited to solving the problem and likely to produce the results desired
3. Convincing evidence of your own *qualifications and capability* for carrying out the plan properly
4. Convincing evidence of your *dependability* as a consultant or contractor

5. A compelling reason for the client to select you as the winner—a winning strategy

Each of these items is discussed in much greater detail in the pages to come. In fact, to a large degree, the remainder of this book is devoted primarily to discussing these items and how they are implemented, as well as how, where, and when to utilize proposals as a prime marketing tool. Nonetheless, some preliminary discussion is likely to prove helpful.

Understanding of the Client's Problem

An amazingly large number of proposals convey the notion that the writer of the proposal did not understand the problem. In some cases, the writer truly did not understand the problem. Sometimes the consultant, eager for business, is stretching things a bit too far, undertaking to try for a contract and project that are not really in his or her field. Sometimes the consultant has simply been in too great a hurry to write the proposal and has not given enough thought to the expressed need—The consultant has not studied the need at length and has not planned thoroughly enough to offer a convincing presentation. Often, however, the primary weakness is neither of these: it is careless writing. That is, the consultant understands the problem and has a worthy approach but fails both to demonstrate that understanding and to explain the virtues of the consultant's approach and proposed plan or design.

You may argue that the client should be able to perceive your understanding of the need and worthiness of your approach in your project plan or design, but that is expecting the client to make a specific extra effort—study and analysis—to make up for a deficiency in your proposal. (That argument also assumes that the client has the technical capability to evaluate your design without your guidance, and that may be an erroneous assumption too.) It simply won't happen. In fact, unless your proposal establishes and demonstrates your understanding of the need quite clearly in the introductory portion (and in terms that do not require much technical expertise to understand), the client may decide after the first few pages that time is better spent on the next proposal. Often, as many as two out of three proposals are disqualified and discarded as a result of the first reading or even partial reading.

Program Plan or Design

The portion of the proposal that establishes clearly your understanding of the client's problem should bridge logically—make a transition—into a discussion of your program plan or design. That discussion must convince the client that yours is the best approach and best design or plan for satisfying the client's need.

This is a crucial place to sell your ideas, for unless you manage to convince the client here that you offer what is probably the best plan (and the meaning of the word "best" in this context is discussed later), you will already have lost. You are going to need both sales ability and rationale for this portion of the proposal.

Qualifications and Capability

Once you have proposed, explained, and marketed your plan or design as the best one, you must prove that you have all the necessary qualifications for carrying out the plan or implementing the design. What's more, establishing those qualifications beyond a reasonable doubt only partly depends on establishing your own technical and professional credentials. Those qualifications may include specific experience that relates directly to the need because general, indirectly related experience may not be acceptable to some clients.

Some projects require certain physical resources, such as access to computers, laboratories, and other capital items; clerical labor; people to do field surveys; and other such necessities. Finally, you may require other professionals to support you for larger projects. Vague or general assurances that you have access to necessary resources and/or associates or others you can turn to are often not acceptable as proof of necessary resources. The typical client is likely to want some rather solid and specific evidence of adequate and assured availability of any necessary resources, including supporting professionals when the project obviously requires such support.

Dependability

The dependability of a contractor is always a concern, but it is particularly so for any client who has ever contracted with someone who proved to be less than totally dependable. Given a superb project plan or design, and given a superbly qualified consultant to carry out the plan successfully, the project can still founder quite easily if the consultant is not highly conscientious and properly dedicated to the project. This consideration is no less important than that of technical/professional capability, for neither is of use without the other.

All clients want some kind of assurance that they can depend on you if they award you the contract, but promises and pledges alone are not enough to provide that assurance. Something more substantial than soothing syrup is needed. This subject is also explored and studied in later pages.

Winning Strategy

There are numerous strategies possible in proposal writing, all of which this book discusses. However, there is always the question of the major strategy, the winning strategy (also referred to as "capture strategy," "win strategy," or "main strategy," to distinguish it from other, subordinate strategies) on which you base your entire argument and your hope of capturing the contract.

To put this another way and possibly to clarify the meaning immediately, the winning strategy is your explanation to the client of why the client should favor you with the award.

In simple terms, sales techniques are based largely on giving the prospect a reason for doing business with you. The proposal you write is not a solicitation or an entreaty, and it certainly should not be written as though it were. It is a sales presentation, but it should be presented as an offer, a business offer, an offer to *do something* for the client. Don't expect the client to think out reasons for accepting your offer; you must do your own selling. You must always furnish the reasons, make the client see why it is in his or her own best interests to accept your offer. That is what strategy is all about—the right reasons and the right way to present them.

THE EVOLUTION OF STRATEGY

Strategy was mentioned last in the series of five elements of effective proposals, but in fact, the other four items are closely linked to strategy and even stem from it. Strategy should drive the entire proposal. In fact, the evolution of your strategy, for even the simplest and most informal proposal, should proceed similarly to the steps in Figure 1.

The following greatly simplified explanation is expanded and presented in increasing detail later, but it does capture the main steps in the evolution

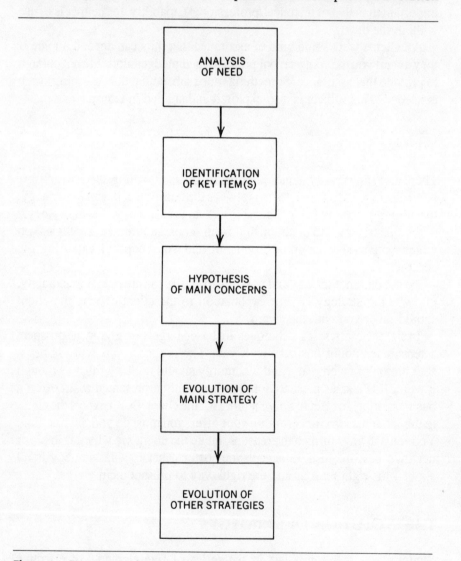

Figure 1.   First steps in devising a strategy for a proposal.

of basic program or design strategy: Begin by analyzing the client's need, based on the client's own description of the need, as filtered and interpreted through your own knowledge and experience, and add any independent observations you have been able to make. Next, you must define the client's need in your own terms, which might not coincide and agree with the client's identification.

As a result of this beginning analysis, you must form some kind of hypothesis about the client's primary concerns that inspired the client to request proposals. (Regard this request as an opportunity.) Your success in evolving an effective main (capture) strategy is usually tied closely to the accuracy with which you are able to hypothesize the client's major worries.

The major beginning steps are (1) to identify the problem, (2) to determine the key points of the problem and the client's basic reason for seeking consulting help, and (3) to hypothesize the client's chief worries, at least tentatively. You can then begin to devise some sort of main strategy that addresses the client's principal worries while assuring the client that the need will be entirely satisfied.

At this point, the strategy does not yet include or embrace the first four items enumerated earlier in this discussion. Those are obligatory items that must be present in every proposal, whereas the strategy is uniquely devised and developed especially for the individual proposal and based on the circumstances surrounding that proposal.

Understand also that the entire process is not truly as linear or entirely sequential as charts and other presentations describe; instead, it is almost always an iterative process characterized by many repetitions. However, it is necessary to idealize the process—to project it as though it were the orderly and sequential process described—because it would be impractical to attempt to show all the feedback loops that reflect the reality of most proposal development, even those of rather modest size. When actually developing and writing a proposal, with only rare exception, there are many feedback loops, trial fits, and modifications. Tentative theories or hypotheses are assembled, tested and sometimes discarded, reshaped or otherwise molded to suggest possible plans and approaches until a final approach and design is chosen. Usually, this is as true for the proposal written by a single individual as it is for the proposal written by a large team of consultants.

The foregoing primarily concerns the evolution of the main or capture strategy. Inevitably, however, strategies must be evolved for several other proposal elements, areas that might not coincide with the main strategy. The other elements include at least these:

Program
Cost
Presentation
Competitors

You should concern yourself with each of these elements in any proposal you write, although the main strategy usually only has to address one of these. That is, the client's chief concern will usually be about one of the first three areas, or your chief problem in winning will be to outshine your competitors. Still, each of these areas makes its own contribution to the client's decision, and the surest way to be successful is to be thorough in attending to all details and so maximize the odds in your favor. Hasty and careless proposals rarely win anything but a quick discard.

FORMAL VERSUS INFORMAL PROPOSALS

The chief difference between formal and informal proposals is size and format. Logically, the presentation of information and ideas follows the same sequence in each. However, the formal proposal is usually only submitted for a sizable project, and it is a discrete document, with headlines, cover and title page, and other publication formalities. The informal proposal is usually in the form of a letter of several pages. (It is often called a "letter proposal.") Nonetheless, the letter proposal and the formal proposal are written similarly: Whatever has been or is said later about the formal proposal applies equally to letter proposals.

Letter proposals are usually used for small projects that do not merit the cost of developing formal proposals.

A RECOMMENDED PROPOSAL FORMAT

Occasionally, a client will mandate a proposal format, specifying the order in which information is to be presented, as well as precisely what informa-

SECTION I: INTRODUCTION

ABOUT THE OFFEROR

UNDERSTANDING OF THE REQUIREMENT

SECTION II: DISCUSSION

THE REQUIREMENT

ANALYSIS

APPROACH

SECTION III: PROPOSED PROJECT

PROJECT ORGANIZATION

MANAGEMENT

PLANS AND PROCEDURES

STAFF

DELIVERABLE ITEMS

SCHEDULES

RESUME(S)

SECTION IV: QUALIFICATIONS AND EXPERIENCE

RELEVANT CURRENT AND RECENT PROJECTS

RESOURCES

MISCELLANEOUS

FRONT MATTER

APPENDICES

Figure 2. General proposal format.

tion is required. This is fairly rare, however; usually, the client explains
what information is required but leaves the format up to you.

I recommend a proposal format (Figure 2), with brief explanations
following those items that require some explanation. (Later discussions are
based on the presumption of this format and elaborate extensively on these
brief introductory explanations.) The reasons for the recommendation of
this particular format are several:

1. It was developed over years of practical experience with proposals.
2. It reflects many useful practices of others observed over the years.
3. It is quite similar to many mandated formats.
4. It offers a logical development of ideas and information.
5. It is quite flexible, adaptable to most needs and readily modified or
    expanded.
6. It works. Many of my clients and I have used it successfully many
    times over many years.

This is a four-part format, which can be easily expanded to five or even
six parts, as the occasion requires. In some cases, such expansion is
desirable and beneficial, even required. It is even readily adaptable to the
multivolume approach required for some large proposals. The modification
of this format is described later, as the need arises, in relation to the various
needs and situations under which you must or should offer a proposal.

I call each of the four parts a "section," I use a few generic or descriptive
titles and sideheads (most proposals of any size use many more), and I
number them with Roman numerals in the example here. Of course, in your
proposal, you can call them "chapters," and you may name and number the
headings any way you please; make whatever changes you wish. Those
superficial matters do not affect the outcome. Moreover, these format issues
are elaborated later, when I also furnish some specific examples of proposal
contents for each of these sections or chapters. Some brief explanations of
each section are in order here.

Section I

The first section should be brief because it is only introductory. I recommend only two subsections, although you may, of course, use additional

subject subheadings, such as your proposal's specifics and concrete examples (discussed later).

The first subsection has three aims: (1) to introduce yourself briefly (who and what you are—name and field of specialization); (2) to give some very brief idea of your credentials and experience, to establish your qualifications quickly (perhaps the names of a well-known client or two); and (3) to offer something that captures attention and arouses early interest, motivating the reader to keep turning pages.

The second subsection's purpose is to demonstrate your true understanding of the client's requirement. However, because it is to be brief, it should summarize that requirement and should focus on the essence of the requirement, making it clear that you are discriminating between the essential need and the extraneous or less-important details.

Section II

There should be a direct transition from that second subsection of Section I to the first sentences of Section II. Section II starts by expanding on your discussion of the requirement to explore and probe all aspects of it, persuading the reader to take your view, with your analyses and rationales. This leads to the clearly defined and logic-based approach with which this section should end. This section should prove your approach and sell it to the client.

Section III

This is the section in which you present your plans for implementing the approach and the plans described in the previous section. The section is a natural transition from Section II, and the major headings listed are essentially self-explanatory. (Again, you may wish to add many subheadings.) Moreover, you may present the subjects in any order you deem appropriate, but all the subjects shown in Figure 2 should be included in this section. For major proposals, this section is usually split into two or even three sections (or even separate volumes), most commonly offering the subject of management separately and sometimes listing deliverables and schedules separately. This section is, in effect, the contract, or what you are offering to contract for.

Section IV

Like Section III, the major headings of this section are generally self-explanatory, may be added to and/or supported with subheadings, and may be presented in an alternative order if your sense of order is somewhat different from that suggested here. These are, however, the typical subjects for this section.

Miscellaneous

Several other elements are referred to under the general heading of "front matter"; they are discussed in more detail in the appropriate chapter. For a formal proposal, the typical front matter includes a title page, a table of contents, an executive summary, a foreword or preface, a frontispiece, and a response matrix; many proposals also include other items in the front matter.

Many proposals have an appendix, or even several appendices. These are also discussed in later pages.

APPLICATION OF FORMAT TO LETTER PROPOSALS

Philosophically, the chief difference between the formal and the informal (letter) proposal is that the latter does not have the title page, the table of contents, the multiple levels of headings, and other such features of the formal proposal. (Large, formal proposals may even be multivolume; many major proposals have been prepared in four or more large volumes.) The letter proposal, however, has an introduction, a discussion, a proposed program (or procedures), and the qualifications of the offeror. It may have some front matter, principally a summary, and it may have an appendix, as well. Bear that in mind as you proceed through these pages.

Bear in mind one other, equally important fact at all times. Don't wait to be asked for a proposal, formal or otherwise. Whenever you believe that you have a serious prospect or a prospect with a serious need, and you think that you know enough of the need to offer a proposal, do so. Do so even if you have not advised the prospect in advance or asked for permission to submit a proposal. A letter proposal is always an excellent way to follow up an earlier contact with a prospect, and it often is by far the best way to do so.

WHY SHOULD YOU WANT TO WRITE PROPOSALS?

The first question raised in this chapter was why clients should want proposals. To answer that question, I inevitably also discussed why you should want to write proposals—because each proposal is a sales opportunity. Even more significant, it is a unique sales opportunity: No other occasion is quite as ideal to demonstrate to a prospective client what you can do for him or her. Other kinds of presentations offer opportunities to present your general capabilities, but only in proposals and/or follow-up formal oral presentations do you get the opportunity to present a thoughtful analysis and plan specific to a prospective client's stated needs. That is one of the chief reasons even to create opportunities to write proposals by offering them voluntarily, as a standard marketing practice.

CHAPTER 2

What It Takes to Write a Good Proposal

A *good proposal* is, by definition, one that wins the contract. There are other measures of proposals, however, and you must examine and understand these other measures if you are to become expert in writing and using proposals.

IS IT REALLY PROPOSAL *WRITING*?

Because the proposals discussed in this book are written presentations, it is natural to refer to their development as "proposal writing." Yet, what is the significance of that word *writing* in this use? That is, how important is the skill of writing in the process of producing a successful—contract-winning—proposal? To develop a sensible and reasonable answer to that question, it is necessary to analyze just what a proposal is, why you would write one, and what you expect it to do for you.

You have already looked at this briefly from the client's viewpoint, to judge what the client expects or should expect, and why the client wants or should want proposals as part of the process of selecting a consultant. Understanding the client's purposes and intent is the key to understanding why you write proposals, how you should write them, what should be in them, how you should use them, and what you should expect them to do for you.

To paraphrase a government contracting officer, the client's purpose in requesting proposals is to select the best possible consultant, with the best possible plan, at the best possible cost. This description of the client's purpose assumes that the client has a true insight into his or her need.

Clients may know or may think they know precisely what the problem is and how it must be solved, but that is not necessarily so. Quite often, the client may be aware only of symptoms and might not recognize that these symptoms do not necessarily define the problem. The client then depends on the consultant who wins the contract to determine precisely what the problem or need really is.

Given the likelihood of this situation, unless you are quite sure that the client has correctly identified the problem or need, you must assume a responsibility to educate—that is, counsel—the client accordingly. You must also somehow not only persuade the client that you are right in your analysis and evaluation, but also do it diplomatically enough to avoid criticizing or belittling the client or the client's views.

In short, you must manage somehow to be several things in writing proposals, and the writer hat is only one of several you must wear. You must also be a marketer, a sales expert, a diplomat, an analyst, a subject-matter expert, a designer, and perhaps even one or two other things, with everything those terms imply. A deficiency in even one of these areas or functions can easily cost you the contract. As Dave Hamilton, operations manager for the Quadrex Corporation's Tulsa division, wisely observed, proposals must be reviewed and revised continuously to ensure that they include selling statements, and that they are not confined to being straight technical dissertations. The technical explanations and arguments are necessary, but they alone do not and cannot sell the project.

SKILLS NEEDED TO WRITE WINNING PROPOSALS

Were I were to rank-order the major skills required to turn out effective proposals—that is, proposals that win contracts—I would say that they are these, in descending order of importance:

1. Marketing and sales skills
2. Analytical and creative skills
3. Subject-matter expertise
4. Writing skills

This is not to say that skills not at the head of the list are unimportant. All contribute heavily to success, and strength in all is most important for success in proposal competitions; weakness in a single area may easily defeat your proposal. Writing should not be underrated, despite these observations: Writing is important as the vehicle for implementing these other skills effectively through skillful integration of all. It is therefore with some trepidation that I list writing at the bottom of the scale, for fear that you may gain the wrong impression. However, despite some exceptions, even the most skillful writing alone rarely, if ever, wins proposal competitions, while marketing and sales skills alone have often carried the day, even with weaknesses in the other areas. Hence, the chief purpose of the rank ordering is to establish an appreciation of all the several skills and capabilities that make up successful proposal writing. Therefore, the term *proposal writing*, really refers to the entire proposal development process, with writing skills playing only a part in the process.

A new element today is the swift propagation of desktop computers. The most common use of these computers, and the most common reason for acquiring them, is word processing. Word processing has revolutionized the office routines for producing business documents. It can also revolutionize writing itself, especially proposal writing. In addition, the computer offers several other kinds of help in proposal development. What the informed and wise use of computers can do for the process is discussed later.

Marketing and Sales Skills

A later chapter is devoted entirely to the subject of sales and marketing, but it is almost impossible to discuss even the basics of proposal writing without casting the discussion in the reference framework of sales and marketing. Therefore, I preview that later chapter here to establish the ground rules for the discussions in this chapter, although I discuss sales principles more than those of marketing here, and do not go much beyond basic principles.

Some Typical Kinds of Fumbles

Bear in mind at all times that whatever else it may be, a proposal is first and foremost a sales presentation. (Other objectives of the proposal, if any, are in addition to and subordinate to that main goal.) One of the most common underlying causes of proposal failure is the result of failing to recognize this simple fact. Following are a few examples of proposals written to other objectives and thus failing to become winners:

1. The Aggressive/Defensive Proposal.   Some consultants write proposals with a main focus on the terms they expect to impose. They often tend to have a tone of aggressiveness, with a definitely defensive stance. These writers tend also to hedge all promises and commitments with numerous escape clauses, casting doubt on the client's integrity and intentions to deal honorably.

2. The Loud-Claims Proposal.   Some consultants appear to labor under an inability to distinguish claims and laudatory self-appraisals from sales arguments. Their proposals contain few facts and are characterized principally by hyperbole, that is heavy with adjectives, adverbs, and superlatives alleging the writer's great accomplishments, highly respected place in the profession, and marvelous abilities. The strategy apparently is to overwhelm the client by outshouting all the other proposers. It is usually not a successful tactic.

3. The "Me Too" Proposal.   Some proposals appear to mumble only that the writer can do the job as well as anyone, so why not make the award to that proposer. Such proposals almost inevitably succumb to the competition of other proposals, which are based on legitimate sales arguments and strive to be originals and not carbon copies.

4. The I'm-Not-Really-Sure-I-Know-What-You-Want Proposal.   One common type of writer, usually a neophyte in proposal writing, believes that the client knows exactly what he or she wants to see proposed, and that the client will award the contract to the fortunate writer who succeeds in guessing exactly what that is. This consultant is very much afraid that whatever he or she proposes will not be exactly what the client wants. Therefore, the writer is completely evasive and general, never says anything very concrete, and especially never proposes a detailed plan of action or even a clear-cut analysis of the problem. (In fact, this is the underlying reason for many "me too" proposals.)

5. The Canned Solution Proposal.   Some consultants have one or two canned solutions, old reliable standards they offer every potential client, no matter what the client stipulates as the need. Some of the writers of this genre even have preprinted proposals, with a few blanks for the client's name and address and other minor variables. They manage to win an assignment once in a while, when the need happens by chance to coincide with the canned solution, but they don't win contracts very often.

The Problem's Importance to the Client

All of these fumbling approaches, and others that are as bad, ignore the client's interest. They reflect indifference to the client's need, intended or not, and they suggest that the consultant who writes them doesn't really care what the client's problem is, or at least does not consider the problem serious enough to merit much study and thought. Whether the causes for all these almost-certain-to-lose approaches is fear, laziness, indifference, arrogance, or simple lack of understanding of what is wanted and needed, all radiate the same philosophy: Just give me the money, and I'll do whatever it is you want done, but your problem does not merit much of my time now, before I have a contract. Whatever it is, I'll take care of it when the time comes.

Of course, the problem *is* important to the client, who would not be seeking or even considering consulting help if the problem were not important. It is therefore a fatal error to convey to the client, directly or indirectly, any suggestion that you belittle the importance of the problem. If you do happen to hold that opinion, it will almost surely manage to show, to shine through your writing.

To avoid undervaluing the client's problem, you must be deeply conscious of the client's feelings and respect the seriousness of the problem. To write anything effectively, but especially to write a successful sales presentation, you must be able to perceive the problem from the client's perspective, to understand and even actually feel the client's concerns and earnest desires. That is the essence of selling. Your own perceptions are of no importance here; only the client's perspectives matter. Because everyone acts in his or her own self-interest at all times, the client does not care what you want, except as your wants are necessary as an avenue toward achieving his or her own wants. The client's wants are first and foremost, and the way to sell anything is to identify what the client wants and then to show the client how to satisfy that want.

Analytical and Creative Skills

Needs and Wants

Marketing people sometimes refer to needs and wants as though they were
different things. They are not. In an earlier time, *want* meant lack of (e.g.,
"for want of a nail . . . "), but it is used today to mean *desire*, whereas *need*
is generally used to refer to a necessity. Practically, however, when a client
decides to want something, that want becomes a need, and the sales/
marketing problem is one of how to persuade the client that the best or most
desirable way to satisfy the need is to accept your offer. Simple? It is that
simple—and that complex.

A common failure in marketing is failing to identify the client's need
accurately. You cannot sell the client something the client truly does not
want—that is, does not identify either as his or her need or as the best way
to satisfy the need, which is essentially the same thing. A brief example may
help to ensure your understanding of what may seem to be a hair-splitting
point, but such understanding often makes the difference between success
and failure in the marketplace:

> Let us suppose that the client has announced a perceived need for a better
> inventory-control and -management system to replace the one currently in
> use. The client's objection to the existing system is that it wastes both
> warehouse space and capital, with too much stock in too many slow-moving
> items. Several consultants have offered proposals. All the proposals offer
> more or less standard or classical solutions to the problem through computer
> control that bases ordering of each item of inventory on complex calculations
> involving required lead time for ordering, history of traffic in the item, current
> orders, anticipated orders, and estimates based on trend lines and what those
> trends project.
>
> All of those approaches or solutions appear suitable enough for satisfying
> the client's perceived need, at least as the client's request for proposals
> defines or identifies that need. You, however, do not accept the client's
> definition of need without question. Instead, you study it carefully and in
> greater depth, either to validate the definition as described in the RFP, or to
> amend and correct it before writing your own proposal. You decide that the
> client's definition of need is a bit shallow and needs more careful thought.
> You redefine it accordingly and then offer a somewhat different approach,
> one that is considerably more sophisticated than the one just described and
> that better suits the need as you perceive it.

Sensible though others' approaches are, they are conventional, while your approach goes a step or two beyond them and recommends the addition of equipment and software that will enable the client to keep close track of the supply situation in real time and to order items accordingly, via computer-to-computer connections, thereby reducing the lead time by days and thus reducing total costs for the client. You might also even propose a study of suppliers to identify those with whom such computer-to-computer monitoring and ordering is possible, thus maximizing the use of the method and paving the way for a turnkey project.

The client now decides that this—ordering all inventory via computer to reduce the lead time and minimize the time items stay and age in storage— is really the need. For all practical purposes, you are now the only consultant offering the right solution—the one that satisfies the real need, as you have now persuaded the client to perceive the need.

In one sense, you have created a need, a new need, by showing the client a better way. (Many marketing and sales successes are the result of skillful education of the client, helping the client to discover the true need.) In another sense, however, there is no such thing as a new need, for basic needs never change. Only the ways of satisfying those basic needs change.

Many new products and new services struggle for success in the marketplace. Some succeed in becoming large successes after a long time. Some become only modest successes, no matter how long they struggle for preeminence in the marketplace. And some never find success. On the other hand, some become instant successes. Television is one such example, as are videocassette recorders, microcomputers, pocket calculators, and xerographic copying machines.

In contrast, all those other xerographic copying machines that had to use specially treated paper cast hardly a shadow in the wake of Xerox® because only Xerox Corporation could make its copies on plain paper, at least until its protective patents finally expired years later.

The need, then, was defined by the public in all of these cases. While you may argue that the invention of TV created a need for TV, the fact is that the need for home entertainment always existed, and TV was one of a long series of steadily improving means of home entertainment, the latest of which is the videocassette recorder and the predecessor of which was the radio.

Copiers that required specially treated paper were modest successes because plain-paper copying was (and is) a clearly and dramatically better way to satisfy the need for copies: It is swift and convenient, and it has produced copies of steadily improving fidelity, until the most modern copier models produce copies that sometimes are even better than the originals. So Xerox was immensely successful, in contrast with its rivals. (There had been several earlier types of office copiers, none of them very convenient or very efficient, and hardly an improvement over carbon paper, in fact. They succeeded in finding acceptance, for a time, because there was nothing else available to satisfy the need for copying, but they all disappeared from view almost overnight when xerographic copying on a practical basis made its appearance.)

Examine the apparent need, then, in terms of (a) the basic and classic need it really represents (which is not always readily apparent), and (b) the way in which you can satisfy that need better than it has ever been satisfied before or, at least, in a better way than your competitors are likely to offer. *Better* can mean faster, cheaper, more conveniently, with better reliability, or with any other benefit.

Marketing/Salesmanship Considerations

An ingenious home-workshop inventor, Fred Grisé, had a great idea, early in his career. (He has created a great many successful inventions since.) He invented a solution to a problem that vexes a great many of us: He devised a way to make the ketchup flow easily out of that traditional narrow-necked bottle. So off he went to sell his invention to the leading manufacturer of ketchup, convinced that his fortune was assured.

To his dismay, he found himself all but thrown down the stairs by the horrified officials of that firm when they heard his proposition. They could not get him off their premises fast enough. Later, a disappointed and disillusioned Grisé philosophized that he had learned his lesson: He would henceforth offer clients only what they wanted, not what they needed.

Brilliant and imaginative inventor that he is, he was slightly off target in his ruminations about a lesson learned. The ketchup manufacturer's whole advertising and marketing campaign is based on that "slowest ketchup in the west" theme. Grisé's invention would have totally destroyed that carefully crafted and slowly built-up image of quality, which was based on a message strongly implying that the thicker the ketchup, the higher was its quality. From a marketing and sales viewpoint, the ketchup executives not only did not need that new invention, but they needed to bury it as quickly as possible, as a direct threat to their existence or at least to their commanding position in the ketchup market.

Lesson: To write a good proposal, you must have a good understanding of marketing, and often, as in the case cited here, you must also understand the principles of sales and marketing from the client's viewpoint. You must find the best way to provide what the client *needs*.

Creativity

Finding or devising a new and better way to satisfy a need is a creative process, and it should be recognized as such. Though the nature of creativity is explored in some depth in a later chapter, I must mention here a basic principle or two about the subject because one of the characteristics required to write a really good proposal is creative imagination.

First of all, creativity is rarely, if ever, the result of a truly new or revolutionary idea. Instead, it is generally a new combination of ideas, an extrapolation of what is already known. TV owes its basic circuits and technology to the earlier radio sciences, for example, but it did not become a practical reality until the picture tube was added as the means for displaying the output of the system. (Early models used unsatisfactory devices called "flying spot scanners.") However, the picture tube was not really a new invention, either. It was an adaptation of an established device, the cathode ray tube used in a laboratory instrument, the oscilloscope.

Nor was the transistor a brand new idea because its predecessor devices and basic technology go back to 1870 at least. Even the modern personal computer is a new combination of radio, TV, early computers, the telephone, and other communications technology. Creativity is, thus, largely a matter of reassembling known ideas into new patterns or adapting established ideas, devices, and methods to new uses.

One of the obstacles that inhibits creativity is the all-too-human resistance to change. Giving up established, familiar, and comfortable ways and accepting the hazards of the unknown, give rise to a sense of insecurity for many, especially for those who are considered to be experts in the known. Thus, Thomas Edison, Louis Pasteur, Charles Kettering, and many others were assailed for their "ignorance" and "stupidity" in attempting to achieve what the experts knew were impossible goals—the incandescent electric light, proof that microorganisms do not emerge spontaneously out of inert matter, and the automobile self-starter, respectively. These creative people are only three of literally hundreds of such possible citations, not the least of which was Admiral William Leahy's confident assertion that the atomic bomb would never detonate, which he qualified with the assurance that he spoke as an expert on explosives.

It requires a sturdy and dedicated individual to proceed in the face of such sneering, condescending condemnation by those regarded as known and acknowledged experts. Courage was not the least of the characteristics that enabled such creative individuals as Edison, Pasteur, and Kettering to press on with their efforts. The courage to ignore conventional wisdom and to be unmoved by criticism, no matter the source, is almost an absolute prerequisite for creativity. In addition, creativity requires knowledge—deep and broad knowledge of one's field and related areas.

Subject-Matter Expertise

Many breakthroughs are based on original ideas by individuals who are not regarded as qualified experts in their fields; in fact, many originators are sniffed at somewhat disdainfully as amateurs. If Thomas Edison were starting out today, he probably could not get a job as a scientist or engineer in any organization, and he probably would have trouble even being hired as a lab technician. When I was employed at Philco-Ford's government communications and weapons division some years ago, the engineer there with the greatest number of patents to his name (some 65, if memory serves me) had never seen the inside of a college. Moreover, the engineer who was designing some of the most sophisticated digital-data secure-communications devices was likewise from the "old" (noncollege) school; what's more, he did not know how to draw up a functional logic diagram or to use Boolean algebra for his designs (both considered by others to be a sine qua non for the work). Instead, he drafted everything laboriously in complicated electronic circuit diagrams.

This is not to decry the need for conventional formal education and experience. It points out that it is the knowledge and ability per se, no matter how and where acquired, that makes the difference. You can hardly be creative without knowing what you are doing—without, that is, knowing your field thoroughly and examining the problem or need *objectively*, no matter what others say or think. Kettering was himself widely quoted as saying that education was all right if one did not permit it to interfere with thinking. (Nor does this denigrate or make light of instinctual urges, which are probably the logic of the subconscious mind, that characterize many acts of creativity.)

Today, because the desktop computer is a reality and has invaded offices everywhere, from the most elaborate corporate headquarters to the most humble at-home office, millions of individuals have been adding computer skills to their repertoires, many even becoming outstandingly expert in the various computer arts and sciences.

Being computer knowledgeable, if not expert, is not a sine qua non for proposal writing, but it is certainly a great asset in many ways. Take only the example cited earlier of the proposal for solving inventory-management problems by offering an entirely new approach. Conceiving that technical strategy could stem only from a competent appreciation of computer capabilities. The author of that idea was able to formulate an imaginative new approach only because he or she had learned something of what can be done in this new computer age, especially in routine and efficient computer-to-computer communication available at the press of a button.

Writing Skills

The subject of writing, per se, has been relegated to last place, despite the use of the term proposal *writing*. Briefly, the main significance of writing skill is this: Writing is the means by which we implement and exploit all the other work that has gone into devising a program and a set of sales/marketing strategies. Strategy has two parts: the concept and the implementation. The latter is a function of the writing: Ineffective writing means ineffective strategy, and even ineffective design.

Consider, for example, the situation postulated earlier, in which you did not settle for the client's description of the need but decided to study the need in some depth—to validate the need or to correct the definition. Having decided that the client had not probed deeply enough in defining the need, you redefined it in your proposal and offered what you thought was the best possible solution.

Handled properly in your written presentation, this can be the basis for a powerful strategy. It demonstrates your own sincerity and perceptiveness, and possibly even a superior approach and greater ability than other proposers have demonstrated. It also almost compels the client to reconsider all other proposals to see how others measure up by comparison. (Inevitably, much of the proposal evaluation must be a comparative one.)

If you do a proper selling job and convince the client that yours is the way to go, you knock out most, and maybe all of your competitors without making a direct reference to any. Later, in a chapter dealing with writing persuasively, I suggest wordings and arguments to maximize these effects without "knocking" competitors.

The strategies you devise will depend heavily on the quality of your writing. The "quality of your writing" does not refer to your literary elegance or grammatical perfection, but to the persuasiveness of your prose. The factors that achieve persuasiveness are also discussed in a later chapter. In addition, that chapter describes the use of the computer and certain types of software, including but not restricted to word processors, to help you achieve great impact with your writing.

DEVELOPING THE NECESSARY SKILLS

The first step in developing and/or honing existing skills in these several areas is to recognize and accept the need to do so. All good writing is rewriting: Even the most expert professional writer accepts that as the secret of writing well. Rewriting is one of the great benefits of using a computer for writing: Computers encourage rewriting because they make rewriting enormously easier to do than ever before.

A major purpose of this book is to help you further develop your skills in the several areas necessary for writing successful proposals, even in your subject-matter knowledge. Some of these areas are actually closely intertwined, and separating them into separate discussions in earlier paragraphs was a purely mechanical device. In the following discussions, I make no great effort to so separate the topics, so that you can see their close interrelationships. In regard to subject-matter knowledge, you may believe that you do not need my help, but I propose to begin there, by showing you how you may increase your own knowledge, through your own efforts.

I freely acknowledge that you almost certainly are already far more expert in your technical or professional field than I am, intend to be, or ever could be—that is, in that field or those fields in which you specialize as a consultant. I therefore cannot impart to you any subject-matter knowledge per se, nor do I intend to try to do so.

On the other hand, do you really know as much as you should about your own field and—think carefully about this—about other, closely related fields? Are you keeping up with your field? Reading at least some of the literature? Active in a relevant association or two? In touch with others in your field? Attending conferences and conventions? Making at least occasional contributions to the literature, even if only in a trade journal or two? Do you think that you need to know more about what is happening currently in your field and related subjects?

Please also note the earlier remarks about becoming acquainted with modern desktop computers. That is a "horizontal" field we all must become at least "literate" in. (Note: Any consultant today ought to be more than merely literate in computers.) Finally, are you taking full advantage of the research and other information-furnishing assets that the computer has helped to make available?

If you are not answering "yes" to at least a few of these queries, you are in danger of becoming a dinosaur in your field. The world won't wait for you to catch up; you have to keep up, even if that means a lot of running. If you are not more expert, more imaginative, more enterprising, and more dedicated to your profession than are the nine-to-five masses in your field, you are probably not truly suited to the consulting profession, and you are not likely to become a good proposal writer.

Your creative output is related quite closely to and is proportional to your information input. However, that input does not occur automatically as a result of reading the daily literature of your field; it may require that you make special efforts, such as conjuring up questions to which you need answers and then seeking out the sources of information, such as public databases accessible by computer. What's more, seeking existing information is only one ingredient necessary to create new ideas. Another required ingredient is *introspection*—thinking about things in general, about what they mean and how they can be best understood.

Creative people constantly seek more and/or new information about a great many things, but they are also quite aware that the information they seek may not exist anywhere. That is, they may have to generate that information themselves through creative thinking. Professor Charles H. Townes, for example, was reportedly ruminating on a park bench when he conceived the *maser* (microwave amplification by stimulated emission of radiation) and, soon after and more significantly, the laser (light amplification by stimulated emission of radiation), both major scientific breakthroughs. However, he had been working on the problem with other scientists for a long time, and he had been gathering relevant information and pondering the problems during all that time, as had the others, before his introspection finally produced the seminal inspiration for the breakthrough.

The point of some earlier discussions was that new and better ways themselves create new needs. That is, you can address a client's stated need in either or both of two ways:

1. Study the need itself, as defined by the client, and decide whether that is the true definition of the need or whether you must redefine it. That is, decide what is the true need, the *result* that the client really wants.

2. Study the various ways in which the need can be satisfied (the result achieved), and identify the best way, redefining the need in terms of that best way.

In many cases, the second approach works best and is really used. Here is an example of how that might work:

The client says he or she wants a rapid-delivery service. However, the client's thinking is restricted by his or her perception of reality—that is, the delivery services available. The client does not define the need beyond the term "fastest possible delivery," when in fact the client really wants to be able to deliver documents to the opposite coast on the same day. The obvious method for delivery is express air service, which can do the job within 12 hours. However, another transmission method can do the job in a fraction of that time: *electronic mail*, a method in which the report is recorded on some magnetic or other machine-readable medium and sent via computer-to-computer telephone-line communication. The availability of the second method makes the first method obsolete and thus becomes a need by the simple virtue of its availability. If the client did not know that it was possible, the proposer who explains and proposes it creates a new need simply by making the client aware of the possibility.

But wait: Fax (facsimile) transmission is even better than electronic mail because it is as fast (almost instantaneous) and far simpler (any layperson can do it, whereas electronic mail requires some special skills). That changes the need further.

Note that what changed the need here was not even the creation of a method not heretofore available, but simply making the client aware of that method.

If the client did not know that the method (fax) existed, educating the client changed the client's definition of need. It is not truth but the client's *perception* of truth that makes the difference. Is fax, then, the final answer?

Not necessarily. Depending on the size of the document to be transmitted, electronic mail may be less costly, and just as fast—even faster—for a lengthy document. Fax transmission involves some sacrifice in quality, so the client must consider the importance of the quality of reproduction. There are also a few other technical considerations.

Technological, economic, and marketing or business factors are involved in evaluating the three basic options. How do you write an effective proposal if you are not reasonably knowledgeable in all three areas?

A MASTER STRATEGY

Educating the client is a general master strategy available in many proposal situations. Sometimes, you can devise a totally different and better way to satisfy a need simply by knowing much more than the requester knew. You often succeed then in changing the rules—in essence, writing your own. This means that you have actually succeeded in changing the specification of the need, invalidating all proposals that limit themselves to responding to the need as defined in the RFP. Often, you wind up with a clear field if no competitor knew of a better way, made the effort to develop a new and better way, or was forthright enough to educate the client accordingly.

There is a qualifier in all this, however: For practical purposes (as a winning strategy, that is), your new and different innovation is better only if the client agrees that it is better. Your allegation that it is better does not automatically make it so in the client's perception. To change the definition or specification of need, you must succeed in persuading the client to agree with your definition. That is, you must *sell* that idea to the client.

Moreover, you must never assume that the client can or will easily see for himself or herself that your solution is by far the best one; you must explain your rationale carefully, making sure that the reader is able to follow your reasoning completely. For even if the client is knowledgeable enough to make the analysis without your help—and that might not be so in all cases—there is no earthly reason for the client to go to that much trouble. (To expect that is to expect the client to do your selling job for you; it won't happen.)

Finally, in addition, you have at least one other consideration: The client, like most other people, probably almost instinctively resists new and different ideas. The client is not likely to hasten to embrace your new and different idea unless you succeed in your persuasive arguments for it. Most people are not visionary at all, and they tend to reject new ideas, especially those that are revolutionary and call for casting out old ideas and old prejudices. Alexander Graham Bell was unable to sell his telephone to Western Union, whose officials thought the idea of people talking to each other over a wire was ridiculous. (Of course, they also saw the telephone as contrary to their interests.)

Kodak and IBM, among others, reportedly were offered and rejected the new xerographic copying invention that tiny Haloid Corporation embraced, which sparked its growth into today's giant Xerox Corporation: Those who rejected Chester Carlson's invention could not foresee much of practical value in this idea of xerographic copying. Thomas Watson, head of IBM, which was later to become by far the leading computer firm in the world, was originally highly unenthusiastic about computers. In 1943, he estimated a world market for computers of about five buyers.

There are, of course, legions of similar stories. The platitude about the better mousetrap is a myth. The world will not beat a path to your door, no matter how good your mousetrap is unless you manage to sell it to the world. Do not be misled by the occasional exceptions. Exceptions to all rules are inevitable, but they do not invalidate the principle.

Evidently, almost no one is immune to the human tendency to wear blinders. Ironically, even those who ought to know better because of their own experience have the same frailty: As late as 1922, Edison expressed the opinion that radio was a passing fad. Lee DeForest, inventor of one of the basic breakthroughs in radio (the "audion" tube) and considered to be at least one of the parents of radio, assured any who would listen that TV was probably a technical possibility but could never be a practical success because it was not feasible commercially or financially. And H. G. Wells, acclaimed writer of visionary science fiction novels, predicted that submarines would succeed in nothing but suffocating their crews to death.

The tendency of most of us to resist new ideas is proportional to how different or revolutionary those new ideas seem to us. Those ideas with which we are most uncomfortable are those that require us to discard the familiar notions and opinions we already hold, so we are far more resistant to *revolutionary change* than we are to *evolutionary change*. Evolutionary changes are new ideas we can accommodate side-by-side with those we already hold or by minor modification of the latter, instead of requiring us to cast them out totally. We are also uncomfortable with new ideas that we do not really understand, and so we tend to reject new ideas for that reason as well.

The means for presenting and selling new and different ideas to clients must also take these principles into consideration, to avoid traumatizing the client with new ideas that the client will find extremely difficult to accept. There are several means for so doing, and a later chapter explores some means for coping with these problems successfully. For now, bear in mind these principles in the following discussion of the various kinds of strategies that can be and should be embodied in most proposals.

CHAPTER 3

The Development of Effective Strategies

In marketing, as in waging war, strategy is a prime factor of success and failure. Also, as in military matters, discriminating among the many possible strategies and tactics to identify the one most likely to effect success is much more art than science.

THE GENERAL ANATOMY OF STRATEGY

It is not easy to define the word *strategy*. Even lexicographers have difficulty with it. They tend to cast its definition in terms of artifices for conducting war. Here, *strategies* are methodologies for inducing prospective clients to find our proposals more persuasive than those of our competitors, and so to win contracts. However, that is an oversimplification, too.

The Goal Versus the Objective

Winning the contract that is at stake in the usual proposal contest is a general goal, rather than a direct objective. I use the word *goal*, rather than *objective*; because *goal* suggests the long-term target, whereas *objective* refers to the short-term or immediate target. Therefore, *goal* is more apt because most proposal competitions do not result in a contract award directly and immediately. In most proposal contests, and especially in the case of the large contracts, proposal evaluations are followed by such activities as a call for presentations, a call for best and final offers, and discussions and other kinds of negotiations or preliminaries to negotiations. Typically, the process for all but the smallest purchases entails distinct phases:

1. Selection of the most suitable candidates to be included in the lists of those invited to submit proposals and compete; issuance of the request
2. Reading and evaluation of proposals, selecting all nominally acceptable as "within the competitive range"
3. Follow-up discussions, oral presentations, and best and final offers, by selected proposers; narrowing and rank-ordering of candidates
4. Negotiations leading to the award of a contract

In short, it is rare that a contract award follows proposal evaluations directly. In most cases, that evaluation is one of the preliminary steps to the final choice. The proposal is thus a mechanism for narrowing the field to the acceptable candidates, from whose number the client will eventually choose a contractor.

In the case of the large contract, the several phases or steps are likely to be formal procedures, with each top-ranked proposer invited to attend a discussion of his or her proposal ("orals") and usually also invited to make a formal oral presentation (the "dog and pony show"). This usually includes an invitation to submit relevant amendments to both the technical proposal and the cost proposal. (The latter is a broad suggestion that paring the price is likely to be helpful.)

In the case of the small contract, these are likely to be informal procedures: exchanges via letter, fax, telephone, or even telegram, but the effect is the same: proposal follow-up to reach final decisions.

Identifying the True Strategic Approach

What this means is that there are already two clearly implied broad strategies: For the small contract, the broad strategy is usually direct pursuit of a contract award, whereas in the case of the large contract there is an implied strategy of pursuing an invitation to a best-and-final offer meeting as the main objective.

A go-for-broke win strategy, conceived in the hope of winning the contract directly and immediately on the basis of the proposal itself, may thus be a mistake, distracting you from what ought to be your true objective: getting over a first hurdle and in line for the next procedure. A true win strategy anticipates the several phases and the needed responses to each.

Theoretically, you cannot know whether the client will choose a winner without that usual postproposal activity; there are exceptions. However, should the client bypass those usual postproposal steps, having based your main strategy on the objective of getting into that next-stage phase will not hurt you in any way. The reverse is not true. Shooting for a direct win means a go-for-broke attack, and that can hurt you because it leaves you unprepared for the next phase. You may need to save something for that encore.

The Advantage of Face-to-Face Presentation

Even the preceding rationale is not the entire essence of the matter. Most marketers consider it a handicap to be restricted to writing alone to make their presentation. Many firmly believe that they can do a far more effective marketing job in face-to-face discussions with prospective clients. For them, the most important objective of their proposal writing effort is to win the opportunity for such discussions—to "get to the table," as many put it.

This is probably true for everyone. There are some advantages in making a written presentation, and there are some others in an oral presentation. For most of us, the ideal is often the combination of both: the powerful written presentation, followed by the face-to-face meeting and discussion. It is so much in your interest to do this that the wise marketer of consulting services does not even try to guess whether the client will issue that invitation to orals or other discussions. Instead, if you are such a marketer, you will do everything possible to induce the client to find a meeting necessary. You will set a clear and unambiguous objective of inducing the client to call for a proposal follow-up, and you will structure and design your win strategies to include this objective as the first step.

The objective is nothing by itself. What can you do to bring that about? You need some kind of plan to put your strategy to work and produce that result, as the following consultants did.

Case History No. 1

An organization was being overwhelmed with mail requesting highly technical information regarding their activities in wind energy utilization devices, so it invited consultants to propose a program for handling that overload. One consultant responded that the consultant could easily help them to handle the overload, but that preparing to handle future overloads without subcontracting out some of their work was a potential problem for the client. He could solve that and could enable the organization to handle the mail problem in-house with a design strategy he had developed, and which he would gladly disclose.

Obviously, the organization could not afford to do other than hear him out, and so they invited him to make an oral presentation. He did so and was awarded a contract of far greater scope than originally contemplated.

Case History No. 2

Invited to devise an on-the-job training program for technicians, a training-systems consultant proposed such a radically new and different approach to the design of the system that the client could hardly help but ask the consultant to visit and explain his ideas. The consultant, a wise marketer, had deliberately withheld key details of his plan, while issuing a clear invitation to request a formal presentation of the plan. He knew he had piqued the client's curiosity enough to ensure that he would be asked to appear and be cross-examined by the client's staff.

DEVISING STRATEGIES

A successful strategy is often the result of inspiration, which is a somewhat subconscious process. However, you cannot afford either to be at the mercy of uncertain and unpredictable inspiration and subconscious processes, or to accept any premise that requires such fortuitous circumstances for the development of effective strategies. You must have something much more dependable and controllable, something that can be employed methodically and produce effective strategies on demand. You must therefore analyze strategies and find those elements that are the basis for all successful strategies. However, there are several strategic arenas in which you must compete with your proposals, and these subdivide into major and minor strategies.

Before looking at these, however, note and remember this: The most effective strategy is one suggested by the client. It is built around whatever appears to be of the greatest importance to the client. The search for a strategic approach must therefore be based on a quest to identify the client's prime concerns and priorities, even when the client has not consciously stated these. Always be watchful for clues to these.

THE MAJOR STRATEGIES

It is necessary to have a master strategy (known variously as "capture strategy," "main strategy," "win strategy," etc.), but there are at least four other major strategic concepts to consider, as well as some minor ones, which are discussed here, too. First, however, a few introductory thoughts about these major strategies, suggested by the identifying names assigned them:

Technical or program strategy
Cost strategy
Competitive strategy
Presentation strategy

The win strategy must be sharply focused. It is usually one of the preceding four, but never all of them. The remaining strategies support, but must never eclipse or cast shadows over, the main strategy. At the same time, these strategies may be linked in some manner, and the linkage must be clear. It may even be essential to the strategy.

For example, if your win strategy is to offer the lowest costs, you must prove that you can do the job properly at the promised lowest costs, and that may entail showing how your innovative and clever technical or program strategy makes the low cost possible. Most effective win strategies have cause-and-effect links to more than one of these, but one clear strategy must dominate. The process of deciding what that strategy is to be should be a major objective of the preliminary requirements' identification and analysis.

Whatever the specific situation, it is always essential that you identify your selected win strategy as early in the proposal process as possible, because it has such a great effect on all elements of the proposal—the program design strategy, the presentation strategy, and perhaps even the competitive strategy. At the same time, you need the flexibility to modify or even change your win strategy if later developments suggest that as the sensible course of action. Therefore, try to identify a tentative win strategy at an early time, but look at it frequently as you develop your proposal, and do not hesitate to refine and sharpen it continuously.

IDENTIFYING A WIN STRATEGY

The main (win) strategy many inexperienced marketers employ is to try to use and maximize all the strategic ideas, in a kind of "buckshot" approach. This is based on the hope that the more buckshot or strategic attacks scattered by the proposal, the more likely it is that some will strike the target in a vital spot and thus produce some kind of salutary effect.

Alas, it rarely happens. Trying to be all things results in a dissipation of your effort. You scatter not only your strategic ammunition but also your energies. The lack of clear focus, that vague meandering around the subject without ever coming to grips directly with it, characterizes many unsuccessful proposals. That weakness reflects the lack of commitment to a main strategy as a base for the proposal. It is probably the reason for failure of about two thirds of all proposals.

To be maximally effective, strategy must have a clear focus. It cannot help your cause to argue the technical merits of your proposed method or the virtues of your specialized experience when the client has shown concern for costs only. You must have decided which is the most critical concern (in the client's perception), crystallize your strategy around that specific idea, and suspend your entire presentation from that superstructure. If you decide that the client is especially concerned with keeping the cost low, you must seek means for doing so in every aspect of the program you propose, while developing evidence to demonstrate that the cost saving is not at the expense of performance and quality. The reader should never have the slightest doubt as to exactly what your principal argument is. Nor should you.

There is, of course, always a hazard in the decision that commits you to a specific strategy, the hazard that you will make the wrong decision and waste all your efforts in pressing home the wrong strategy. It is undoubtedly that danger that impels so many proposers to try "polypharmacological" proposals, offering many kinds of "medicine" to cure the client's ills.

The danger of making the fatal error is real, but the proper approach to avoiding that error is to do whatever is necessary to identify the proper win strategy. It is far more a matter of doing the right thing than one of avoiding the wrong thing.

This is not to say that the many other strategies are not to be used. They can and should make their own contributions, but they should be most definitely in supporting roles, linked to the main strategy, and clearly subordinated to it. Look at each of these.

Technical/Program Strategy

Technical or program strategy includes such matters as your approach to the solution of the client's problem, satisfaction of need, characteristics of design, procedures prescribed, materials to be used, special features, innovative ideas, use of specialists/special resources, and other features. These may have direct effects and may be closely linked, even in cause-and-effect relationships, with such other matters as costs and schedules.

Cost Strategy

Cost is rarely the sole consideration and often not even the chief consideration in the client's choice, but it is never unimportant. Cost strategy is possible because cost is rarely an absolute term or an absolute amount. In most cases, cost is a relative term and has numerous qualifiers that point this out for various situations—such as, acquisition costs, maintenance costs, installation costs, support costs, total cost of ownership, and life-cycle costs. Even then, related cost considerations should be taken into account, such as the possible effects of the consulting work on other costs the client normally experiences.

In many cases, it is simply not possible to determine what the final true costs will be or, perhaps more significantly, even who the low bidder is among all the proposers or bidders. Within this inescapable anomaly are the conditions for the development of cost strategies.

Competitive Strategy

It is a competitive world, and you are rarely fortunate enough to be the only consultant invited to propose. In most cases, you are one of at least several, frequently many, able consultants vying for the contract.

No matter how capable you are or how well you write, it is likely that at least some of your competitors are as able as you and write as well as you. To believe that none of your competitors approach you in competence or capability for presenting their credentials is an almost certain road to disaster. Remember at all times that with only occasional exception, the client judges the capabilities and competence of the proposers primarily by what they say in their proposals and how credible those statements appear to be. Therefore, as far as the client is concerned,

Proposal quality = Consultant quality.

True or not, and justified or not, this is the client's perception.

That means that you must have some kind of competitive strategy so that you help the client find reasons to rate your proposal higher than those of competitors. In fact, competitive strategy should ideally be based on one prime factor that somehow dramatizes the issue in your favor.

Presentation Strategy

Your proposal is a sales presentation. Many presentation strategies are possible; these techniques can make your proposal more effective by increasing its impact, by capturing the client's attention in some special way, or by otherwise maximizing the benefits through various artful methods.

Don't underestimate the contribution to success that a good presentation strategy can make. It is often only in the presentation strategy that the other strategies are implemented successfully so that you can gain the benefits of those other strategies.

STRATEGIES IN A MINOR KEY

Many problems require the development of minor strategies to cope with them successfully. In fact, these strategies deserve a special category: "assets and liabilities strategies."

You are not often so perfect for a requirement that your qualifications represent 100 percent assets and 0 liabilities, with regard to the requirement. More often, you must weigh your assets and liabilities, vis-à-vis the requirement, in evolving some kind of strategy. However, aside from the question of a win strategy and those other major strategic factors, there is the question of exploiting your assets and overcoming your liabilities.

For example, suppose you must write a proposal to offer your services in an area where you have little or no specific experience to present as your technical/professional qualifications. How can you cope with this? Some requirements may clearly call for the services of a sizable team, one considerably larger than your own staff. How do you satisfy the client that you can meet this need successfully without risking failure? A requirement may be for services primarily in your field, but it still requires special capabilities for some aspect of the project, special qualifications you do not possess. How can you overcome this liability?

On the other hand, you also need to evolve strategies for maximizing the benefits of your assets. If you have extraordinary experience or other resources that are directly relevant to the client's need, you can benefit from exploiting these as an advantage over competitors. However, you gain the benefits of exploiting them properly only by using specific strategies to do so. Such benefits won't come about spontaneously.

How Important are the Minor Strategies?

These latter strategies are referred to as "minor" strategies only because they generally affect only relatively minor matters. However, that is not always the case. Often, the strategy that began as the solution to some apparently minor asset or liability begins to assume more and more importance as the proposal evolves, and sometimes it becomes the pivot on which success turns. One small firm (total staff of four), for example, was among those invited to submit proposals to create and present a training program for a large firm managing a federal (Energy Department) facility in Idaho. The problem was that the schedule was exceedingly difficult to meet because it was so short. However, this small firm pursuing the contract happened by pure chance to have an unusual asset: They had a proprietary program on the shelf that was so close to what was needed that it could be adapted to the need with only a few days' work. This asset translated into both a unique ability to meet the impossible schedule and a cost advantage. However, the schedule advantage was all that was required to win the job easily: no one else could offer a firm guarantee to meet the schedule. Thus, the proposal focused the entire sales argument on this, and this became the win strategy.

Other Objectives

You might find a few other kinds of objectives useful to consider in various proposal circumstances:

- Persuade the client to modify the statement of work.
- Make the client perceive unusually splendid qualifications in you.
- Persuade the client to see extraordinary assets in your proposed design.
- Sell the client a different approach than the request suggests.
- Sell the absolute need for some unique resource you offer.
- Alert the client to the hazards of the project if it isn't managed by you.
- Convince the client that any cost in excess of what you estimate is sheer waste and totally unnecessary.

Of course, there are thousands of other possible objectives, each clearly defining or implying a strategy, which may be a win strategy or only a subordinate strategy. In either case, it is necessary to do more than merely state the allegation of the objective. Strategy is the means of persuading the client to agree with the statement, to perceive the situation as you perceive it. Flat statements are not enough to do the job; they represent opinion or claims, not demonstrated facts or what the client will accept as facts.

For example, if you wanted to alert the client to possible hazards of the project called for, you might validate your allegation (and so implement your strategic objective) by citing case histories, published papers, public statements from prominent authorities, or simple logical analysis. To add weight to your arguments, you might even reproduce some of the relevant published material, drawings, photographs, or other supporting materials.

THE OPPOSITE POLES OF STRATEGY

Two angles of attack are open to you as a proposal strategist; you might call them the "positive" and "negative" approaches. In the positive mode, you might try to better your position by boosting yourself and what you have to offer. With the negative approach, you try to better your position by trying to knock your competitors out. In some cases, you might use one or the other of these two general approaches, but more commonly you will employ both. Both are entirely legitimate in this competitive world, even that of attacking competitors and doing your level best to discredit them in the eyes of the client.

Positive Strategy: Gain

Most of what we have discussed is geared to boosting your own image and ideas. This approach is based on the promise of gain. It argues that this proposal offers the client the greatest gain of all the courses open, for whatever reason the basic strategy dictates, such as better schedule, lower cost, greater dependability, or other such boon.

Obviously, this approach claims that you offer more gain—better results—than do your competitors in general, although it never knocks competitors directly. The implication that competitive offers and competitive capabilities are inferior to your own is subtle or low-key. Of course, all of us have come to expect that every advertisement and sales presentation will necessarily make the claim of superiority of product or service. We would be dumbfounded at any presentation that neglected to make such a claim.

The strategies underlying these kinds of presentations do not qualify as competitive or competitor strategies. Except in that most general sense, they are not aimed directly or indirectly at invalidating competitive claims, and therefore they represent only one of the two basic strategic orientations. Nonetheless, it is possible to draw a bead on competitors without appearing unethical or in violation of good taste.

Negative Strategy: Fear

Boosting your own position at the direct expense of competitors, while avoiding the stigma of directly knocking competitors, calls for delicacy. Probably the most effective way to do this is to use fear motivation. One way to do this is to combine the gain motivation with the provision of a worry item, and present this with a twist: You alert the client to the problems and even disasters that are possible (perhaps even probable) unless certain measures are taken, certain capabilities at hand, certain resources available, certain foresight present, etc. Then, of course, you are the only proposer who has that foresight and can offer whatever it is you say is necessary to avoid disaster.

The immediately preceding sentence holds the root of the strategy. For it to be effective, it must meet certain conditions:

1. The problems or disasters predicated must be legitimate (believable) eventualities. (That is, you must identify real possibilities and make them believable.)
2. They must be things your competitors are not likely to think of or to point out to the client in their own proposals.
3. You must provide some credible evidence of your own unique capabilities to cope successfully with the projected problems.

That third condition is the hardest to satisfy, inasmuch as probably all or nearly all the proposers in any given proposal competition are competent providers of whatever consulting services are required. To succeed with the first two items but fail totally with the third one is probably to make yourself appear somewhat foolish, but, worse still, give your competitors more of a boost than a kick. Therefore, give careful thought to that aspect of this strategy. The following guidance may help.

If you have some special and unique or unusual asset, such as a helpful proprietary resource or some highly specialized experience, you can probably make that the basis of your claim. If you do not have that kind of advantage, there is always one other way to address this, a way that has proved to be successful many times. Base your claim on the need for foresight and advance planning, pointing out that you are now demonstrating that foresight and advance preparation. Be sure that you have identified real problem potentials that probably either no one else will think of or no one else will mention in their own proposals.

To summarize, the essence of this technique is to find or create the worry item that is a legitimate concern and that provides some special advantage over competitors in terms of the image you present in your proposal.

IMAGE STRATEGY AND CAPABILITY BROCHURES

The image you strive to create for yourself is itself a strategic approach, one on which you normally base all your marketing effort. One place you try to create that image is in your brochures, especially that type of brochure that is known in some circles as a "capability brochure."

For many consultants, the capability brochure is almost a standard proposal, often used as a major element of or basis for the consultant's proposals. Of those surveyed in gathering material for this book, 69 percent reported that they employed brochures and other boilerplated material as major portions of their proposals, and only 31 percent reported that each of their proposals was a completely custom-written original.

A well-designed capability brochure is itself based on a major strategic concept, usually one that strives toward creating a specific image for the consultant. Computer Programming Services, Inc. (CPS), a computer consultant in Prairie Village, Kansas, supplied a sample of its capability brochure, which it uses as an integral part of its proposals. The basic strategy underlying the firm's posture is quite evident in that brochure. The clear message is that the firm sells absolutely no proprietary products—neither hardware nor software. It offers only custom services to clients. The firm therefore has no commitments to any proprietary products, and for that reason, it has no difficulty being completely impartial and objective in its recommendations to clients—that is, the firm's stated policy with regard to proprietaries enables the firm to truly represent its clients and its clients' best interests.

The capability brochure is an excellent idea for anyone offering custom services of any kind. It is itself a basis for many, if not all, of your proposals (depending on several factors, discussed later). It is a guide to and aid in preparing individual proposals. Also, a well-designed capability brochure greatly facilitates and speeds up proposal writing. In addition, not the least of its virtues, it is an excellent means of establishing and promoting your professional image, as CPS does with its brochure.

An image strategy should send a message. CPS's image is one of deliberately engineered objectivity to enable unflinching loyalty to the client. The following examples are images that other brochures present:

- "Quick reaction" services, available to support clients on short notice, with impossible schedules, and in emergencies of all kinds
- "One stop" services, a resource to handle almost any related requirement within the general field
- Unparalleled experience in the field, possibly even unique in quality of experience or capability
- Top-drawer; the ne plus ultra of such services; expensive, but the very best

Unfortunately, many of the brochures offered by consultants reflect no strategy at all, image or otherwise. Instead, they pursue the futile allegations of the consultant's superiority in all respects through self-appraisal, with generous use of superlatives. Obviously, the "strategy" intended here is to overwhelm the client with claims and hyperbole, which is, of course, no strategy at all and is rarely effective.

As a consultant, you probably should have a capability brochure of some kind (format and content are suggested later), and it should most definitely be based on some strategy that is designed to create a suitable image for you. That image should be the one that you want customers to preceive about you generally, and it should be the underpinning not only for your proposals specifically but also for all your marketing presentations. Find a niche for yourself.

THEME

The strategy underlying brochures and proposals has still another aspect, a related subject to consider: theme. *Theme* has several meanings, yet it is difficult to define in terms of what it means in proposals and other sales presentations. Theme relates closely to strategy and should reflect the strategy. Properly used, it also reinforces and continuously reminds the client of your image and of your strategy. Some examples may help to illustrate the meaning of them:

Two companies were proposing to design for the Department of Defense (DOD) an airplane that could be used by both the Air Force and the Navy. One company decided that their proposal theme was to be, "an aerodynamic solution to an aerodynamic problem." A competitor presented its own technical arguments for its proposed design and used the theme, "commonality."

The first company used a theme that appealed to logic, assuming that the client accepted the company's technical arguments for its design and its claims of superior technical/scientific aeronautical engineering expertise. The second company used a theme that appealed to emotions, assuming that the DOD had a truly great desire to achieve commonality.

The first proposer was striving to project the image of an organization of superlative technical expertise and unflagging devotion to scientific integrity, offering what it insisted was the only design that made aeronautical sense. The second proposer focused on an image of total devotion to the client's goal, taking the position that technical/scientific competence was a given, with no need to argue it because the company was well known in its field. The second company's strategy was to portray a project and staff so committed to the client's desired end-goal—commonality—that it never took its eye off that target, not for a single page.

You probably can identify the winner from the information supplied. You certainly will be able to identify the winner later, if not now, after you have further probed the nature of sales persuasion.

In another case, the client had asked for a computer/data-processing service that was difficult to supply at best. Briefly, the request called for a contractor to supply on demand the services of any of a vast number of computer specialists, each with different expertise in computer languages, machines, kinds of programs, and job functions.

The proposal request suggested that the successful proposer would need to be an organization with all such experts on staff, readily at hand. This obviously would have slanted the requirement toward only the largest of the computer service companies.

One proposer decided that the company's personnel could not make their strongest possible presentation if it were based on that suggested modus operandus, because that approach denied them the opportunity to take advantage of their strengths as an organization. They were sure that they could do the job very well and could make a strong argument for themselves if the approach were such as to exploit their strengths as an organization. They therefore took the sensible course of exploring ways of meeting the requirement through employing those methods that did take advantage of their own strengths. Accordingly, they pursued the proposal presentation along the following lines:

1. They first isolated the desired result from the suggested method and pointed out that the suggested method was, first of all, only one of several possible approaches to satisfying the requirement.

2. They argued against the suggested approach, pointing out its weaknesses, that even if there were a company or two large enough to have all the cited kinds of experts on staff (which was itself a doubtful supposition), there was no guarantee that the one expert required for any given task would always be available immediately, when needed. Quite the contrary, chance being the perverse factor that it so often is (per Murphy's Law, of course), that expert would probably be the only one of that kind in the company and would be already engaged several thousand miles away on another assignment.

3. They suggested a different approach, one that they could employ, using their own large rosters of consultants (a large part of their business was the provision of technical/professional temporaries), and they argued for it.

4. They expressed their conviction that this was an even more responsive proposal than one offering the suggested solution because this would guarantee the same result, which they said was the true test of responsiveness, and it would be a more efficient, more dependable, and less costly approach.

The strategy was to take advantage of their strength by changing the rules of the game—invalidating the suggested approach—thus also denying competitors the advantages of their strengths.

Their theme was that success depended on the contractor's total capabilities, not on any specific design of the system of services. The theme reflected their basic strength as a leading provider of technical/professional temporaries, with an already-in-place staff accustomed to filling such requirements every day. It was the most successful approach.

In still another case, the client wanted to contract with an electronics firm for the design and manufacture of a teleprinter, which in today's technology includes much of the same elements and capabilities of a modern desktop computer, as well as of the printer that accompanies most such computers. One proposer, anticipating that most if not all competitors would propose systems consisting of separate components interconnected by cables, proposed a teleprinter unit enclosed in a single housing as a monolithic unit. Their proposal used that word monolithic as a recurring theme in discussing design pros and cons, arguing for the advantages of their design versus the disadvantages and weaknesses of a design requiring separate units interconnected by cables.

It proved an effective device, helping greatly to support the major strategy, which was superiority of design. The client agreed and became convinced that it reflected an important idea and indicated superior design.

DESIGNING STRATEGIES FROM STRENGTHS

This chapter has barely penetrated the outer skin of the subject of strategies. A later chapter gets into specific tools, methods, and procedures, and it even offers forms for developing strategies. In the meanwhile, remember that one of the basic approaches to developing a win strategy is to first identify clearly the result the client seeks. Then inventory all your strengths and weaknesses—assets and liabilities—vis-à-vis the client's requirement. Next, study all the possible ways to achieve the desired result. Then select a way that enables you to utilize your own greatest strengths as a consultant while still being an effective way to achieve the desired result. Then devise the arguments to sell that approach to the client.

The next chapter probes the subject of selling your approach to the client, and it probes much more deeply both into the nature of persuasion generally as the essence of sales and marketing and into the specific dos and don'ts of sales activities.

CHAPTER 4

Some Basics of Sales and Marketing

> Despite the mystique that sometimes surrounds sales and marketing, the fundamental principles are quite easy to understand and are in themselves a basic explanation of human behavior in sales situations.

NEEDS, WANTS, AND THE GENTLE ART OF PERSUASION

There are many immutable truths in selling. They apply to all kinds of selling under all kinds of circumstances. They are, in fact, truths that apply to all kinds of persuasion, for selling is, of course, an act of persuasion. Sometimes, the buyer is persuaded by an effective sales presentation, sometimes simply by the appearance of the item, sometimes by a description of it, sometimes even by curiosity. Always, however, selling is an act of persuasion, even if the buyer is motivated by self-persuasion. (If someone buys something without being persuaded, that isn't selling, marketing, or advertising; it's simply order-taking.) Thus, to understand selling at its most fundamental level, it is necessary to understand the art of persuasion.

We all want most earnestly to believe that we are totally rational animals, logical thinkers, easily able to behave according to the dictates of reason. That is a truth, but a qualified one. We are, indeed, reasoning creatures, seeking to reach logical conclusions on which to base all our decisions and actions. However, with perhaps a rare exception here and there, we generally subordinate our reasoned conclusions to our emotional reactions and impulses, consciously or unconsciously. Who has never overcome restraining efforts of reason and yielded to an impulse to inflict verbal or even physical violence on someone else? Even when we regret so yielding or "losing control," as we often put it, have we not often rationalized our action and justified it by assuring ourselves that we had been "pushed too far"? Who has not bought something on impulse and regretted it later in that phenomenon that salespeople refer to as "buyer's remorse"?

We usually try to rationalize those decisions and conclusions we arrive at on an emotional basis, and we discard or reverse those decisions and conclusions only if we are unable to rationalize them satisfactorily. This is perhaps especially true in sales situations, as witness an example or two: When television receivers first appeared, shortly after World War II, they were quite expensive, as new luxuries tend to be. A few people bought receivers, but most of us felt unable to afford this new delight, much as we wanted it. The cost stayed our hands, preventing us from acting on that emotional desire to have this new toy. Some even rationalized that it was smart to wait until TV was "perfected" before buying a set. (Some individuals are reluctant to admit even to themselves that they cannot afford something they want and so rationalize even that situation.)

On the other hand, many who may have severely strained their financial resources wanted TV enough, even at those high original prices, to have managed to persuade themselves that they could afford it or that they really needed it. Today, there is still plenty of evidence for unrestrained and unwise buying behavior with the appearance of what some have called "credit card junkies."

Bear this emotional influence in mind, as we examine the subject of sales and marketing, and you will see evidence of this again and again, as suggested in an earlier chapter. Understanding of this is essential both to understanding all selling and to developing successful proposals, for it applies to the business world as much as to the nonbusiness world.

Chapter 2 briefly discussed the subject of needs and wants, pointing out that a need is usually perceived as an absolute requirement that is recognized through pure objective reason, whereas a *want* is something desired, although it may not be absolutely required. For example, owning my own word processing system was a perceived need for me and was the only reason I bought a personal computer, but the word-counting program, the spooler software, the A-B switch and modem, and many other additions were expensive wants because I could have managed quite well without them, as I had for many previous years.

On the other hand, although I did very well without those items for all those years, once I decided to want them, I had no difficulty convincing myself that they were needs and that I must have them. (I did write many books, proposals, articles, and other things on a typewriter before I owned a computer and word processor.) So while I regard all of these as needs, before I bought them they were wants, and as long as I felt unable to afford them, I persuaded myself that they would not really be of much use to me. My reasoning changed abruptly, however, when circumstances enabled me to afford a system of my own: I had no difficulty then in reframing that want as an absolute need, a need that had to be satisfied without further delay.

In fact, there is no practical difference between a want and a need, for marketing purposes. They are the same. The want becomes a need instantly when the individual succeeds in rationalizing the want—or when the effective sales presenter helps the client make the rationalization successfully.

That is the essence of all selling: Identify and stimulate the want, and provide or support the rationalization. The means for doing so, however, are somewhat varied, and these means are what sales and marketing are all about.

WHAT IS A NEED?

Sales experts sometimes identify two different kinds of needs, naming one a "felt" need and the other a need that has been "created." In general, this concept attempts to distinguish between the buyer who sets out deliberately to buy something he or she has already perceived as a need and the buyer who is persuaded to recognize or feel a need. Thus the idea of creating a need assumes that an effective sales presentation can induce a prospective buyer ("prospect") to want an item. There are two things wrong with this idea:

1. There is ample evidence that efforts to create needs by persuading uninterested prospects to become interested are almost always wasted. In fact, it is a truism that you cannot really sell a prospect anything the prospect has not persuaded himself or herself to become interested in.

2. Basic needs are really never new, and they have never changed throughout the course of human history. We have the same needs our ancestors had, even when they were living in caves.

The Felt Need

Some products and services are instant successes. Commercial radio and TV caught on with the public very quickly, as did movies, the personal computer, air travel, xerographic office copiers, express mail and package services, fast food establishments, and a great many other things. That means that the public quickly decided that they felt a need for these things without being prompted by advertising.

Can Needs be Created?

It might be said that these new developments created new needs by the simple fact of their availability. Obviously, one could not have a need (as marketers use the term) for something that did not exist and was not even dreamed of. (Or could they?) So it is valid to think of the rapid acceptance of new items as reflecting a need that had been heretofore unfilled and probably even unperceived.

On the other hand, perhaps there is another way to explain the swift success of these and many other new creations: Is it possible that these items succeeded almost instantly because they satisfied *felt* needs that had either never been satisfied before or they satisfied those felt needs in a far better way than they had ever been satisfied before? Let's consider this by identifying the needs some of these items serve.

Radio and TV are among the latest (the VCR—videocassette recorder—is *the* latest) home-entertainment devices. They were new and better ways of satisfying a long-standing need for entertainment, especially in the home. Witness what these relatively new home entertainment devices have done to theater attendance, public band concerts, public lectures, and many other older forms of pastime for adults.

Computers gained acceptance quickly, despite their great cost, but the acceptance and popularity of small calculators was almost an explosion. And if there is any doubt as to whether there has been a long-standing need for better means of making calculations, consider the Chinese abacus and how long it has been in existence.

The message here is plain enough, even as it was suggested in another context earlier: First determine what the client really wants—the truly *basic* want, that is, because that basic want is the client's need—and then show the client a better way to satisfy that need. If you can persuade the client to accept your argument that yours is truly a better way, success is almost inevitable.

Clients Do Not Always Recognize a Felt Need

Oddly enough, in the face of all that I have said here, the client's felt need is one that is often not felt consciously but only unconsciously. As many people have observed, they "know it when [they] see it," but presumably not until then. Consciously, they feel only a vague discontent, an unrest, an awareness that something is needed, and yet they are unable to actually "put [their] finger on it." That vague discomfort is a sensation somewhat akin to that of trying to recognize a face you know you ought to recognize or recall a name you know that you should know, some knowledge that probably lies deeply in your subconscious but won't come forth on command.

This comes through often in proposal requests and in statements of work written by clients, as they describe what they are unable to identify clearly enough to specify in detail. It is readily apparent in such cases that the client is troubled and feels a need for help (that is indeed the universal reason for seeking the services of a consultant), but often the help needed includes help in deciding what the problem is.

GOOD PROPOSALS HELP CLIENTS IDENTIFY THEIR NEEDS

Your proposal itself is a direct benefit to the client if it is truly a good one. The client is often unable to actually identify and define the problem accurately, and sometimes not able even to describe the symptoms with any great accuracy or detail. That makes your analysis of the client's work statement and resulting interpretation of the need a very important part of the proposal. The presence or the lack of effective preliminary analysis and need identification often becomes the critical difference between successful and unsuccessful proposals. If you do an effective job of identifying and defining the problem in your proposal, you do the client a great service by providing valuable education, improving considerably your position as a contender for the contract.

Many Clients Need Education

Many clients distinctly need education. Educating the client—selectively, that is, in terms of the immediate problem and its solution—is often the key to a successful main strategy. Of course, this must be done judiciously. Often enough, the client would not care to admit such a need as this and may even feel defensive about it. It's important to be aware of this, for obvious reasons, and to exercise a great deal of diplomacy in administering the necessary education. That aside, however, never underestimate the importance of client education; quite often, it is most needed by clients who appear to have the least need for it! Witness my own case, in regard to buying a computer and word processor.

With a fairly extensive technological background in modern electronics, including much experience with mainframe computers in a variety of major applications, I was sure that I fully understood the significance of personal computers and word processing. I thought myself to be in an especially privileged position in this respect. Moreover, as the successful professional writer of a large number of books and other publications, I was sure that I had a realistic grasp on what word processing would and would not mean to me as a writer.

I thought it would be pleasant and convenient to work with this new technological miracle, and I planned to do so eventually, but I didn't think that the use of word processing would contribute much to my efficiency or effectiveness. In fact, I was convinced that it would not greatly increase my productivity because I was already making free and effective use of all the time- and labor-saving cut-and-paste techniques I had learned in my years in the technical-publications industry, and I had even developed a few special techniques and tactics of my own, in this respect. I was thus able to keep the labor of retyping revised manuscript copy to a minimum.

Therefore, I did not see how this new system could do very much to increase the quality or reduce the labor of my writing because I already did what I believed to be at least an adequate amount of self-editing, rewriting, and revision, while minimizing the production labor these required.

I was wrong on all counts. I didn't find out how wrong I was until I began to use a word processor. The chief reason I decided that I could afford a word processor when I did was that I was beginning to write books about computers and their use, and I found it embarrassing, as well as ludicrous, to do so without owning a system of my own.

I believe that I would have bought one much earlier had I been properly educated by someone in what a word processor would really do for me—had I somehow gained a more accurate and insightful grasp of what word processing really is. (In retrospect, however, that is not too surprising, considering how few of the outpouring of printed words on the subject have shown a true appreciation of word processing. Relatively few users seem to understand it yet, and many tend to use it as an automatic typewriter, rather than learning how to gain the more valuable advantages of using it as the revolutionary new, different, and better way of writing that it is.)

When I did buy a system, after fairly extensive research, I bought one featured in full-page advertising in the *Writer's Digest*, that enduring journal of freelance writing that I have read for a great many years. (I think it was at that point, when I read that advertising, that I began to suspect that perhaps word processing offered more for the professional writer than I had previously believed.) Incidentally, inasmuch as word processing is reported as by far the most popular use of and outstanding reason for buying personal computers, it has always struck me as odd that so few manufacturers and distributors of personal computers have focused any significant portion of their advertising efforts on media and means for reaching writers. Further, what has been and is published on the subject tends to stress heavily the technical advantages of the system being touted, rather than its functional advantages. Virtually no advertising is devoted to explaining the true advantages of word processing over the more conventional means of writing. (A later chapter discusses ways to use computers and word processing to add leverage in proposal writing.)

This example reveals quite clearly a shortcoming of many marketers in failing to understand what business they are in.

WHAT BUSINESS ARE YOU IN?

When conducting seminars on proposal writing, I sometimes ask my attendees, "What business are you in?" I get such answers as these:

"We provide accounting services."

"We are marketing consultants."

"I am an interior designer."

"I teach people how to use their computers."

"We help clients design their office systems."

All these answers suffer from the same deficiency: Each definition of the business is focused on "we" or "I" and describes what the consultant sells or wishes to sell. None of these statements reflects what the client wishes to buy or even shows concern for (or is it awareness of?) the probable client want.

As everyone knows today, the railroads represent the classic case cited so often to illustrate the point. Becoming "fat, dumb, and happy," as modern vernacular puts it, the prosperous railroad magnates sneered at change and stubbornly insisted that they were in the railroad business, even as they watched their dwindling freight business being transferred to the huge tractor-trailers multiplying on the rapidly growing network of superhighways, while their vanishing passenger business was flowing to the growing number of airports, large and small. Only when they had begun to founder did they begin to reshape their thinking, but it was too late then to salvage more than a shadow of their former industry.

The problem is that each of us tends to think in terms of what we want rather than in terms of what the client wants. We even rationalize that what we want is what the client ought to want. Even when the subject of educating the client arises, most of us—at least until we come to know better through getting a proper education in the subject ourselves—believe that educating the client means making the client understand why what we want is what he or she ought to want.

Of course, this perspective gets it all backward. It is we who should want what the client wants. It is we who should—*must*—sell what the client wants, and we must identify and define our business in those terms. Even today, many do not understand what the railroads were or should have been selling. Some people who ought to know better believe that the railroads were actually in the "transportation business," but even that is a bit too abstract to come to real grips with what customers want and so to properly orient and focus marketing appeals. Customers do not want to buy "transportation," per se; they want to get their goods delivered to customers (as quickly as possible) and to get themselves to wherever they are going (as quickly and as comfortably as possible). Customers want these services provided efficiently, speedily, comfortably, conveniently, and economically (not necessarily in that order).

Airlines offer much greater speed in actual in-transit time than do railroads, although they do not offer as much convenience in many respects, due primarily to the remote locations of airports and the hassle of transportation to and from those airports. Nor do airlines always offer greater speed in total travel time, especially in short hauls of a few hundred miles where passengers spend much more time traveling to and from airports than they do in the air. Rail travel, in portal-to-portal terms, is often as rapid as air travel, as well as much more convenient, more comfortable, and less expensive. Had the railroads focused on those advantages and concentrated on increasing them, they would almost surely have retained much of their passenger business, especially the short-haul business.

Also, had the railroads thought out and maximized the advantages they could offer in freight forwarding—delivering the goods to customers— they would have kept much more of their freight business than they did. However, the railroads failed even to think out marketing strategies, much less to do anything to put them to work. That is, they did not do so until the damage was done, when it was too late to salvage very much, even with the help of the federal government and heavy subsidies, as the government struggles to prop up this white elephant that is becoming a dinosaur.

Few have learned from that classic case of the railroads, and many of us are making those same kinds of mistakes today, albeit on a smaller scale and in less dramatic industries. Unfortunately, nothing has changed very much.

The business you are in has nothing to do with what you want. It has everything to do with what the client wants. In a very large sense, we are all in the same business: helping the client. The differences among us are in how we help clients, or perhaps more accurately, in what help the client needs.

To help you to gain a firm grasp on this and to apply it to your own case, try your hand at the exercise presented in Figure 3. The idea here is to first study the typical consulting services numbered as 1 to 10, and then match up those services with the kinds of benefits suggested in the second part of

CONSULTING SPECIALTIES

1. Marketing services
2. Interior design
3. Office systems design
4. Computer systems specialist
5. Hypnotist

6. Speech coach
7. Publications specialist
8. Conference management
9. Investment advisor
10. Real estate appraiser

11. Your own specialty(ies) _____

_____

_____

PRIMARY BENEFITS

Maximize profits _____

Stop smoking _____

Save money _____

Be in style _____

Avoid making a mistake _____

Reduce risk _____

Raise efficiency _____

Increase sales _____

Gain personal prestige _____

Improve business image _____

_____

_____

_____

THE BUSINESS YOU ARE IN

_____

_____

_____

_____

Figure 3. Exercise sheet.

the figure by writing in the number(s) of each kind of service you believe can be fairly represented as offering that/those benefit(s). Of course, some of the services offer more than one kind of benefit or the benefit can be represented in more than one set of terms, so you should wind up with many more than 10 numbers written on the lines following the list of possible benefits.

You should also, at whatever point you wish to do so, add both a description of your own services and your own ideas as to benefits offered by any of these services, including your own. (That is the purpose of the blank lines provided.) That, conceiving of additional benefits and words with which to express them, is an important part of this exercise, designed to compel you to think seriously about this. This is an opportunity to orient and sharpen your thought processes regarding this aspect of marketing; the time you spend on this will be well spent.

Finally, go to the third part of the figure and write out a statement of the business you are in, as you now see it. Be sure that this is a statement that emphasizes what you do to help the client directly and in terms of *result*. Do not overlook the emotional element in articulating that main benefit. Don't worry about how many words you need to make your statement, and do actually write it out. Return to it later, and see whether you are still satisfied with that definition or you wish to revise it as you gain more insights into successful proposal-writing strategies and tactics.

Note also the point made earlier that the most basic appeals and motivators are emotional ones, not rational ones. Study those benefit items and note that most have an emotional appeal—to be in style, to gain personal prestige, to make more money, to improve one's business image.

This is not by chance. All experienced marketers and sales experts are well aware that the prime motivator is emotional, and that logic and reason play necessary but only supporting roles in marketing and sales.

MOTIVATORS

Earlier, you read that fear and greed are primary motivators. People act out of the desires both to gain what they want and to avoid what they fear. A great deal of evidence shows that fear is probably by far the more persuasive motivator. That is itself not too surprising, when you consider the ever-greater pressures of modern life and what that inevitably does to increase the sense of insecurity that most of us have to some degree. (In fact, is there anyone who is not insecure to at least some degree in this uncertain world?)

Motivators Are Emotional

Note carefully that these are emotional motivators. Study all successful advertising, especially those appearing on TV as commercials. You can easily tell which are the most successful ones: They are the ones that are repeated again and again, over a long period of time, excellent evidence that they are effective. Study these for emotional content, the common factor.

Invariably, successful advertising is addressed to the emotions, to what people are most likely to want to gain or avoid. Insurance, smoke detectors, burglar alarms, locks, security systems, safes, and many other items are sold principally through fear motivation, often with an appeal to guilt thrown in, as insurance advertisements urge prospects to remember their obligations to provide for their families, even after they are gone from this sphere. Many other items are sold through promises of gain—money, love, fun, prestige, and other such endowments. Sometimes advertisers manage to incorporate both kinds of motivators, as in the case of some securities advisors who promise to reduce the risks while helping you make profitable investments and even offer discounted stockbrokerage fees.

Sell Motivating Benefits—What the Item *Does*

Note how many of these successful advertisements do not even attempt to sell the product or service directly. Instead, they focus the major persuasive effort on the claimed benefit directly and then describe and sell the product or service only as the means to the benefit. Rare indeed are the advertisers who make even an effort to prove their product better than anyone else's product, except to support their claims of what the product does for the buyer. Kitchen or dishwasher detergents are not of better quality per se, in the TV commercials, for example; they simply produce better results, such as literally spotless glassware and dishes that shine so that you can see your face reflected in them.

Once the advertiser has established that claim of beneficial result, the time comes to support that claim with some evidence to help the prospect believe the promise of pleasing results.

"Prove" the Claim

Wherever possible, that "evidence" (which may or may not be legitimate evidence, but which the advertiser hopes the prospect will accept as evidence) is linked logically and directly to the qualities or characteristics of the product or service. For example, claims of better riding quality in an advertiser's automobile might be supported by technical or semitechnical descriptions of the suspension system. This is the best kind of evidence, usually, and it should be used when possible.

In some cases, it is not possible to link the promised blessing with the qualities of the product or with any direct claim to superiority of product. Beer is one such case. Beer advertisers rarely base their advertising on any claim of product superiority in quality. (Not only would that be almost impossible to prove, but beer drinkers couldn't care less about the technology of making beer or the logic of one method over another.) Rather, beer advertisers only suggest broadly that it's more fun to drink their beer by showing their beer being consumed in a good-times atmosphere. As another (less powerful) theme, they try to portray their product as the "in" product through commercials that attempt to prove that "everyone" (or at least everyone with good taste) buys their product.

In another case, where there is no logical basis (and probably no valid basis) on which to lay a claim of superiority, the advertiser might simply claim superiority and "substantiate" that with testimonials by some public figure from the sports or entertainment world. An alternative is to show an actor dressed appropriately as an authority with relevance to the advertised product or service, such as in a white laboratory coat, offering the "expert opinion."

Humans have a herd instinct, too, and they tend to join the flock rather than go it alone. Probably this is another manifestation of our common sense of insecurity, but it can be used effectively in marketing. The influence of testimonials and other data that demonstrates widespread acceptance of your product or service is not entirely logical, nor is it real evidence that yours is a good product or service. It is also an emotional appeal to the human instinct to join the crowd and to agree with the popular view. This may be another manifestation of fear motivation, reflecting the fear many of us have to go it alone.

Sell Only What the Client Wants

I once had the opportunity to observe an outstandingly successful Fuller Brush salesman at work. His technique was really quite simple. He went through his entire case of samples—he carried perhaps 30 to 40 items—showing each to the customer with a few words of introduction, watching the customer's eyes intently. If the eyes remained vacant, he went on. If he detected a spark of interest, he stopped and began to sell that item, usually with great success.

There were many other aspects to his technique, but this was the basic one, and it was the one that most clearly explained this man's basic success. He understood that it was impracticable and wasteful of time to try to sell something the prospect was not really interested in, when the time could be invested much more profitably in selling something in which the prospect showed some immediate interest. His tactic was simply to find out which items stirred the prospect's interest, and to do so as quickly as possible so he could get on to the more important business of getting the maximum-sized orders for those items. (He also had effective techniques for maximizing those orders, but that is not relevant here.)

That's a universal truth. You can't sell the client what the client really does not want. The most effective tactic is to find out first what the client really wants, but remember that clients often do not know what they want or are not fully conscious of that want. ("I know it when I see it!") At least, this is often true in the sense that they do not know precisely how to identify or specify what they want, and they need your help in doing so.

We All Sell the Same Thing

Buyers are motivated by the desire to gain or avoid things. From the sellers' viewpoint, we all sell the same thing: help. And while that is true for everyone who sells anything, it is especially true for consultants because the desire for help is usually the conscious and direct objective of clients who go in quest of consulting services. We sell help in avoiding things, help in gaining things, help in achieving things. Even more fundamentally than that, it is not help itself that we sell, but the *promise* of help.

A BASIC MARKETING PROBLEM

Why is it important to recognize that fact—that what we sell is the *promise* of help? It is important because it illustrates both the basic difficulty in selling consulting services and the importance of the proposal in marketing those services. It is important to have a realistic appreciation of the marketing problem, with all its difficulties. Of course, selling a prospect a tangible object, even such a costly one as an automobile or house, is far less difficult than selling any intangible, such as a service. Also, regarding services, there are sublevels of marketing difficulty too, for it is obviously far easier to sell mundane, workaday services such as automobile repair and accounting services than it is to sell the relatively sophisticated and mysterious services known as "consulting." Further, when the sophisticated services mandate that the client entrust a stranger, no matter how well recommended, with confidential information and perhaps even with the welfare of a business enterprise, clients need a great deal of reassurance before they agree to undertake the risk.

In the face of this almost overwhelming need for gaining the client's complete confidence if you are to win the contract, it is not surprising that conventional advertising does not generally work well for consultants. It also explains why the proposal must be considerably more than a brochure and a quotation of prices and terms. It must satisfy a number of requirements, at the minimum, including the following:

- A persuasive demonstration that you fully understand and appreciate the client's need
- A believable promise of help that is appropriate to the client's perception of need
- Evidence that you can and will deliver that promised help
- Evidence that you are a dependable and trustworthy consultant.

CHAPTER 5

Gathering Market Intelligence

The effectiveness with which the consultant gathers information and the quality of the information gathered often make the difference between winning and losing the proposal competition.

THE BASIC SOURCES OF INFORMATION

The quality of your proposal—any proposal—inevitably depends on the quantity and quality of the information on which it is based. That is true about proposals generally, but it is especially true as it applies to the approaches and strategies on which you base your proposal. It's hard to imagine how you can devise effective approaches and strategies without adequate and accurate information, properly organized and properly used.

Much of your proposal content stems entirely from your own knowledge, judgment, analysis, and creative imagination, but there must be other sources and other information also. In fact, your own cognitive and creative processes also depend on those other sources. This applies equally to the formal and informal proposals submitted in response to specific requests from clients and to the unsolicited proposals you submit as a voluntary follow-up to earlier marketing contacts and initiatives.

Gathering the intelligence necessary to the development of a successful proposal is rarely easy. It requires a great deal of effort, imagination, resourcefulness, and even ingenuity. But that effort and resourcefulness are often what make the difference.

There are many potential sources of information—market intelligence—to support your proposal-writing effort. Following are some of the typical ones:

1. The client's RFP (request for proposal)
2. Conversations with the client
3. Other client materials, such as brochures and reports
4. Other readily available public information about the client
5. Your own experience, knowledge, and judgment
6. Your proposal library and files
7. Study/analysis of the requirement and related research
8. Special methods and sources
9. Public databases

Some of these items are self-explanatory or have been referred to earlier; others merit some special consideration and discussion here.

THE CLIENT'S RFP

Reading a Proposal Request

The sardonic observation that enjoins us, "When all else fails, read the instructions," comes to mind here; we often neglect to take advantage of the primary and most important source of information: the request for proposals and its work statement. Surprisingly often, the answers to questions that arise in your mind and the information you seek in developing a proposal are readily at hand in those documents but are still overlooked.

It is easy to understand why this is so. The client's statement of the requirement and other portions of the RFP are often neither well organized nor fluently expressed, and that can easily lead you astray. Impatient to get on with important work, you are unwilling to engage in what appears to be a waste of time because the quality of the writing suggests that there is little of value to be gained from study of the request.

That is not the only problem. You must also guard against an unconscious tendency to leap to conclusions in reading the request and especially in reading what is not there. (It's quite easy to see what you expect to see rather than what is actually written there, and in reading proposal requests, this tendency must be specifically guarded against.) This often leads to offering the client a ready-made solution that may be a reasonable approach but not the best one and perhaps not even the most relevant one.

Acres of Diamonds

Despite the apparent uselessness of much of the written material that forms the RFP, the contrary often proves to be true. Again and again, after lengthy investigation into other sources, I have found that the information I needed was in the request, after all. Quite often, the search through the formal request is a painstaking one and not at all easy, but it is almost always more efficient than most other ways you can pursue and uncover the information. Moreover, it is almost always more reliable information than any you can gather in any other manner. The time spent in studying the client's representation of requirements and what is wanted in the proposal is usually a worthwhile investment.

One of the reasons many consultants miss so much information of importance in reading the client's request is that they often content themselves with a single reading of the request and an occasional brief review. That is rarely sufficient. The first reading of the typical request normally produces only a superficial understanding of the client's needs and desires. One of the benefits of preparing the checklists recommended in Chapter 6 is the enforcement of a discipline in the reading, compelling you to read with great care, as you deliberately and consciously search out specific items for your lists. (Even if the preparation of the lists did nothing more than that, the time would be well spent.) Additional readings, as you study the problem and begin to develop an approach and design, have greater significance than the earlier readings because you then have specific questions and are in quest of specific information. Ergo, it is quite important to continue to reread the client's request continually, while you are developing the proposal. Regard it as your primary source of information.

Serendipitous Finds

Finding answers to specific questions or finding specific information you believe you need is one reason for that careful and continual study of the request. Another is that without studying the request, you might simply miss some important piece of information, perhaps even something that will spell the difference between success and failure to win the award. Sometimes information that seemed trivial on the first reading assumes great importance after you have worked on the proposal for a while and have developed a much more in-depth appreciation of what you need to know to write the winning proposal. You must therefore satisfy yourself that you have indeed extracted everything of worth to be extracted from the request.

Reading Between the Lines

Another common mistake some consultants make in reading a client's request is to assume that anything not stated plainly is simply not present in the request. That is, they fail even to make the effort to read between the lines, much less to do so effectively. Often, the most valuable information lies there, between the lines, information that is implicit and not explicit but still useful information.

You may have to be something of a detective to read between the lines well, but doing so is often the key to winning. If you do not tend by instinct to think deductively, train yourself to do so. You will greatly increase what you can infer from your reading.

Information often is or appears to be implied, rather than stated plainly. That may be due to nothing more or less than simple weakness in writing or a peculiarity in the writer's style. Some clients are simply unable to express themselves as clearly as we would prefer them to, or they have a difficult writing style—a not-unusual circumstance. In other cases, the subtlety is deliberate; there may be "political" considerations in the client's organization that prevent the client from writing as plainly as he or she would wish, and that compel the client to do little more than hint at certain facts. Also, sometimes there is a specific effort to hold back certain information for such reasons, but the information gap is often quite apparent. The resourceful consultant will often be aware that such a gap exists and may even be able to gauge what it is that is being withheld. There may also be a personal bias in the client's view of a situation—also a not-unusual condition. Whatever the reasons for the obfuscation, it is important for you to gain a clear and objective view.

CONVERSATIONS WITH THE CLIENT

Information received verbally from the client is second in usefulness and value only to that contained in a formal written RFP. (In some cases, it may even exceed that source in importance.) In fact, in the case of submitting an unsolicited proposal on your own initiative, there will be no formal written request, and perhaps not even a verbal one, from the client. It is especially important to have made notes of your conversations, preferably during the conversations, but certainly immediately afterward, while your recall is fresh. It may be possible to tape-record the conversation, but be sure that the client does not object to this: Ask for permission to do so. Be aware, however, that even when permission is given, there may be a down side to recording: Many people are much more guarded in their remarks when a tape recorder is running, and so even with permission to record, it is not always beneficial.

In responding to formal requests, especially with any government organization, it is a mistake to ask questions that you do not truly need the answers to (and you can almost always find a way to write your proposal without asking those questions). You often give away more than you get by asking questions.

In the case of an unsolicited proposal or one that you are asked for informally and are the only one so invited, it is different. It is usually safe to ask questions now. However, first explore all accessible avenues of information, especially that of available client materials. It is embarrassing and often harmful to your image to have the client point out that he or she has already supplied the information you seek or that it is readily available elsewhere.

OTHER CLIENT MATERIALS

Often, regardless of other circumstances surrounding the situation, you can gain access to many kinds of client materials, such as annual reports, brochures, newsletters, and article reprints. Whatever sources you have, you ought to utilize these also, and you should keep such materials in your proposal library and resource files. Study all such materials to learn as much as possible about the client before deciding on your proposal strategy and approach.

OTHER READILY AVAILABLE PUBLIC
INFORMATION ABOUT THE CLIENT

There are often other sources of information about the client, especially if
the client is a well-established organization. There are, for example, D&B
(Dun & Bradstreet) reports, listings and descriptions in various kinds of
directories (e.g., the *Thomas Register, Standard & Poor,* the D&B *Million
Dollar Directory,* and the Facts on File *Directory of Major Public Corporations*) and various other public sources of information, most of them
available in any well-stocked public library. These sources tell you a great
deal about the client and provide valuable input and idea starters for your
proposal effort. Too, if the clients are business firms, read the appropriate
business periodicals, including the daily newspaper financial sections and
the financial newspapers, the *Wall Street Journal* and the *New York Times.*

YOUR OWN EXPERIENCE, KNOWLEDGE,
AND JUDGMENT, AND YOUR
PROPOSAL LIBRARY AND FILES

One marketing resource you should have been building up from the day you
entered practice is your proposal library and files. Work at maintaining this
resource, and it expands and improves steadily; your proposal success
should then likewise continue to expand and improve.

There are several basic elements to a proposal library:

- Swipe files
- Copies of your own proposals
- Competitors' proposals
- Competitor information
- Reference books
- Client information

Swipe Files

Cut and paste techniques have long existed. Once, one kept "swipe files,"
a vast assortment of materials that had potential use elsewhere, in the form
of sheets of typed material, clippings from newspapers and magazines,

handwritten notes, and other such materials. Much of each new proposal consisted of such material arranged in some order and handed over to a secretary or typist to be typed up into a rough-draft manuscript. That draft was then edited, reviewed, revised, and polished for final typing or typesetting. Later, as xerographic copiers became available, original swipe files were left undisturbed, and xerographic copies were cut and pasted together.

Today, that has changed again. Much of the material included in today's swipe files are on computer disks, and they can be printed out for conventional cut-and-paste makeup. However, they can also be handled far more efficiently by electronic cut and paste, such as can be done with any modern word processor. With modern scanners, even clippings and other hard copy—printed materials—can often be translated easily into computer files.

Copies of Your Own Proposals

Those proposals you have written in the past that were successful in winning contracts are valuable as models, because they are models of and for success. However, that does not mean that the remaining proposals, those that did not win contracts, have no value. There is much in them that is useful. They are or have items that are salvageable for other use, so they should not be discarded; they should be filed as permanent items in your proposal library.

For one thing, many of those contain valuable analyses and studies that will save you a great deal of time and money, and they often even make it possible to write a new proposal that would not be viable if you had to write it all from scratch. They also often contain many illustrations, tables, discussions, and arguments that you can use again and again, sometimes with minor modifications, but often without even these.

In this respect, these proposals are part of your swipe files, as well as models for future guidance, and they should be so regarded. They should be stored as computer files, as well as printed copies, for the greater facility in handling and using them that this affords.

Competitors' Proposals

When opportunities arise to get copies of competitors' proposals, take advantage of them, and study those competitive proposals. Become deeply conscious of a need to get copies of competitors' proposals, and opportunities to do so will arise.

Competitor Information

Collect information about competitors as eagerly as you collect information about clients and potential clients. Gather and store competitors' brochures, articles, newsletters, catalogs, capability statements, and other information. Be alert for materials when you attend conferences, conventions, trade shows, seminars, and other such conclaves.

Reference Books

If you maintain an adequate library, you can carry out a great deal of your research without stirring from your desk. *Everything* with potential usefulness for proposal effort belongs in your library.

Client Information

Deposit those clippings about your clients and potential clients, as well as brochures, annual reports, and all other information relevant to clients and prospective clients.

Miscellaneous papers, drawings, price lists, catalogs, reports, and other such items all belong in your proposal reference files as part of your proposal library. Give serendipity a maximum chance to happen.

DATABASE MANAGEMENT

All of this material constitutes a *database*, which is simply a collection of related information. This database is your entire proposal library and reference files. Or it may be several databases if you prefer to organize the material into several such sets of files, such as a *competitor* database, an *own proposals* database, a *swipe files* database, and others. You can do either, but the practical criterion is one of size: When files or sets of files—such as databases—get too large, they become unwieldy and difficult to manage and manipulate. *Manipulate* includes such functions as adding to files, sorting them, and searching them to find what you are looking for, so it is probably wise to establish several database files.

You may not have thought of database management software as a writer's tool; most people probably don't regard it as such. However, it is valuable as a research tool when you have the banks of material organized into files. Once you have built up those banks of swipe files, old proposals, competitors' proposals, resumes, current and past projects, and other such materials, they begin to become somewhat unmanageable if you must rely on your memory or random searching to find what you want. That's when you need the database management software.

Database management (DBM) programs enable you to organize your databases for searching, retrieving, sorting, and other manipulating. The effectiveness of these depends on the wisdom of your design, for DBM software permits you great flexibility in designing the system according to your own ideas and preferences. In a sense, a DBM program is clay that you may shape and mold to your own preference. Therein lies its great power.

If you design your database properly, you can sort files by competitors' names, by types of programs, by types of skills, or by any parameter for which you anticipated a need and provided tags. You can also print out a variety of reports, tables, and listings of various kinds, again largely dependent on your own ideas and preferences. Database management is therefore almost essential for the maintenance of an effective proposal library.

STUDY/ANALYSIS OF THE REQUIREMENT AND SPECIAL RESEARCH

Naturally, you will be studying and analyzing the client's requirement. Sometimes, special studies and research are required to carry out a proper analysis of the requirement. It may not be possible to do this yourself, if the effort requires an excessive investment in the proposal. As an alternative to dropping the proposal, you may wish to consider an arrangement with another consultant, one whose field enables him or her to handle the special study as a routine analysis. You can be coproposers and partners in any resulting contract, one of you may subcontract to the other, or you may be able to find some other mutually agreeable business arrangement.

SPECIAL METHODS AND SOURCES

There are many situations where special and even unorthodox methods of intelligence-gathering are necessary to maximize your probabilities of winning. These problems call often for imagination and resourcefulness, and the contracts tend to go to those who gather the information they need.

Advertising for Information

One project called for operating a client-owned installation that employed a number of people. The grapevine reported that the client was unhappy with the incumbent contracting firm and would like to make a change, if the client could find someone suitable.

The RFP, while not cryptic, was not enlightening either. It did not specify, for example, how many people were employed by the incumbent, and it did not furnish much information about those employees' specialties, the total payroll the contractor would have to handle, or any of a number of other details one would usually want to have to support a proposal development.

The successful proposer ran carefully worded help-wanted advertisements, designed specifically to draw responses from those currently employed in the project, and specifying that respondents must submit up-to-date résumés.

Résumés resulted in abundance, with a satisfying number coming from those working on the project in question. The résumés received were a motherlode of priceless information, but the proposer also invited some of the respondents—those who appeared to be key people and therefore knowledgeable of important details—to visit and be interviewed. These interviews produced even more useful information. The proposer reported later that she had never had more precise or more accurate information, and she had little difficulty developing a powerful proposal that won the contract.

In a somewhat analogous but different case, a consultant found herself invited to propose an on-premises project several states away. The project required the hiring of several local people to do certain specialized work on the client's premises. Uncertain as to local rates for the kinds of specialists required in the client's area, the consultant placed advertisements in a local newspaper and arranged to travel there to conduct interviews. As a result of those interviews, she acquainted herself with the local supply of qualified labor for the project, learned what rates she would have to pay, made tentative arrangements to hire several people, and got permission to incorporate their résumés in her successful proposal.

This is not uncommon. Many small consulting firms, and even some not-so-small firms, use this method for gathering résumés of qualified individuals to be included in their proposals. In the course of doing this, the truly alert proposal writer manages to gather a great deal of useful information, even if that is not the specific reason for requesting the résumés.

Clipping Services

To avoid the time-consuming work of the reading and clipping you would have to do to build files on clients and prospective clients, you can buy the service from any clipping service. For a per-clipping fee, such agencies scan newspapers and magazines for you and clip out items you specify. (PR [public relations] firms, for example, order items about their own clients, to check on their own effectiveness and to provide clients with proof of results.)

PUBLIC DATABASES

Computer Online Database Services

One way to get a great deal of research done without leaving your desk is to order information from any of a growing number of online public databases. This can be done with almost any personal computer equipped with a modem, which permits your computer to "talk" to another. In one case, I was able, for about $100, to carry out in an hour research that would have cost me several days otherwise, and even then, it would have produced less precise and less reliable data as a result. With the right equipment, this becomes as convenient and easy as an ordinary telephone call.

There are many online databases available to anyone equipped to reach them via modem-equipped computer and dial-up (touch-tone) telephone line. Several popular and well-known online services serve the general public, such as The Source and CompuServe. Many specialized ones, however, are designed primarily to serve the needs of specific interests, such as lawyers, engineers, retailers, government contractors, bankers, investment brokers, the medical profession, and others. The fees charged for subscriptions and access to most of these are relatively modest as an ordinary business expense.

Here are just a few suggestions for using your personal computer in the intelligence-gathering effort:

- General information
- Online programming services
- Machine-readable files
- Collaborative efforts
- Electronic bulletin boards
- Fax services

Gathering Information Generally

Proposal writing is almost always done under difficult, impossibly tight schedules. So there is often not enough time to wait for information to arrive via the mails. There are other ways to get information: It is often possible to get information immediately, via access to some of the online databases. For example, D&B operates its own online database service, and there are many others; the number has been growing. Following are just a few of the kinds and names of databases made available by the online services. (These were selected from a list of GTE Telenet users, which alone includes some 300 different databases offered by over 100 information services, still by no means a complete listing of such resources, which continue to grow steadily.)

APTIC—air pollution control	Dialog Information Services
AVLINE—AV programs on health sciences	National Library of Medicine
BOOKS INFO—data on books in print	Brodart Co.
CITIDATA—financial indicators	Citishare Corporation
DRUG INFORMATION—data on 1,100 drugs	GTE Telenet
GRANTS—federal, state, local grants	SDC Search Information Services
HAZARDLINE—2,000 hazardous substances	Occupational Health Services

MANAGEMENT—business/ management literature	SDC Search Information Services
MERLIN—technical database on securities	Remote Computing
MNT—literature on mining technology	TEXT Information Services
MORT—mortgage amortization program	QL Systems Limited
PATSEARCH—patent information	Pergamon InfoLine

Online Programming Services

One service offered by a number of online systems is that of assistance in running computer programs, in those cases where the consultant's personal computer is not suitable for the task.

Computer conferencing	Electronic mail
Financial analysis	Job costing
Inventory control	Pension management
Econometric modeling	Communications network design
Energy auditing	Simulation and modeling
Flowcharting	Market research
Mapping	Media research

Machine-Readable Library Files

Your proposal library does not necessarily consist solely of ink and paper. Quite the contrary, in many ways it is more useful to have as much of your library as possible in machine-readable ("machinable") form, which means that it's in some form that your computer can scan—usually magnetic recordings on tape or disks. The advantages of putting as much of your library as possible in machinable form are several:

- The files are more readily accessible—much more easily found because the computer itself helps find the right files quickly.
- The information in individual files can be found more quickly

because, again, the computer can help with this through its search
functions.

- It's easy to copy and/or print out files or portions of files for use in
your research studies.

It is not suggested that you "computerize" (convert to machinable form)
those library materials that you acquire as ink-and-paper materials. The
labor involved in doing so is usually too great to be a practical option.
However, much of the information you accumulate for your library, such as
your own prior proposals and data files acquired earlier in prior information
searches via computer and online databases, should be saved and filed in
their original magnetic form, rather than in hard copy (printout) versions.
And that points out another advantage machinable files offer: Paper files
become so voluminous that finding or making space for them often
becomes a problem in itself and compels you to consider whether it is
worthwhile to keep them at all, much less whether to devote valuable live-
storage space to them. (And, of course, the minute you place old files in dead
storage, you have need for them and must go in search of them.)

That is not a problem with computer storage media, for a desk drawer and
even a desktop can hold many thousands of pages worth of information
when it is in magnetic form. (The equivalent of approximately 8,000 pages
of typed material resides within arm's reach on my own desk, as floppy
diskettes stored in two convenient disk "trees," with several times that
amount of recorded data within a step or two of my desk.) The storage case
alone makes it possible for most of us to maintain a much larger resource
library than we would be able to do without the aid of the computer.

Collaborative Efforts

When you undertake a joint effort with another specialist to help you write
your proposal, as suggested in an earlier paragraph, the problems of
proximity and schedule coordination sometimes arise. Working together on
a proposal requires frequent discussions and exchanges in a close coordination. It is rarely that each of you can work independently on portions of
the proposal, in relative isolation from each other, and find that it all fits
together properly in the end. The personal computer can solve problems of

schedule conflicts and long distances between you and your collaborator. Even incompatible systems can communicate with each other via modem and telephone lines, so you can work closely together without either of you leaving your own office. Through intercomputer linkage you can exchange copy, comments, ideas, and almost anything else you might otherwise do in a face-to-face meeting.

Broadcasting Requests

With the great number of electronic bulletin board systems (BBSs) in operation today, it is possible to reach many individuals rather easily and inexpensively by posting messages on a number of boards. I have used this approach a number of times in researching information for projects. In one case, I wanted to conduct a survey among independent consultants, so I placed a message on a number of BBSs inviting interested individuals to participate. I sent questionnaires to those who responded, and I was able to do my survey without leaving my desk! (The results were part of the input information for this book.) I have also used this method many times to gather anecdotes, opinions, and case histories for other projects.

Using Fax Facilities

Your resources should include a fax (facsimile) machine or, at least, a fax board in your computer. (The standalone fax machine is probably more convenient and more versatile.) Fax enables almost instantaneous transmission of printed materials. There have been occasions when my request, transmitted by fax, brought back a magazine article or other response within an hour. There have also been occasions when a client has sent me materials by fax for my comment, so I was able to read them and respond within an hour or two.

Fax machines range widely in price. My own is a Murata 1200, a simple "low end" model of good repute that is quite efficient, if it is also devoid of "features," such as automatic dialing and automatic paper cutting. It is a $900 (list) machine that I was able to buy at $600. At the other end, there are fax machines selling for as much as $4,000, offering many convenient features.

GETTING INFORMATION FOR DEVELOPMENT
OF GOVERNMENT PROPOSALS

The government issues many contracts for consulting services, although most of the contracts are not characterized as consulting services for a variety of reasons. The problems of writing proposals to government agencies are similar to, and yet in some respects somewhat different from, those of writing proposals in the commercial markets.

The Freedom of Information Act

These differences and similarities apply to the gathering of intelligence, as they do to all other aspects of proposal development. A great deal of information is readily available about government agencies and their programs, and you can gather up a large library of materials, much of it free. However, there is also one significant difference between intelligence-gathering for the development of proposals to government agencies and that for developing commercial proposals. A federal law makes it mandatory for government agencies to release, on demand or of their own volition and initiative, all information that is not classified—affecting national security—and/or does not infringe on individual privacy or the right to hold certain information proprietary and confidential. That law is, of course, the Freedom of Information Act.

Under that act, you have the right to demand certain information that is properly public information—bought with tax money. The following are typical items of information you can and should normally request:

- What the government is now paying for a given service (in the case of a competitive procurement to continue a service now being provided)
- The name of the incumbent contractor
- A copy of the successful proposal (Confidential and proprietary data will be excised from the copy you get.)
- Copies of reports and/or other documents generated earlier in the performance of the contract or related contracts

- Records of work required and performed under the existing or earlier contracts

In connection with these items, you can often get these even without invoking the Freedom of Information Act by visiting the agency's library and reading some of the reports and other documents on the shelves. And in some cases, a visit to a Government Printing Office bookstore will produce a great deal of useful information available in publications of the Government Printing Office.

It should be noted, in connection with using the Freedom of Information Act, that you may run into difficulties on occasion if you do not specifically invoke the act when asking for the information. Some bureaucrats take advantage of the technicality that unless you specifically state that you are invoking that law, they still have the right to refuse the information. There are also some who will insist that the request must be in writing, so be prepared to meet this challenge too. If you are unfortunate enough to encounter such an individual, remember that you are not asking for a favor; you are asking for what must be provided under the law. You have the right to insist on it.

Government Publications

The Government Printing Office today has nothing free or even inexpensive. Every publication they sell in their bookstores costs money. However, every publication in their bookstores was originally ordered and paid for by a federal agency. (It is when the GPO—Government Printing Office—thinks the publication to be salable to the public that they run extra copies and stock them in their bookstores.) In many cases, the agency that ordered the printing has copies available on request free of charge. If you can determine which agency ordered the printing of any publications that interest you, you can ask the agency for a copy.

You can also write or call federal agencies and ask for publications by their general nature, such as publications on purchasing and procurement. Do this with the DOD (Department of Defense), the General Services Administration, and other agencies.

Check also with the Department of Commerce and the Small Business Administration for their publications, many of which are free or sold at nominal prices.

Government Electronic Bulletin Boards

Many federal agencies operate their own electronic bulletin boards today. In the Washington area, for example, there are bulletin boards operated by or for the Department of Commerce, the DOD, the General Services Administration, NASA (National Aeronautics and Space Administration), and others. (Listings of these are supplied in a later chapter.)

CHAPTER 6 _____

Making a Beginning

Success in marketing rarely occurs by chance. It comes to those who think
ahead, plan ahead, and act accordingly.

WHEN IS THE RIGHT TIME TO MARKET?

I have no doubt that the single most common cause of failure in consulting
enterprises is the failure to market effectively. One reason for this is a failure
by many new to consulting to understand that consulting is not a "one-call"
business. Marketing success results only from steady, persistent, long-term
effort.

What this means, practically, is that you can never afford to neglect
marketing. Most assignments result from spade work done many moons
earlier. If you are the typical newcomer to the field, you began or will begin
practice with a single client, or perhaps even without an initial client. Once
working on your first project, you will give little or no thought to the day
when you must find new clients. Instead, as one new to the field, you wait
until you finish that first assignment to begin looking for another client and
another assignment. However, the marketing of consulting services normally produces clients and assignments only months, sometimes many
months, after making the marketing contacts. Unfortunately, while waiting
to land that next client, you may find yourself unable to survive. This failure
to understand marketing is responsible for a great deal of turnover in the
ranks of independent consultants.

This situation is not inevitable; there is a way to prevent the problem from arising: advance planning—prevention, rather than cure. The time for marketing is today—every day, starting with the day you decide to launch an independent practice. As an independent consultant, you cannot afford ever to be too busy to maintain marketing activities. It's part of the price for being an independent consultant. Make time for it.

Proposal writing is an important part of marketing, but much work must precede the proposal writing. For example, the successful marketer reviews many opportunities to write proposals, more than you can or should respond to. That raises the question of the need to make the inevitable bid/no-bid decision. This decision is an important element of marketing.

BID/NO-BID DECISION MAKING

Every proposal represents a serious commitment by you. In fact, it really represents two commitments: One is the pledge of what you propose as a firm offer to the client. The second is the time and money you spend in writing the proposal. In many cases, the latter is by far the greater commitment; while many proposals are relatively minor efforts (e.g., the simple and informal ones known popularly as "letter proposals"), many others are major undertakings, with large investments of time and money.

For this reason, large organizations that write many major proposals and get all or most of their business in this manner often have formal systems for analyzing each bid opportunity and making decisions on whether or not to submit a bid in each case. Many of these firms have standard forms with which to document and report the results of each such analysis. Figure 4 typifies such designs and is the basis for the following discussion of bid/no-bid analytical procedures.

Analytical Procedure

The RFP head data on the form are self-explanatory, serving merely to identify the bid opportunity and list its basic characteristics. The significance of some of the other entry blanks provided may not be as apparent now, but it should become so as the discussion progresses.

First of all, such an analysis is rarely cut-and-dried but is almost always

RFP HEAD DATA

Title: _____ Due: _____

Client: _____

Requirement summary: _____

_____

Formal proposal [ ] Ltr. proposal [ ] With pricing [ ] Separate pricing [ ]

EVALUATIVE ESTIMATES

Est. value ($):_____ Est. bid/proposal effort (hrs): _____

Probable competition: _____

_____

*Rank order (vis-a-vis other bid opportunities available now): No. _____

Our major strength: _____

_____

Our major weakness: _____

_____

RATIONALE

*Arguments pro: _____

_____

*Arguments con: _____

_____

CONCLUSION AND RECOMMENDATION

Est. win probability (%):_____ *Recommendation: Bid [ ] No bid [ ]

*REMARKS

_____

_____

*Consider all related factors.

Figure 4. Bid/no-bid analysis and reporting form.

linked to conditions of the moment. That is, the bid opportunity that you might eagerly seize on one occasion, you may turn down on another occasion, depending on such variables as your current in-house workload, how urgently you need new work, and spin-off benefits (e.g., getting a foot in the door with a new client or diversifying experience and market possibilities). Therefore, on one occasion you might invest time and money to write a proposal for which you rate your chances at only 25 percent, whereas at another time you would not undertake any proposal unless you rated your prospects for winning at 75 percent or more.

It is largely for these reasons that a relatively large section is provided at the bottom of Figure 4 for remarks, immediately following the space provided to record your conclusions and recommendations. In that remarks section, the evaluator or evaluators (in larger organizations or where you are working with other consultants and considering a cobid, there may be several people making independent evaluations and then meeting to discuss them) record pertinent observations and recommendations. Motivation also may vary and is not always profit for its own sake: On some occasions, an organization undertakes a project at cost or on a very narrow profit margin because the work is needed to keep the organization going or there is some spin-off benefit that makes the risk worthwhile.

Measures to Increase the Likelihood of Success

The uncertainties and the transient conditions that have such profound effects on decisions are realities over which you do not always have any control. However, you can pursue a few marketing measures that will help you to increase the odds in your favor and to vastly improve your proposal "batting average" over what it might otherwise be:

   1. Do everything possible to receive a maximum number of opportunities to prepare and submit bids and proposals. The more such opportunities you have, the more selective you can be in choosing only those that appear to offer you the greatest possibilities for success. However, do not confine these efforts to getting yourself on as many bidders' lists as possible. Instead, take advantage of every opportunity to submit unsolicited proposals either where you believe you have a fair chance of winning a contract or where, at least, the cost in time and money is relatively insignificant. Proposals that do not win contracts are not always a total waste: If they are truly superior proposals, though they still may not win a contract, they do win the client's attention and often lead to other opportunities. Therefore, almost every well-written and well-thought-out proposal is a worthwhile marketing activity.

2. Maintain constant intelligence-gathering to maximize your knowledge of competitor activities. Gather as many of your competitors' brochures as possible, and be alert also to opportunities to acquire copies of their proposals. (Such opportunities do arise, but you must be alert for them.) Remember that the quality of any proposal is linked directly to and dependent on the quality of the information on which it was based.

3. Build the most extensive proposal library you can manage, including competitor literature, copies of your own proposals, useful boilerplate materials and swipe files, reference books, rosters and résumés of specialists you might need for future projects, and whatever else might help your proposal efforts. If you are using a computer and word processor, you should also have a disk library, with as much material in disk files as possible.

4. Try to evaluate the possibilities of follow-on work with current clients so that you can consider this too in assessing your probable need for new contracts and project assignments. You often get surprising benefits by simply being honest and direct. Try telling your clients frankly that you are planning your schedules for the near future and need help in anticipating your probable workload.

5. Keep in touch with clients you did work for in the past. Conditions change in client companies. People move about. Departments are reorganized. It is easy to be forgotten or overlooked, even by those who were most enthusiastic about the work you did. It's your job to see to it that they do not forget you. Keep them on your mailing list for brochures, sales letters, and announcements. Call on the telephone and in person to say "hello" and remind them that you are still in practice and available to help solve problems.

PREPARATIONS FOR PROPOSAL WRITING

One of the most common mistakes in proposal writing is that of beginning to write too soon, before doing the necessary advance planning and preparation. The consequence of that haste is often a rough-draft proposal that requires more work to revise than it is possible to do in the time allowed for proposal submittal, compelling you to submit a proposal that is not your best possible presentation. In some cases, the cost of the revision is far too great with respect to the size of the contract.

The only way to minimize rewriting and revision is to plan ahead before you begin to write so that you know your precise objectives in advance and you have planned the route to reach them. Proposal writing exemplifies the superiority of prevention over cure.

Planning Essentials

The main elements and steps of planning a proposal are simply these:

1. Define the major objective.
2. Identify your approach.
3. Develop your grand strategy.
4. Prepare an itinerary (outline).

Of course, all of these are closely related to each other, and rarely does anyone have these fully detailed in advance when writing a proposal because the time and the cost of writing proposals bars that excessive degree of advance planning. However, if the proposal writing is to be accomplished with any degree of efficiency and economy, some planning along these lines ought to be done before investing any large amount of time in serious writing efforts.

The First Input

Obviously, the data required to establish these elements must come from somewhere before the serious proposal writing begins. If you have carried out a bid/no-bid analysis and recorded your estimates, you already have some data that ought to be the first inputs for your proposal planning. Most of the items you will have recorded are of direct interest in writing a proposal, and you should be conscious of this probability as you develop the estimates and judgments that you record in that initial analysis. Following are some notes on each of those items that are not completely self-explanatory.

Data Needed

RFP Head Data. Aside from identifying the request for proposals, the client from whom the request comes, and the due date for the proposal, there are some items here of direct interest in reaching a final decision. One is the kind of requirement; an accurate summary of the requirement is important here. Another important item is the type of proposal required, especially as compared with the estimated size (dollar value) of the contract and the estimate of cost in labor hours required to write the proposal, and recorded in the next item. (You might, for example, decide to write an informal or letter proposal, even when you do not rate your chances for success very highly, because the proposal is easy and inexpensive to write.)

Estimated Value. This is a measure of the size and importance of the proposal. It should thus indicate the approximate amount of effort and size of proposal that are justified and necessary. This is only a rough indicator, because it is only one of several ballpark estimates you will have made in analyzing the RFP, but it is nevertheless a guideline.

Probable Competition. Your ability to judge this depends on several factors. One is your familiarity with your special field. If you have been in your practice or have been working in the field for someone else for some time, you probably have a very good idea of who are all the general competitors in your field. That gives you some beginning idea of probable competitors for any given contract. If you have a great many acquaintances in your field, you may be in touch with a kind of grapevine that exists in all fields and is often a source for information. Also the client may have held the a preproposal conference, and in attending that, you may have had the opportunity to observe and note the other attendees. Sometimes, you can even persuade the client to tell you who else was invited to propose.

Whatever the case, the information is usually useful and may affect your strategy decisions. Certainly it will affect your decisions as to what competitor strategy to use.

Rank Order. This calls for you to consider the other bid opportunities that are available to you and to make your best estimate of how you would rank this one in comparison with the others. This automatically also enters into the estimate the factor of the total number of bid opportunities available at the time. If this were your lowest-rated choice, for example, it would be number 35 in a field of 35 opportunities, but number 1 if there were no others available at the moment.

Major Strengths. This is critically important. It may even be the basis for your grand strategy. Caution: This item refers to your major strengths vis-à-vis this contract only. It has nothing to do with other major strengths you may have. For example, you may be a computer expert, but if you are pursuing a project that doesn't entail computer work as a major element, this is not a strength in this case.

In all cases, it is important to be as objective as you can. If you find it difficult to be objective about this estimate, get someone else to play devil's advocate for you to help you make an objective evaluation.

Major Weaknesses. Everything said about your major strengths applies to your weaknesses also. In some respects, however, this is even more important. You must be sure that any weaknesses you perceive will not be fatal ones, and you must have some reason for believing that you can offset or overcome any weaknesses, if you decide to develop a proposal.

Arguments Pro. Here, you should summarize the logical arguments for going ahead with the proposal and trying to win the contract even if you have found persuasive arguments con. This is a polemic exercise, recording the logical arguments for proposing, without regard to the arguments against proposing or to your decision to propose or not to propose.

Arguments Con. This is the other side of the coin, and it should be recorded according to the same philosophy as arguments pro.

Estimated Win Probability. This, like the arguments pro and con, should be as objective as possible. It has nothing to do with your final decision or recommendation regarding the development and submittal of a proposal. On the other hand, your estimate of win probability just might affect your final decision or recommendation.

Recommendation. Here, you simply summarize what you believe to be the logical conclusion of all the data you have analyzed and recorded, and you make your recommendation to bid (propose) or not to bid.

Remarks. This area is used to supplement or explain any of the previous items or to add comments that are germane but not covered by any preceding item. Obviously, this may be supplemented by additional sheets of paper when necessary. The footnote is a reminder to consider all factors, also suggesting that while some of the items can be estimated without regard to other factors, many cannot be estimated on an absolute scale. Instead, many items are necessarily estimated only after taking into account other items or specific conditions peculiar to the specific situation. Obviously, the final recommendation is the total of many factors considered together.

Rough Estimates and Drafts

There is a rough logic in the order in which the items are listed, but this is not absolute and is not necessarily the precise order in which you might enter your estimates and appraisals. Too, there is nothing sacred about your initial estimates, and you may find it wise to make rough preliminary guesses first, making up an initial, rough-draft form as a worksheet. There is absolutely no reason for not revising that form several times until you are satisfied that you have reached as accurate a set of estimates as possible. In fact, the probability is that you are far more likely to make a realistic and dependable appraisal by doing this than by trying to create a do-or-die first effort. (This is an excellent application for your personal computer because the revisions and updates are immeasurably easier when done on-screen and on-disk.)

Unsolicited Proposals—Data Inputs

This discussion has been predicated on the assumption of a rather formal request for proposals having been made by a client, whether at the client's own initiative or as a result of your suggestion to a prospective client to write out a description of the requirement. However, it is not only when you have received a written request for a proposal that you are faced with the task of writing one. (Actually, it should be regarded as a marketing opportunity, not as a task, when you have a prospective client willing to accept and consider a proposal from you.)

If you perceptively and aggressively market your services, you will always be alert for opportunities to offer a proposal to a client or prospective client. Your input information may sometimes be only verbal information

gathered informally in conversation with the client. That does not make the
bid/no-bid analysis any less a valid and sensible procedure to follow,
although the information may have to come from your verbal exchanges
with the client and perhaps from other sources, such as the client's
brochures and annual reports, from your own library and files, or from calls
to other people who can supply useful information.

In such a case, the form shown in Figure 4 can usefully guide you in
gathering information on which to base a proposal. However, one question
does not appear on the form, which may be pertinent in the circumstances
described here. In the case of your volunteering a proposal to a client with
whom you have had informal conversation, the missing item is this:
"Probability of award," which refers to the question of whether there will
be an award to anyone. That is, has the prospective client merely humored
you in agreeing to consider your proposal, or is it likely that the client is
serious and will, indeed, make an award to someone? Sometimes a client is
really asking for a quotation to see if management will approve an
appropriation for the project and cannot guarantee that there will be an
award. On the other hand, this probability of award is usually a consideration only when the proposal is a fairly costly effort because it is possible in
many circumstances to submit an informal or letter proposal at hardly more
cost than that of sending the prospective client a printed brochure. If so, the
question of how serious the client is about making an award is of no real
importance.

The Second Input

With the basic data of the bid/no-bid analysis at hand and a decision to
proceed with the proposal, specific data gathering and organization are the
next steps. The places from which to gather these are the client's request and
specifications for the work to be done, where there are such documents, as
well as from whatever other sources you can find.

Some requests and their work statements are well organized and in
logical order; many others are not. Many are vague, rambling, even almost
incoherent. The same consideration applies to gathering information from
other sources. Sometimes you can get a wealth of reliable and helpful
information from other sources, whereas at other times, the information is
scanty and of doubtful accuracy or usefulness. Nevertheless, it is necessary

to manage somehow to cope successfully under all these conditions and circumstances. A tool that has proved to be helpful in doing so is the checklist, which you should be developing as you study the requirements.

Figure 5 suggests one format for such a checklist. Actually, there are two or three lists: (1) a list of items specified as requirements in the proposal itself, (2) a list of items that must appear as elements of the project or program called for, and (3), in some cases, a list of evaluative criteria specified by the client. (The third is a requirement of federal agencies requesting proposals, and it may be found in proposal requests from other clients as well.) The same format may be used for all three lists, merely changing the heading in each case. Or you may prefer the design of Figure 6, which lists all the items on the same page, in parallel columns, with notes at the bottom or on a separate sheet. (Note that "DAA" refers to "days after award.") The advantage of this arrangement is that having the items side-by-side helps you to perceive correlations among the various items, and that can be a useful contribution. However, the format is not the important matter; the completeness of the listings is.

WHY USE A CHECKLIST?

For even the small or informal proposal, there are several reasons for making and using a checklist, such as the following:

PROPOSAL REQUIREMENTS CHECKLIST

Item	Page Par Nos.	Notes
State major project objectives	pp 2, 11, 33–37	Milestone chart?
Describe relevant experience	p 7, par 2.3, pp 8, 9	List specific contracts, clients
List, describe entire staff proposed	p 12	Needs 6 or more professionals; offer resumes of associates

Figure 5.   One possible format for a proposal checklist.

REQUIREMENTS CHECKLIST

Proposal	Project	Evaluation
1) State major project objectives, pp 2, 11, 33–37	1a) Must be in place in 30 DAA	1b) Understanding: 10 pts
2) Describe relevant experience, p 7, par 2.3, pp 8, 9	2a) Must be validated at 90/90	2b) Resumes: 20 pts
3) List, describe entire staff proposed, p 12	3a) Final report & manual due 120 DAA	3b) Viability of design: 30 pts

NOTES:
1) Milestone chart? 2) specific contract clients 3) Needs 6 or more professionals; offer resumes of associates

Figure 6.   An alternative checklist format.

1.   For the vague or haphazard request, the checklist helps to bring order by revealing the focal points—what the client really requires—which are otherwise often buried in and obscured by the verbiage. In short, it helps you to identify and define the true need of the client, even when the client is not entirely clear on just what that need is.

2.   The checklist often brings anomalies to the surface, especially when various items are compared and correlated. These are important to you from more than one viewpoint: They are the basis for the identification of "worry items," and creation of strategies. It is necessary to identify and recognize these to design a practicable and efficient project; they are potent ammunition for the development of competitor strategies, as you point out problems that competitors often miss.

3.   The lists are a valuable aid in identifying the most critically important points in both the project requirement and the proposal requirement, offering you an opportunity to see all items arrayed.

4.   Every requirement entails a deliverable item of some sort, though it is not always clear precisely what that is. In fact, it is sometimes unclear whether the client knows exactly what is to be delivered. The checklist helps in identifying this and even in helping the client understand precisely what it should be.

5. The list has another use, to be described later when discussing front matter of formal proposals, in creating a "response matrix," a device that is instrumental in maximizing the technical rating given your proposal.

GRAPHIC EQUIVALENT

The use of graphics in proposals is generally highly desirable for a variety of reasons, not the least of which are these:

1. It makes study and understanding of your proposal much easier for the client. The desirability of making things as easy as possible for the buyer is a basic objective of all enlightened sales and marketing activity.
2. Used judiciously, graphic devices displace more than the amount of space required by equivalent text, thus reducing the labor of writing and the sheer bulk of the product.
3. The "right" graphics can help you, the writer, gain a better understanding of the requirement and the best approach to satisfying it.
4. With good graphics, the writing job itself is made far easier for a few reasons. It is much easier to "write to" graphic illustrations for explanations are made much simpler and require far fewer words. Also, the graphics help you, as a writer, to get things into perspective, which also facilitates the writing process. For this reason, creating graphics can be a useful step in *preparing* to write the proposal.

In some circumstances, described later in this chapter, it is better to precede the development of the checklists by designing a graphic. The specific graphic device referred to here is usually referred to as a "functional flowchart." The concept underlying such a chart is that the work of the project is a flow process, a series of steps arranged in some logical sequence wherein each step, proceeding from left to right, is a necessary prerequisite to the next step, and each "next step" is a step closer to the goal or objective of the entire flow. There is thus a "why" logic in such charts as you examine the flow from start to finish, and a "how" logic as you study it in the opposite direction.

Starting at the beginning (the leftmost box), ask "why" of the information in the box, and it should be answered by the information in the next box. In Figure 7, for example, the first box calls for the gathering of data. "Why" is answered by the next box, which explains that the data are needed to make an analysis of test procedures; why the analysis is needed is to validate the test procedures, and so on. Starting at the other end, "how" final delivery is accomplished is by getting client review and approval, which is gained by validation testing of the manual, and so on. These checks enable you to verify that your chart is complete and coherent, or to find out what its deficiencies are, if they exist.

While not exactly an equivalent of the checklist, a well-conceived functional flowchart summarizes the project in the most efficient presentation possible—a single drawing or, in some cases, a set of several drawings—revealing all the significant steps of the project, together with the logic of the design and delineation of the extremes, from the starting first step to the final step and the final deliverable items.

In fact, the functional flowchart of the project often comes to the client as something of a shock, helping the client gain a much deeper insight into the requirement than he or she had before, and often revealing that the consultant has a better view than the client has. The development and presentation of a really good functional flowchart is thus usually an impressive performance, and the client is often somewhat awed by the consultant's demonstrated x-ray vision, which can pierce to the heart of the requirement.

Figure 7 is a simplified example of such a functional flowchart. (For many projects, such charts extend six feet or more in length, and include more than one stream of information.) This simple chart explains how the consultant proposes to develop a set of maintenance procedures and appropriate accompanying documentation. In the actual case, such a project requires many more steps than those shown here.

There are two ways to graph functional flowcharts. One is to develop a fully detailed single chart that reveals all the steps in a single flow representation. The other is to offer a set of several functional flowcharts, with one top-level chart showing only the main phases or functions, and the others each showing one of those main phases or functions in greater detail.

Figure 7 shows the flow as we normally read, from left to right, descending a step as we run out of space on the right, as we do in reading text. However, some individuals, especially those who work with comput-

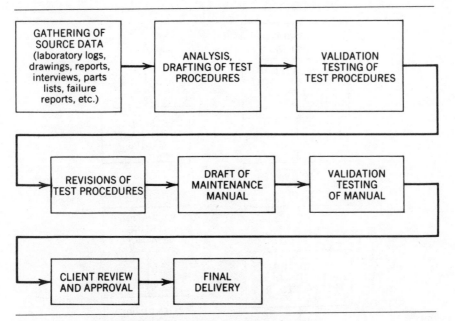

Figure 7. Simple functional flowchart of a proposed project.

ers, prefer to show the flow from top to bottom, as shown in the next figure, Figure 8. This has a some advantages, as well as some disadvantages: It's easier to create, especially if you do not have a professional illustrator available and must create your own charts, and perhaps it is more efficient in its use of space. Also, because this is somewhat "cleaner"—less cluttered and perhaps less confusing—than is the left-to-right presentation. On the other hand, since we all learn to read from left to right, it takes a little more adjustment to learn to read charts using this alternate orientation.

The chart shown as Figures 7 and 8 is a functional flow in its simplest arrangement, as a purely linear and unambiguous process. In fact, few projects are that simple. Most processes entail iterations, options, and/or feedback loops, as in Figure 9. Though Figure 9 is still relatively simple, it demonstrates that illustrating is a parallel or concurrent function, and editing creates a feedback loop for corrections and revisions.

A further refinement makes the proposal easier to write and easier to read and understand: It is usually possible to add a milestone or schedule chart to the functional flow, as in Figure 10.

Although these graphic representations aid both in writing and in reading

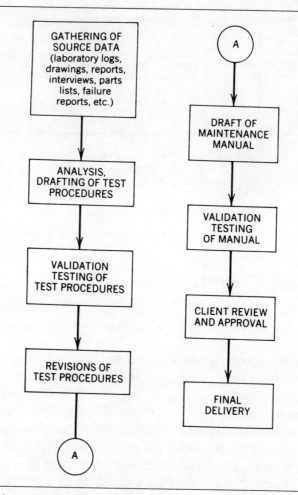

Figure 8. Alternative flowchart presentation.

the proposal, the initial goal of developing the overall functional flowchart is to aid you in at least four ways:

1. It is an analytical tool, helping you to understand the requirement.
2. It is a design tool, helping you in designing the project to be proposed.
3. It is a planning tool, helping you plan your presentation—the proposal itself.

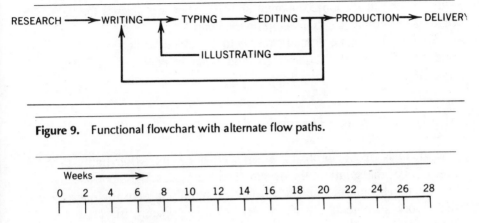

Figure 9. Functional flowchart with alternate flow paths.

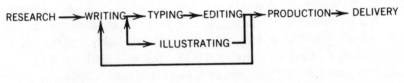

Figure 10. Functional flowchart combined with schedule chart.

4. It is a presentation tool, greatly simplifying and easing the writing task.

Let's consider and explore each of these advantages briefly, after which we'll go on to discuss the alternative approaches to creating the overall functional flowchart.

The Flowchart as an Analytical Tool

Whether you develop the first draft of the overall functional flow of the project before, after, or concurrently with the development of your checklist, compelling yourself to depict the project's process flow graphically, enforces discipline upon your thinking. It is relatively easy to generalize in verbiage and even easier to deceive yourself about your understanding, but it is much more difficult to do so when you attempt to portray the process graphically, depicting the logical order in *how* and *why* sequences. (That will become much more apparent shortly, when we discuss the several options of approaches to developing the chart.)

The result of that enforced study is to achieve a far deeper and clearer understanding of the requirement and what is necessary to satisfy it properly.

The Flowchart as a Design Tool

The analysis of any problem, when well done, leads inevitably to the synthesis of the solution: the design. The anomalies, the inconsistencies, and the non sequiturs that can be found so often in proposal requests and their work statements are not always readily apparent in verbal form, especially in lengthy and complex statements. This is because perceiving these kinds of problems in text requires (a) that you mentally picture the processes while you read, and (b) that you attempt to visualize all the phases and functions in relation to each other. This is obviously difficult for any but the simplest situations and requirements, so it is not surprising that so many such logical absurdities elude us in reading proposal requests.

Once committed to paper (or computer screen) as a functional flowchart, those things show up quickly, simply because the flowchart is inherently a logic-based presentation. Redundancies, dead-end flows, and "you-can't-get-there-from-here" anomalies fairly leap from the graphic presentation, all but guiding your hand in making the changes necessary to a successful and efficient design.

The Flowchart as a Planning Tool

In a sense, the flowchart has already been discussed as a planning tool, in considering its utility in planning the project design. In addition, it is a tool for planning the proposal itself, for it is the representation of the proposed project, and almost everything in your proposal that pertains directly to the project is geared to that flowchart. The flowchart should be the unifying theme, and everything your words say should be entirely consistent with what the chart says graphically. You should therefore plan and outline your proposal with an eye on that chart so that your proposal "proves" your design and *sells* it to the client as the most dependable, most efficient, lowest cost, or most whatever your chosen strategy dictates as sales arguments.

The Flowchart as a Presentation Tool

The benefits of using a well-designed flowchart as a presentation tool have been touched on already and are fairly obvious in any case. Properly designed, the flowchart (or any other graphic representation, for that matter) should require little explanatory text, or it fails in its basic purpose. On the other hand, it should also serve as a reference for much of the related text, also easing the burden of textual explanations. In fact, the really well-designed functional flowchart does far more than explain and support the basic design and schedule presentations. It also explains and supports arguments for the proposed design, for the features, for the costs, and for the many other factors that must be explained and sold to the client if the proposal is to be persuasive enough to be successful.

CREATING THE FUNCTIONAL FLOWCHART

The flowchart, like the text, must go through at least one rough draft stage before being finalized, but there are alternatives to the creation of the first rough draft, usually depending on the quality and the abundance of the information initially available to you. In some cases, the client has furnished such detailed information and ideas about what is needed that a rough-draft flowchart can be constructed by the simple expedient of translating the words into their graphic equivalent. However, in many other cases, this is not a practical option because the available information is imprecise or inadequate in other ways. In these cases the rough-draft flowchart must be constructed by other methods. These other methods are considerably more difficult and more time-consuming, but they are probably even more necessary if the ultimate proposal is to be at all effective.

First Steps

There are at least three alternatives available for creating a functional flowchart in the case of imprecise or inadequate data. The easiest case is that in which the requirement is totally conventional and uncomplicated, involving well-established routine procedures and processes. For example, if the requirement is to develop a manual, conduct a survey, or write a computer program, the expert consultant who specializes in the appropriate field knows in advance what all the major steps and procedures must be. If you are faced with a requirement of this nature, you begin your flowchart by first depicting the typical functions and phases of the work and then seeking out any special conditions, problems, or requirements and modifying your draft chart accordingly.

In another case, you may have little useful information beyond a definition of the required result—a manual, report, computer program, installed system, training program, or other product. In such a case, you usually find the most practical approach to be one that starts at the terminus of the chart with a symbol or box depicting that product. You then must work backward, asking *how* you arrive at that point, to determine what must be the preceding step. To check and verify your chart, ask yourself *why* you should take the next step you've taken instead of taking another course. Figure 11 illustrates this. The requirement is for a survey to support a marketing campaign. The product required is a report of a survey. The details of the survey report can be resolved later, but now a draft chart must be constructed.

The preceding steps are obvious, at least in general terms, although they will have to be elaborated to fit the specific application and circumstances. The specific details can be supplied later, in revising the chart. The present need is to begin, to take the first steps.

The steps leading to the development of the deliverable item are logical necessities. The survey report is created by analyzing the survey data; the data are analyzed by gathering and compiling them; the data are gathered and compiled by conducting the survey. In the other direction, the survey is conducted to gather and compile the data; the data are compiled to be analyzed; and so on.

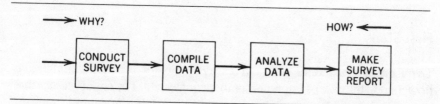

Figure 11.   Beginning a functional flowchart: developing the chart from the end.

Asking these questions helps you construct the chart, and answering them helps you examine the chart to be sure that all necessary steps are there.

Working from Both Ends

In most cases, you know what must be at both ends of the chart because (a), you must know what the required result is to be, and (b) you usually know what you will have to start with. In the case hypothesized in Figure 11, the assumption was only that of a requirement to conduct a survey. Obviously, a client requesting proposals to conduct a survey must have given at least some basic information about the requirement, such as where the survey is to be conducted, whether a survey instrument (e.g., a questionnaire) is to be supplied or must be constructed by the consultant, and at least some other beginning information. Consequently, the actual case is likely to be more along the lines of Figure 12, where you can work from both ends to first define the requirement in at least broad functional terms, and then go on to refine the chart with all the details necessary to carry out a custom project. These charts are obviously so general that they can apply to almost any such projects, and the typical consulting job is a custom project that is shaped and characterized by individual, often unique, needs and considerations.

Working with Open Ends

Despite this, the situation may very well arise wherein you do not have definite information as to a desired outcome or even a specific starting point. This might well be the case, for example, where you have met a prospective client, discussed a problem the client is experiencing, and either been

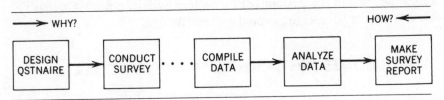

Figure 12. Developing the flowchart from both ends.

invited to or volunteered to and obtained agreement from the client to submit a written proposal for solution of the problem. In such cases, the client may simply say something to the effect, "I really don't know how to proceed, but I am willing to listen to any ideas you have."

This is a completely open-ended opportunity, and it is left almost entirely up to you to propose a project, based on your expert knowledge. You must decide where the project begins and where it ends, and you would presumably have asked the right questions to serve as guides in designing a project. This, however, does not change the basic situation: You still have the problem of both making your prospective client understand what you offer and selling it effectively through a persuasive proposal. Also, you should still develop a functional flowchart to explain your plan and point out its merits.

The open-ended proposal is a double-edged sword. On the one hand, you have carte blanche to propose, and it may well be that you have no direct competitors for the work. However, you are still in competition, for you are even then competing with other possible expenditures of available dollars, and possibly with other departments and their needs. You must still convince the client that the project is of great enough importance to earn a priority for funding. If you go overboard in what you propose, you may thus price yourself out of the job. You may not necessarily lose it to a direct competitor, however, but the client may decide to postpone having the work done or forego it entirely. (However, it is also possible, if the client believes your proposed project too extensive and costly that some of your direct competitors will then be invited to propose, despite the fact that the proposal opportunity resulted from your lead.)

If your work is such that you do essentially the same kind of work on each assignment or project, although tailored for each client, you may find it practicable to construct one or more standardized functional flowcharts that can be adapted to and customized for each individual project. Obviously, there is a great advantage to you if you can do this.

WHICH COMES FIRST, CHECKLIST OR FLOWCHART?

There is an apparent anomaly here, in that I have suggested both developing a checklist and developing a draft flowchart as a first step. The fact is that there is no flat rule possible for this because circumstances vary so much from one case to another, and circumstances often dictate what you must do first. If you have enough information to develop a substantial checklist of items, it is usually advisable to do that first, and then use that checklist as an information source and guide in drafting the functional flowchart. However, if you have in hand a request and work statements that are specific and detailed enough to lend themselves to direct translation into a functional flowchart, it may prove more fruitful to do that. In the actual case, I find it possible quite often to do both concurrently, developing them as I study the request, and correlating the two sets of results as they unfold. Doing both concurrently is probably the most effective, and I recommend that to you for all cases where you find it a practical possibility. (The opportunity to correlate the two sets of results is especially helpful both for finding potential problems as incipient worry items and for devising stratagems therefrom.)

A COMMON DILEMMA

One question almost always arises at my seminars during discussions of making and presenting such analyses as these: How much information can the consultant afford to offer in proposals? That is, won't unscrupulous clients steal the ideas and information from the consultant who is too generous with such detailed information and use them in ways that are contrary to the consultant's own interests, such as doing the job themselves? Or, once the consultant has revealed how to go about it, won't unscrupulous clients pass such information on to competitors whom they favor?

Risks in Giving Free Samples of Expertise

This is a legitimate concern; such unfortunate exploitations of consultants have happened, and this creates a serious dilemma: How much of your expert knowledge and analysis—the knowledge and skills that you normally sell—can you afford to reveal gratuitously without "giving the store away," while still offering that minimum necessary to persuade the client to opt for your proposal?

It is worth noting here, before going on, that many consultants worry about giving away any information free of charge, and some who write and lecture on the subject of consulting even offer specific lectures on "how to avoid giving away free consulting." Going to an extreme with this concern is the result of some sense of insecurity, the notion that your security lies in being secretive about your special work. (Some writers and lecturers who purport to teach consulting even offer lectures on how to make clients dependent on the consultant for all time to come!) These attitudes bear the seeds of their own defeat within them. If you are going to be effective in marketing your services, you cannot avoid giving away a few samples of your knowledge and consulting skills. Those samples are the very best evidence of your abilities, and it is difficult to convince any prospective client that you are the consultant to retain simply on the basis of broad claims to excellence as a consultant. You must get down to present-case specifics to be effective in selling yourself.

Giving specifics is especially important when it comes to submitting proposals. The typical client wants to compare you and what you propose with your competitors and what they propose. That comparative evaluation goes far beyond a comparison of the universities you attended, the organizations who employed you, and the positions you held in the past. It is focused largely on what you have to say about the client's expressed requirement and what you propose to do to satisfy that requirement—That is obviously the client's primary concern. If you avoid entirely a technical discussion and a projection of your approach to satisfying the requirement, and you ask the client to settle for a personal bio and a set of claims to excellence, you might as well forego writing the proposal entirely and save your time and money. You cannot completely avoid the risk of having your "brains picked" unfairly. It's an occupational hazard, and you can only minimize it, at best.

This is rarely a serious problem when dealing with clients in the public sector—government agencies—but it can be a real hazard in marketing to the private sector, even with the largest companies. (I confess to having been so victimized twice, in dealings with large corporations in both cases.) In all fairness to such companies, however, it should be noted that when such things happen in dealings with large corporations, they are almost invariably the unscrupulous acts of individuals seeking personal advantages in their companies and are not sanctioned by management. Management, in fact, would be outraged by such actions and would probably make a serious internal investigation if charges of such depredations were made by any proposer. (Do note this for future reference, if you are or think you have been so victimized.)

Risk-Reduction Strategies

There is no absolute safeguard against this danger, but following are several measures you can take to reduce the danger of such unethical appropriation and misuse of your proposal. They are written here with formal multipage proposals in mind, but they are equally valid for application to informal, letter proposals, and they can be easily adapted to use in those kinds of proposals:

Limit the Proprietary Information. Try to gauge that minimum amount of information necessary to demonstrate your competence and sell your approach/design to the client, and don't go beyond that minimum. At least, try to hold back the most specialized and most proprietary information, information that is critical to success in the project.

Copyright Your Proposal. Place a copyright notice on your proposal, and make the notice prominent. Here is how to establish a common-law copyright:

Near the bottom of an early page, usually the title page, type the words: "Copyright (date) by (your name)." The date used is usually the year or the month and year, although nothing prevents you from using a more specific date. You can use the abbreviation "Copr." or the symbol © instead of the full word "copyright," but the soundest practice is to spell out the word. One note: Many people follow this notice with other words, such as, "All rights reserved" and "Not to be duplicated without express permission." This adds no statutory protection, but it does advise readers what that copyright means and what your position is with regard to it. It won't protect you in a literal sense because copyright covers only a specific construction of words and not the ideas (you can't copyright the information), but it may discourage anyone tempted to misuse the information.

You can register your copyright with the Copyright Office of the Library of Congress, but you are not required to do so to get common-law copyright protection. (You do need to do so if you get into litigation with anyone over your copyright. However, you can register the copyright at that time, if such an eventuality ensues.)

Use a Notice of Proprietary Information.   Because the Freedom of Information Act has given anyone a legal right to demand and get a copy of a proposal submitted by someone else, the federal government has urged proposers to advise readers of any proprietary information contained in their proposals so that such proprietary and confidential information will be excised from any copy of a proposal made available to requesters under the Act. It's a good idea to do this in the private sector too. Here is what to do:

On the title page of your proposal, type a notice along the following general lines:

> The information contained in pages _____ and so noted is proprietary and is not to be revealed or used except for evaluation of this proposal and/or in performance of the services proposed herein. This, however, in no way inhibits the revelation and use of this information in behalf of the client in the event of award to this proposer.

Then you must indicate on each of those pages listed that material you claim as proprietary and so mark it "proprietary" and/or "proprietary and confidential."

Do not attempt to claim that the entire proposal is proprietary, as that would weaken and possibly invalidate totally any later claim of rights to recourse, in event your admonition was totally disregarded because there is always some material in your proposal that is obviously not proprietary.

In this connection, however, it does not hurt to mark your entire proposal "confidential," and to make this marking a prominent one.

None of these are absolute guarantees against violation of what most of us believe to be an ethical code of behavior, but they do seriously lessen the danger in two ways: One, they advise those who might act innocently in revealing information the readers did not even suspect was confidential or proprietary; and two, they serve notice on and should give at least some pause to those who might act wrongfully with full knowledge, but in the hope that their action will go unnoticed or that they might be able to plead ignorance, if detected.

APPLIED PLANNING FOR LETTER PROPOSALS

All of the foregoing pages of this chapter were written with formal proposals in mind. The informal proposal written as a letter of several pages is ordinarily written to propose a small project. It is often written as a follow-up to an earlier contact, with no real assurance that the client will award a contract to anyone. These are necessary marketing activities and should be carried out as energetically and as often as possible, still recognizing that in such cases as these, an elaborate study is not warranted and should not be undertaken.

On the other hand, you should not go to the other extreme and simply "dash off" a quick letter carelessly, for disaster can result from such a hasty action. Rather, you must judge the real prospect of winning some business and estimate the possible benefits, both immediate, as reflected in the probable size of the contract, and long-term, as reflected in the probabilities of other, follow-on business and/or other benefits.

Therefore, do take advantage of all opportunities you encounter or can create to offer a prospect a proposal (for it is a marketing opportunity, and one you can often create by offering an unsolicited letter proposal to prospects). Do prepare these proposals according to the same principles and philosophy followed in developing formal proposals for major contracts, but scale the effort to the size and nature of the proposal. Finally, do not make the mistake of one nationally known electronics/defense-industries engineering company that all but bankrupted itself by continually spending more to create the proposal than the total size of the possible contract that might result.

CHAPTER 7

Program Design

Program design, a must of proposal writing, calls for clear, independent, and original thinking if the design is to be effective in creating a persuasive proposal.

EVERY PROPOSAL MUST BE DESIGN BASED

Clients do not request proposals when they want to buy proprietaries or standard services; they ask for proposals when they need a custom service. Custom design is thus inherent in the concept of proposals, as in consulting itself. It is inevitable that a proposal is based on and built around a specific program design. Also, it is usually the service that is the prime item proposed, although a product—such as a computer program, manual, or report—is also often required to complement the service. In such cases, the design of the product, as well as the design of the proposed program to produce it, must be considered in the discussions. However, even when research and development (R&D) is itself the principal service required, acceptable preliminary design goals and approaches must usually be proposed. Success in proposal competition depends heavily on the client's reaction to the proposed design approaches.

Proposals Usually Describe Programs

Many proposals call for services that do not involve products per se or, at least, do not involve products directly. Nevertheless, there is still a need for clear designs or, at the minimum, clearly defined approaches to design of the service program and products or by-products, when appropriate. Even simple or apparently simple services, such as the provision of technical/ professional temporary staff, generally must present a design for carrying out the obligation. There are such matters of concern to the client as assurance of an adequate supply of qualified individuals and the ability to replace any without delay, if necessary. Sometimes, the consultant organization must provide supervision and manage the individuals assigned, although they are working on the client's premises. (In federal contracts, this is required by law.) It is also not unprecedented for the client to request evidence of the consultant's ability to recruit specialists to be assigned to the project, whether they are themselves individual consultants or are to be new hires.

Program Designs Must Consider Possible Problems

You must think out all the possible problems, especially those that are likely to have been already perceived by the client, and you must provide for their solution in your design. Even when the client has not thought to ask for many of the specific details, the greater the number of pertinent details you include in your proposal, the more impressive and more foolproof your design appears to be. The provision of detail is usually accepted as testimony to capability, which is itself the beginning of a design or program strategy.

What this means is that the design, or at least the factors surrounding it— approaches, design philosophy, and design logic—must be clearly apparent to the client. Mysticism and generalizations are not convincing or persuasive; they are not the evidence you need to sell your proposed program to the client; only the details can show the merit of what you propose.

FRESHNESS AND ORIGINALITY

Design Versus Strategy

Comparing program design and program strategy to determine which is cause and which effect is like the chicken-and-egg question: There is no firm answer. You may develop a brilliant design concept and derive a strategy from that. Or you may do it the other way, evolving a strategy first and basing your design on that. The two are almost inseparable and evolve together in an iterative creative process, each consideration influencing the other. However, the question of creativity does enter into it, for it is possible to create pedestrian designs based solely on one's technical or professional discipline, rather than on true creative inspiration. They are usually the classic designs taught in formal training courses and often to be found in various texts and reference works, from which they may be borrowed.

Such ready-made, standard designs exist in abundance, which is not always a fortunate circumstance. Ready-made solutions tend to arouse little enthusiasm on the part of clients, most of whom have retained a consultant because they are convinced that they do need custom services, which call for original thinking and a good measure of creativity. (Is that not essentially a trait that characterizes consultants?) Standard designs also bear little relationship to anything that might be fairly called a strategy.

The Old Versus the New

In proposal competitions, clinging to yesterday's solutions is likely to be effective in only those cases where no proposer has offered anything more imaginative than the tried-and-true design bromides of yore. The client who was hoping to find something refreshingly new and different will generally sigh and select a proposal reluctantly. In fact, there are many cases where a client, disappointed by all the proposals, simply rejects all and cancels or postpones the procurement. You cannot depend even on being selected as the best of a bad lot.

This is not say that every proposal must be a display of creative genius or a bold departure. Quite the contrary, many clients prefer old, established approaches, regarding them as the low-risk, tried-and-true methods. Still, even they are attracted to fresh ideas, and it is possible to have it both ways—to be refreshingly original and yet not represent radical departures from convention. In fact, from a marketing viewpoint, it is far wiser to be evolutionary than revolutionary in your design: Being too different is likely to alarm any client, but especially the conservative one.

CREATIVITY

In 1899, Charles H. Duell, Commissioner of the U.S. Patent Office under
President McKinley, recommended closing down that office, saying that
everything that could be invented had been. Ludicrous although that may
seem today, the thinking of many has not changed greatly: Many show that
same mental torpidity. Those lacking in creative imagination appear unable
to understand creativity at all, even as exhibited by so many others. That,
however, is not the only startling aspect of the subject. Many also show an
almost inexplicable tendency to cling stubbornly to old, long-established
biases, despite mountains of contrary evidence. Many people believe with
certainty many things that are not so. There is a great reluctance to give up
long-held beliefs; many must be weaned from those beliefs slowly and
carefully. This is a factor to consider also in developing proposals.

Education Versus Creativity

Studies of creativity turn up many surprising facts. One is that almost all of
us are far more creative as children than we are as adults because our educational systems and societal standards tend strongly to stifle our creative
instincts and to actually wean us from them as we grow up. In fact, it has
been shown that in general terms, creative imagination is inversely proportional to levels of formal education. We tend to rely on what we were taught
over all those years of inculcation in formal doctrines and beliefs. We thus
tend strongly to mistrust instincts and independent judgments, and to resist
new ideas, no matter their origin. Probably a great majority of us operate on
an unconscious conviction that having completed our formal education we
have all or nearly all the learning we shall ever need. In fact, we are quite
sure that most of the answers reside in those textbooks, reference books,
professional papers, and other such formal documentation.

Ironically, most such documentation is heavy with bibliographic notations and citations of many sources, so that it begins to reach the absurdity
of an endless circle of scholarly authors quoting and citing each others'
work, each to prove the soundness of his or her own work. This, presumably,
enables an author to escape culpability (in the event of challenges) by
assigning it to those presumably authoritative sources so painfully reported
in the endless footnotes and other bibliographic annotations. This only

supports the tendency to resist new ideas, which for this purpose can be characterized as any ideas for which one cannot find suitable bibliographic citations to defend its use!

Sadly, scholarliness is thus represented more often by knowledge of and research into other writings than by independent and original thinking.

Conventional Wisdom

All of this is conventional wisdom with a vengeance, relying unquestioningly on consensus, rather than on independent reasoning. It is certainly the antithesis of innovation and originality. New ideas cannot survive in such an atmosphere. New ideas spring from a seedbed of questioning and seeking better ways, from a basic philosophy that there is always a better way. We need merely to seek it energetically enough, with an open mind, and we shall find it, but comparatively few of us even make the quest.

Conventional wisdom bears within it its own negation, for in this fast-changing world—and the *rate* at which changes take place is itself increasing steadily—those ideas and methods that become conventional wisdom are already obsolete by the time they begin to assume that status. Thus, anything that is recognized as conventional wisdom may be regarded with some skepticism.

Even the acknowledged thinkers of the world, our scientists, are susceptible to such human frailties. It was once a widely circulated idea that not more than six of the world's scientists understood the theories of Albert Einstein. That was something of a distortion. Most of the world's true scientists understood Einstein's equations, theories, and their subsequent implications well enough. What was probably true was that not more than a handful of the world's scientists *believed* Einstein's ideas and accepted the conclusions to be drawn therefrom. Those ideas were radical departures from old scientific beliefs. To accept Einsteinian physics meant giving up many treasured notions, tantamount to starting over in some areas of scientific thought and speculation. For example, accepting the new physics meant abandoning a law that said that matter could neither be created nor destroyed. (The atomic bomb, for example, compelled changing that physical law to recognize that matter is a form of energy, and the two are interchangeable.)

Even scientists, supposedly objective thinkers, have difficulty abandoning their conventional wisdom to embrace new ideas. Who wants to admit that he or she has been wrong for years, pursuing false gods?

VALUE MANAGEMENT (VM): METHODOLOGY FOR CREATIVE THINKING

Value management (VM) is a discipline known also and perhaps more popularly by such other names as *value analysis* and *value engineering*. It sprang into existence in the engineering field as a result of *serendipity*, that mysterious art of finding what you didn't know you were looking for. (It is characteristic of creative minds that they tend to recognize opportunities in sudden and chance discoveries.) The problem with the name *value engineering* is that it tends to mask the fact that VM (value management) is applicable to almost all human activity, that value can be managed in fields other than engineering.

The Origin of VM

During the Second World War, while using substitute materials as a typical result of wartime shortages of strategic materials, a General Electric Company executive made the rather curious discovery that often the substitute material was better than the original material for which it substituted, and it often was less expensive in the bargain. He observed this to be a fact often enough that he dismissed the idea that it was a freakish exception, and he thought it a phenomenon worthy of serious investigation. That serious investigation, carried out by General Electric engineer Lawrence Miles after the war, produced the original VM methodology, to which a number of enhancements and improvements have since been made.

The Essence of VM

In its barest essence, VM is an organized method for creative improvement. Unfortunately, it is too often used only on existing products and systems in which so much investment has been made that it is often impractical to implement improvements. For example, in many manufacturing processes, the initial investment in tooling (and sometimes in parts and raw materials inventory) is quite enormous. In such cases, any saving offered by design changes would be negated because the changes would require retooling and the scrapping of inventoried materials. To this extent, the benefits of value engineering have some built-in limitations, at least when practiced after the fact. (VM can often tell you how it *should have been done originally*, but with cold comfort now.)

Obviously, the better time for value studies (by any name) is early in the design or predesign stages, long before front-end investments are made. This makes the method nearly ideal for application in the proposal process, where designs and design approaches are being "penciled in" as a matter of course. However, you need learn only a few of the principles and methods, for proposal purposes, and I confine this discussion to those.

WHAT IS VALUE?

The most difficult and least precise idea with which you must come to grips in making value studies is that of value itself—of what it is. Dictionary definitions require several column-inches of fine print, and yet they do not firmly grasp the definition, and they certainly do not produce an unambiguous definition.

Value is neither an absolute nor a constant. It is an abstraction, in fact, a notion, an idea. It changes frequently, with changing circumstances. It is a noun that must be qualified by an adjective to have any substantial meaning at all. The value of the American dollar, for example, is quoted on financial exchanges every day because it is changing constantly as a *market value*.

Artwork and many other objects have an *esteem value*, as well as a market value. Those values may be poles apart. You may, for example, have such esteem for the house you wish to sell that you place a far higher value on it than the market says it is worth. Or you may esteem and want something badly enough to knowingly pay "over the market" to get it.

A piece of jewelry may have an *intrinsic* value, which is the market value of the materials in it—such as gold, silver, and precious stones, for example—but it may also have an esteem value that is greater than its intrinsic value and that equals its market value, as long as others esteem it equally.

Thus, value is an elusive idea, and yet we do need to arrive at an agreement as to what we mean by the term if we are to agree on ways of managing value. Fortunately, VM does not require that we agree on or even establish any absolute definition of value, whether intrinsic, market, esteem, or any other variety. VM can deal with value as a *relative* term only, without regard to its original idea, for the entire idea of VM is to increase or improve value, by whatever yardstick value is measured. VM can be used to improve esteem value, intrinsic value, market value, or whatever other kind of value you wish to apply.

VM does this by making beneficial changes to one or more parameters of the item under study. The parameters of value are *cost* and *utility*. If we can make beneficial changes to either or both so that the result is greater utility, at the same or lower cost or lower cost at the same or greater utility we have increased the value of the item. We might, that is, express value as a ratio of utility to cost. If we were to use a formula such as

$$V = \frac{U}{C}$$

where V = value, U = utility, and C = cost, V becomes a figure of merit, directly proportional to the ratio, utility:cost. (More on this shortly.)

Neither of those two terms, *cost* and *utility*, are as simple or absolute as they appear, however, as the following discussions make abundantly apparent. There are many kinds of cost and utility, and an agreement on what these are is essential to an understanding of VM principles and methods. However, before we attempt to come to grips with these terms and ideas, we must look at another fundamental of VM: the idea of *function*.

THE IDEA OF FUNCTION

The heart of VM lies in the understanding and analysis of functions. It is on the basis of function analyses both that VM studies begin and that improvements in value are predicated. However, experience has demonstrated that many people with nontechnical backgrounds have difficulty with the term *function analysis* and its significance. This may be due to the tendency of many technical professionals to speak in the jargon of their professions, rather than in everyday lay English. Whatever the cause, it seems necessary to discuss this term and its meaning.

Like the term *value, function* is multifaceted in meaning, and this discussion examines these several facets. However, function is not as difficult to define as value is. It is fairly well defined by stating simply that *function* is what the item *does*. In fact, analysis of what an item does is at the heart of VM, at the heart of value itself.

The first question VM asks of an item to be studied is "What is it?" The answer to that question may be simply the proper or generic name of the item, so that it describes the primary purpose of the item. The purpose of the question is to identify the item and make its general purpose clear, in preparation for addressing the question of general function: "What does it do?"

How Many Functions or Kinds of Functions?

Only the simplest of items do only one thing—have only one function. Most items have several functions, even many functions. A wristwatch, for example, indicates the time of day. But many of today's watches also indicate the date, act as stopwatches, are miniature calculators, and even are fine jewelry. Some have other, additional functions. So, "What does it do?" is often not easy to answer unambiguously.

Identifying the Main Function

In the practice of VM, the question is taken to refer to the main (sometimes called "basic" or "primary") function of the device. In the case of a watch, that is not difficult to discern: There is not much question that the main function of a watch is to indicate the time of day. All those other things it does are secondary functions.

Unlike the watch, it is not always easy to determine the main function of some things. Consider the typical accounting system used by businesses. Ask business people what they think the main function of the system is, and you will probably be advised that it is to "keep the books," "keep tax records," and other such ideas. The problem with these definitions is a common one: They strike all around the main function, but they never come to grips with it because the analyst has failed to first answer the more basic question of *why*—Why does the system exist at all? What is the basic *purpose* of the system? What *need* does it satisfy?

The fact is, in this case, that "keeping books" answers *how*, not *why*, and keeping records for tax purposes is a secondary issue and has nothing to do with the main purpose of accounting. (The test is simple: Suppose there were no taxes to pay. Would you not still have an accounting system?) One does not keep a costly accounting system for the convenience or enrichment of government tax bureaus (although it sometimes does appear to be so), but for the benefit of one's own enterprise. Accounting is a management function and exists to aid management by providing information necessary to make sensible management decisions. Relevant information is a need of management. Even the fact of record-keeping is not highly significant here, for that, too, is part of the means and not of the purpose, and the main or basic function always reflects the main or basic purpose.

Aids to Reaching Function Definitions

VM methodology includes measures that help in defining functions and expressing them properly so that they will be useful in the analytical process. Two important measures are these:

The Verb–Noun Rule.   Functions must be defined or identified by two words only: a verb and a noun. (Occasional exceptions are allowed when the verb or the noun must be a compound word to be clear and definite.) The purpose is to enforce discipline and compel the analyst to make firm and unequivocal decisions. Otherwise, the definition of function is not at all useful.

Identification of the Purpose of the Item.   Ask yourself what is the true purpose of the item? Why does it exist? Why has someone gone to the expense of creating or acquiring the item? What is the need that must be satisfied by the item? This requires clear thinking and is at the heart of the discipline. Everything hinges on doing this properly, for everything that follows is based on this definition of main function.

Where the main function is not readily apparent, as in many but not all cases, the most useful first step is usually to identify that purpose by determining the desired result of using the item. In the case of accounting systems, that is useful management information, information that enables managers to make wise and useful management decisions.

The second step is to find the verb and noun that express the definition most accurately and most usefully. And that may entail choosing either word first, depending on the individual circumstances of each case.

In this case, we have already decided on information, and it may be wise, in this case, to use a compound noun, management information, because the unqualified word *information* is not likely to convey the full and proper meaning. In this case, it is also important to choose the verb carefully, for accounting is perceived by most people as a recording process, which is misleading for our purposes. Again, the recording and the recordkeeping are part of the means, rather than the end, and it is important to take note of this. In fact, the most significant aspect of accounting's function vis-à-vis management information is that it is an active function and that it *reports* that information to the executives of the organization. Thus, the definition ought to be "reports information" or perhaps "reports management information."

Secondary Functions

Secondary functions are of two kinds. Some are supporting functions, functions that are necessary to and that support the accomplishment of the main function. Others are supplementary functions, not directly related to the main function.

In the example cited here, if the main function is to report information (to management), recording and recordkeeping are secondary functions, but they are also supporting functions. They are supporting functions because they are the means by which the information is accumulated and recorded steadily, day after day, so that it can be reported to managers periodically. (Monthly, quarterly, semiannual, and annual recapitulations and other derivative reports are made up for transmittal to the managers of most organizations.)

Other secondary functions, such as making up payroll checks, paying bills, invoicing sales, and calculating taxes, are not support functions because they make no direct contributions to the main function, although they are necessary functions and may make some indirect contributions to the main function. (The figures explaining and describing these activities are included in the reports, but the physical processing of the payments and other paper does not support the main function.) In all cases, you, as the analyst, must make a decision about which are the support functions and which are other secondary functions not directly related to the main function.

THE SIGNIFICANCE OF DISTINGUISHING SECONDARY FUNCTIONS

The purpose of the analysis is to prepare for the synthesis of a better way to satisfy the need. The front-end analysis is itself means and not end. Synthesis of improvement—a better system to propose to the client—is the end. It is thus critically important to identify the need that is to be satisfied if you are accurately to identify and define the main function and to evaluate the contributions of support and other secondary functions.

More specifically, once all of this is done, (1) you can begin to judge how well the item performs its main function and satisfies the need; (2) you can judge the usefulness or efficiency of supporting functions; and (3) you can decide whether other secondary functions are necessary and make satisfactory contributions of some kind to the satisfaction of the need, for value improvement can result from a great number and wide variety of changes. There are many deficiencies that you can find among existing systems and for which you would be wise to keep an eye open. Here are just a few of the more common ones:

Unnecessary Frills. American designers especially appear to have a weakness for loading all their designs with "bells and whistles"—numerous secondary functions that have nothing whatsoever to do with the main function but only do the double damage of increasing cost and reducing reliability.

Reluctance to Change. In this jet/space/computer age, many almost Stone Age designs are still appearing everywhere, reflecting the reluctance to change and, to a large extent, the reluctance of many to learn new things and to keep up with their special fields.

The Need to be Clever.   Unfortunately, many individuals design items as monuments to their own cleverness, rather than as the most effective and most efficient designs possible. The ego trip is understandable enough, but are efficiency and effectiveness still the goals?

The Need to Appear Innovative.   Many individuals build designs that are Potemkin villages, in that they have the facade of smart modernity, but they still show early 19th Century thinking. They recognize that times are changing, but they try to disguise old designs and old thinking with new paint.

Conversely, here are just a few of the ways to improve value in the synthesis of better methods and better designs:

1. Eliminate unnecessary, trivial, unneeded, redundant, and/or non-contributing secondary functions.
2. Improve efficiency/effectiveness of main and support functions.
3. Reduce the number of steps required to carry out a function.
4. Reduce the human effort—labor—required to perform a function.
5. Automate functions and systems.

THE IDEA OF UTILITY

The foregoing suggests clearly that value is represented by the ratio of cost to function of the item. Varying either, while holding the other constant, increases or decreases value. But there is more to consider than the main function alone, in most cases. There are such items as convenience or ease of use, efficiency, dependability, durability, and other factors that have to do with the quality of the item. Improving efficiency at a sacrifice in one or more of the other characteristics may actually represent a decrease in value. In fact, the term *function* is not entirely satisfactory as one of the terms necessary to define value. We really need another term, one that considers these other factors that refer to quality and efficiency, which cannot be ignored when trying to assess value, absolute or relative. The term I choose to use here is *utility*, and it is to include the main function, with necessary support functions, if any, and those other characteristics of quality and performance referred to here.

That poses another kind of problem, however: How does one manage somehow to quantify these other factors? Without quantification of some sort, VM cannot have even the semblance of a science.

COST IMPLICATIONS OF PROGRAM DESIGNS

It was with this kind of need in mind that the Department of Defense (DOD) some years ago created the measure they called *cost-effectiveness* (which the popular press quickly explained to the public as a means of measuring the amount of "bang for a buck" a weapon or weapons system produced). One way in which VM attempts to cope with this problem of quantification is in "life cycle" cost measurement, which contemplates the estimated total cost of ownership over the entire life of the item, as distinct from the acquisition or purchase cost.

That life-cycle cost must include all the following costs:

Acquisition or cost of initial purchase
Operating cost
Maintenance cost

Operating cost may include the cost of labor, which is usually the highest cost factor in today's economic environment. It is always important in evaluating and estimating cost consequences of a design to project the probable volume and level of labor required to implement the design operationally.

That does not necessarily mean that it is always possible to substitute equipment for human labor, even when it is technically possible to do so. Equipment entails its own acquisition costs, along with operating, maintenance, and depreciation or amortization costs. These need to be considered and evaluated versus labor costs.

Maintenance cost is not confined to machines and equipment. Even management systems and computer programs often require maintenance to correct "bugs," to update the systems, when conditions call for updating, and often to adapt the systems to new developments and circumstances.

Another factor to consider where it is applicable is the end-of-life salvage value of an item—what the remains of the used-up or obsolete item are likely to bring in the marketplace—as an offset of those costs. Estimated with any accuracy, that total cost takes into account the other factors lumped earlier under the general category of "utility."

IMPACT ON PROPOSAL STRATEGIES

The possibility of designing your program for lowest life-cycle costs without sacrifice of convenience, quality, or utility is important to consider in any proposal planning. Such a possibility points to a proposal cost strategy that can be highly effective: (1) Explain the idea of life-cycle costs, (2) apply the concept to what you propose, and (3) help the client assess the *true* costs of what you offer versus the costs proposed in competitive proposals. If you analyze and present your case well you can demonstrate convincingly that the cost of acquisition is not the true cost of ownership. In this manner, you can often overcome a competitor's advantage in offering a lower acquisition cost. Moreover, this concept of life-cycle costs is not confined to physical (hardware) items; it also has validity when applied to many computer programs, management systems, and other varieties of software.

To make the case effectively, you must do more than demonstrate the validity of the principle; you must apply it to the specific case you are proposing. You must somehow manage to quantify the various cost elements by identifying and unitizing each, and you must do so convincingly. Here, perhaps more than in any other place, you must present good evidence to prove your case, to show a logical and persuasive basis for your projections and claims.

PROPOSAL TACTICS

If designing for a low life-cycle cost is a possible strategy, you still must develop tactics to sell the concept to the client. These tactics would normally proceed along the lines of any sales presentation, first offering the overall emotion-based promise of the desired results, and then building the structure of evidence.

A strong way to build the evidence is a logical argument. A first premise in such an argument might easily borrow VM's basic idea that the item in question (whether it is a system, a service, a product, or anything else) is valuable only in what it *does* for the user, not in what it is. That's not a difficult premise to establish, and it helps to set the scene and tune the client's awareness to the need to weigh results or utility in judging value.

The general evidence of an established idea and widely accepted truth is often a viable second premise. In this case, it might well be the well-known principle of trade-off, sacrificing one thing to gain another—that is, acquisition costs versus life-cycle cost.

The economics of developing a computer program illustrates the benefits of acquisition versus life-cycle cost. One can develop the program for either low acquisition costs—fastest, easiest way of writing the program—or for low operating costs—tightly written, hence economical of running time. One cannot have both, and if the computer program were to be run only once or twice, it would be sounder economic sense to write it as swiftly as possible for the lowest acquisition costs. However, if it were to be run many times, as a relatively permanent element of the system, it would pay to spend more on its development so as to write a tight program and minimize the operating cost.

The mere fact of thinking it through and presenting this careful analysis and explanation is impressive to most clients, as it reveals the consultant's knowledge and thought given to the client's need. However, as noted earlier, for maximum effectiveness, the presentation must go on to apply the principles to the case at hand.

Suppose, for example, the requirement is for the development and presentation of a training program to be presented a dozen times. This presents the familiar acquisition-versus-life-cycle problem. The program can be developed as an instructor-dependent course, one that requires presentation by highly qualified (but costly) instructors. That makes the course relatively inexpensive to develop (because it requires only a lecture guide, lesson plans, and a syllabus, usually, and it depends on the instructor to provide the course content), but it is expensive to deliver.

The reverse is possible. You can develop a course that depends on autoinstructional audiovisual programs, using videotape and other audio-visual materials, and bearing a light instructor load thereby. It requires relatively little "live" instruction and, in many cases, the instructor(s) need not be especially well qualified. Such a program would be costly to develop and costly to produce, but it would be relatively inexpensive to deliver.

There is often a third possibility, one that is normally a compromise between these extremes: A paper-based autoinstructional course, as distinct from an audiovisual one, is thus relatively economical of both instructors and development/production costs, with a cost falling between those of the other two options.

Given such a case as this, your tactics would be to project and present the total estimated costs for each option and propose the one you think most economical, if achieving low cost is, indeed, your strategy. However, to be completely convincing, you must present your design factors and cost analyses in the greatest detail possible, even to the extent of validating your figures by citing the sources (e.g., quotations by vendors) and by offering specific physical evidence, such as catalog sheets and written quotations.

A cry usually comes up in the room when this strategy is offered to a group of seminar attendees: *What do I do when the RFP doesn't reveal how many times the course is to be presented?* (Actually, in many cases the desired information is at least plainly implicit if not explicit.)

The lack of specification of usage is a typical problem, but it does not invalidate the tactic suggested here, and it does not call for asking the client to clarify the point. (It's always risky to ask such questions, especially when proposing to a public-sector—government—organization because the clarification is provided to everyone invited to propose, and you may be thus giving away to competitors much more than you get. Those are poor tactics, and there is a better way: Explain the options and the considerations important to the choice. Then you can pursue either of two courses: (1) Explain that owing to the lack of certain explicit information, you cannot urge any specific choice on the client, but invite the client to choose one of the options, using the criteria you have provided to help guide the client in making the choice. (2) If you think you can infer the information you need, explain the basic problem, recommend one of the options, but still offer the client the final decision or choice of options.

The opportunities to pursue this overall design and cost strategy are more numerous than you may imagine, for with a little imagination the idea can be adapted and applied to many custom developments.

This demonstrates a principle to bear in mind when developing a program design: Always consider the different possible approaches to the program, especially in terms of cost of each alternative, but consider *all* costs.

Giving the client a set of options and suggesting the need to make a choice often has another beneficial effect: It greatly increases the probability that you will be invited to visit the client for a discussion, possibly a presentation. My own experience has been that clients do not make independent choices easily. Once alerted to the options and alternatives, the typical client is usually motivated to want to know more—to discuss these with you, the proposer, to learn more, ostensibly—although I have always suspected that the client is really seeking guidance in making a final choice. In any case, your chances for success have suddenly increased many times!

DESIGNING TO COST

Although VM has too often been used to close the barn door after the horse has escaped, one of its spin-off developments has been the idea of designing to cost. That is, instead of permitting the design ideas to drive the cost, cost drives the design by basing the design studies on the premise, "How can the program be designed to achieve its goals for X dollars?"

This poses another possible proposal strategy, suitable for certain circumstances. For example, when the client has specified the available budget—and even government requests for proposals sometimes do that, to guide the consultant—design studies can be based on the question, "What is the maximum program/benefits we can deliver for this figure?"

Designing to cost uses VM in a special way, probably in the way it is used most effectively: VM considerations dictate the design by restricting it to the indispensable functions and the cost goals.

THE PAYOFF QUESTION IN VM

Mechanical although it may appear when rationalized, the practice of VM is most definitely a creative exercise, and it is generally carried out by a team, working together in a brainstorming session, which I believe is more accurately referred to as "ideastorming." One of the several benefits of such a collective effort to evolve ideas is the *synergy*—a result greater than the sum of its parts—that normally results from this free exchange of ideas, generated spontaneously and often triggering one another.

Having arrived at answers to such questions as "What is it?" and "What does it do?"—that is, "What is its main function?"—there are other answers to be sought. The most significant other questions, the ones that address the main objective of the exercise, are "What else would do that?" and "What would that cost?"

The answers to those questions point to the most effective and most efficient alternatives to the existing item. These questions are from the original value-engineering/VM methodology, which was predicated on the assumption that the study was of an existing item, seeking to improve its value by reducing its production cost without losing any important function or characteristic—without, that is, losing utility or quality. However, your case is different: You are trying to apply VM-like methods to the development of original design. That requires a different approach. If we are to ask, "What else?"—that is, "What should be improved?"—there must be some hypothesized design to improve or some alternative method for using VM principles in developing an original design.

SELLING THE VM-ANALYZED DESIGN

The idea of comparative VM analysis gives you a basis for sales arguments simply because it is much easier to sell against competition than to sell against prejudice. Merely offering something new and different and trying to prove its worth in an absolute sense is very difficult. You are flying directly in the face of well-substantiated resistance to change, especially to change that means accepting new and perhaps revolutionary ideas. If you are a pioneer, many clients shrink from your choice reflexively.

Instead it's much more effective to compare your own proposed design with less-desirable options in order to demonstrate your superiority and sell your design. Obviously, you cannot demonstrate superiority without comparison. However, when you are selling something unique—custom designs—you must create your own competitive item with which to compare your design. You must create what is sometimes called "a straw man" to be knocked down so as to validate your claim of superiority.

There are two ways to create or hypothesize the competitive model against which to sell your own ideas: One is to summon up some conventional design or method long used and make that the basis for your comparison. The other is to estimate one or more approaches you expect your competitors to take.

That second course can be a bit dicey unless you have some substantial reason to believe that you know what your competitors will offer. (That is the case in many situations.) Unless you are reasonably sure of that, you will be well advised to follow the first course, a much safer avenue and usually a quite effective one. If your competitors are following the conservative convention and offering conventional designs, you are selling against their designs. Further, even if they offer innovative ideas, you are asking the client to compare theirs with yours, and you're still selling against competition.

A FOR-INSTANCE

The following example shows how this strategy can be applied successfully: One consulting organization responded to an invitation from the U.S. Postal Service to develop on-the-job training (OJT) for electronic and mechanical maintenance technicians in bulk-mail centers. (The students would have had training in basic electronic and mechanical technologies at U.S. Postal Service schools.)

The successful contender devised a training-development plan, the most attractive features of which were those that departed from the conventional design and from the most disadvantageous methods of developing such training. Conventional maintenance training tends strongly to go overboard and provide far deeper and far more wide-ranging technical training than that required for maintenance: It characteristically overtrains the learners. The winning proposal identified that as a typical weakness of most maintenance training, pointing out the several disadvantages of doing that, and it promised to provide a design that would eliminate that problem. It proposed to train the technicians only in the precise needs of the equipment to be found in bulk-mail plants.

To make that proposition convincing and persuasive, the proposal had to offer some credible method for doing what it proposed. It therefore offered a highly innovative idea, the application of a methodology it called "failure probability analysis" (invented spontaneously for the proposal), explaining what that was, the rationale for it, and how it would be used to identify and define precisely what training was required and how the training program should be weighted. To convince the client of the need for identifying and defining and prioritizing the training needs, the proposer developed another worry item for the client. The worry item was itself the rationale for the proposed model of failure probability analysis, which was necessary to convince the client that the innovative method was needed.

The worry item was based on the fact that much of the equipment in the bulk-mail center was hardly beyond the prototype stage and so had no operating history on which to base the maintenance-training design. The proposer stressed this problem and used it effectively to persuade the client to buy his solution. That points up another factor: You must "do your homework"—gather information on which to base your approach, as this successful proposer did in learning that most of the equipment in the bulk mail center was of recent and untried design.

Suggesting innovation has two potential hazards: (1) The client may be conservative and apprehensive of change that appears revolutionary, or the client may be fond of conventional design and may be fearful of any but the slightest changes for other reasons—perhaps the client has a comfortably familiar existing system to be improved on or replaced but not changed seriously. (2) The client may interpret what you say as an attack on or criticism of his or her existing system or of the method he or she believes in. Hence, you must be careful in your presentation that you do not unintentionally give offense by saying things that the client may interpret as an attack or criticism. (In general, avoid the appearance of criticizing, preaching, lecturing, pontificating, etc.)

You must also be careful to avoid appearing revolutionary. That threatens the client's sense of security, and you must never underestimate the prevalence of insecurity. It lies buried not far beneath the surface in many of us, and it is quite easy to arouse, usually with disastrous results. In fact, you want to strive for the opposite effect of helping the client to feel quite secure in doing business with you.

There is something of an anomaly built into this. On the one hand, you want to be innovative and offer what someone else does not or cannot offer, selling your innovative design on the basis of advantages offered by the innovations. Yet you want also to avoid being too innovative or appearing to be revolutionary. What's more, there is still another consideration: how to gain the advantage of presenting your innovative design in a manner that commands attention and makes your proposal outstanding in that respect.

The excellent example just cited of a proposal to the U.S. Postal Service shows how this typical problem of reconciling these conflicting needs was solved successfully, and it is examined later in regard to the methods used for doing so.

A CLOSER LOOK AT THE CREATIVE PROCESS

There are various theories of how the creative process works, and it probably works in more than one way. Some individuals, such as many prolific inventors, can often come up spontaneously and consciously with useful new ideas on a regular basis. Others can do the same thing, but only through laborious and lengthy processes. Still others develop new ideas occasionally and usually neither know how it was done nor even think about it a great deal. (Unfortunately, many other people develop great new ideas but never do anything about them, either through inertia or because of the common fear of being different to even a slight degree and risking possible criticism thereby.)

Those who have studied creativity and drawn conclusions from their studies advise us that creativity is much more often a new combination of known ideas or components than it is a completely original idea or creation. (Some even maintain that creativity is always a recombination of known factors or components into new patterns.) There is a great deal of evidence for this notion. Certainly, examination of existing devices bears it out in many cases, for there are few inventions or other new developments for which the antecedents are not quite apparent. (It was, for example, quite a long time before automobiles ceased to resemble "horseless carriages" and that epithet vanished from the language.) There is also ample other evidence for this view of creativity.

There is also much evidence that a major element in the creative process is the contribution of one's subconscious mind. In studies of creativity, three main stages appear to exist in most cases of creative breakthrough, stages that can be fairly described by the following terms:

1. Concentration
2. Incubation
3. Inspiration

Again and again, we learn from many of those who have demonstrated great creative powers that first they focus consciously on the problem until they have exhausted all possibilities that occur to them to be worth pursuing. Then they go on to other things and incubate the problem, which means that the subconscious mind takes over and works on the problem. Finally, usually when they are relaxing at something with no particular heavy thinking going on, the inspiration comes or the solution suddenly flashes into their minds.

We are told that your subconscious never forgets anything. That appears to account for its great ability to work on problems: With greater recall, it has far more referents—relevant ideas—to consider than does the conscious mind.

How often have you been frustrated by an inability to remember a name, title, address, telephone number, or other item that you think you ought to be able to recall easily, and then had it pop into your mind much later, when you are not thinking about anything related to it? That is an example of the unconscious mind at work, as is hypnotism and its effects.

There is no readily accessible direct link between the conscious and unconscious minds. Intense concentration is one way to establish linkage. Hypnosis is another way. Hypnosis is based on maximum relaxation of the conscious mind. Evidently, it is that relaxation that opens the gate between the two and permits communication both ways—thus, the need to concentrate on the problem, incubate it, and then ignore it, allowing for inspiration. For example, you may wake up in the morning with the answer to something that has been troubling you, a widely reported experience.

OTHER ANALYTICAL TOOLS

The checklists, the functional flowcharts, and the VM methods are all useful analytical tools, but they are not the only tools available to provoke thoughtful analysis of requirements and formulation of strategies and approaches. Several others are commonly used for this purpose.

Why-It-Can't-Be-Done Analysis

One used by many in proposal development is called informally the "why-it-can't-be-done" analysis. It can be used in almost all cases, although more appropriate in cases where the problem is complex or difficult than in simple or straightforward ones. When the requirement is rather straightforward, it calls more for management and dependability than for complicated problem solving.

One major objective of why-it-can't-be-done analysis is the development of worry items by unearthing problems not readily discerned. (This, you may recall, is also one of the objectives of analytical tools and methods discussed earlier.) Addressing the requirement from this unusual perspective calls for deliberately seeking out problems and looking for potential obstacles to the successful accomplishment of the mission, as you imagine the client or competitors might see them. This discovery process provides the seeds for technical and sales arguments (which are often the same in proposals) by anticipating the objections and responding to them.

Personification

Some analysts find it useful to try to project themselves into the problem to gain greater insight into it. Inventor Charles Kettering (inventor of the automobile self-starter and the electric cash register, among other things), when he was working on improving the diesel engine and making it a more practical prime mover, imagined himself in the inner chambers of the engine, as he asked himself what he needed to work more efficiently as a diesel engine.

FAST Diagramming

VM has developed its own special kind of functional diagramming, which it calls FAST diagrams, for function analysis systems technique. It consists of making a diagram in which the leftmost block represents the main function, followed by a "why" block, and supporting functions are represented in boxes proceeding to the right in order of priority. Other secondary functions, not essential to the main function, are placed above or below the line of flow in locations suggesting their roles in the operational system. Figure 13 illustrates this. Note that the main function must correlate with the purpose of the item.

To further illustrate this, a simplified FAST diagram of the U.S. Postal Service proposal idea is offered as Figure 14. Note the *How? (left-to-right) and Why? (right-to-left)* progression, including the *why* of the main function, answered by a block that describes the purpose of the item. The *How/ Why* questions verify the validity of the diagram, as they do in any other functional or logical diagram.

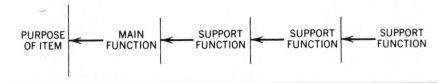

Figure 13. Principle of FAST (function analysis systems technique) diagramming.

Figure 14. FAST diagram of the Postal Service training proposal discussed in text.

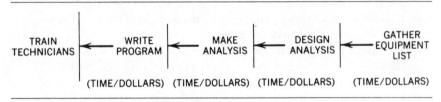

Figure 15. Further use of the FAST diagram.

This is not all of it. There is more utility to the FAST diagram than appears here. Figure 15 illustrates this. A figure for whatever parameter is being addressed—money, time, materials, labor, or other—is measured or estimated for each function in the chain. This is done first for the original model or the one to which the proposed model is to be compared, and then to each alternative model. This enables the analyst to make comparisons and decide which is the best alternative.

Note that it is not necessarily greatest efficiency of cost in dollars that is the objective of the study. This kind of study may be undertaken to find the maximum design for the conservation of time, labor, materials, waste, or almost any other parameter. You can use this to devise the shortest schedule when that is what the client seeks, or to achieve any other parameter of effectiveness and efficiency. To that end, there is a useful technique you may use to develop FAST or any other kind of diagrams with greatest convenience and efficiency. A case history will illustrate this, while it also illustrates the utility of VM to conserve schedule time:

An EPA Problem

The Environmental Protection Agency of the federal government (EPA) was having trouble spending all the $10 billion it was authorized by Congress to give away in grants to communities whose water systems needed to be repaired, improved, and/or updated. There was a time limit on the program, but there were also requirements for grantee qualifications and for engineering/technical specifications. A Vermont engineering firm had been retained to help the communities make the engineering studies the program required with each grant application. Still, each grant application was taking far too long to get through the system, and it was almost a certainty that unless something was done soon, the money would not be spent within the statutory time limit set for it by Congress.

Something had to be done to prevent the program from foundering. The Vermont firm was expert enough in the technical work that had to be done, but they did not have the kind of capability required to help EPA speed up the program. Consequently, EPA decided that this was a case for VM, and it assisted the Vermont firm by arranging for the services of three VM experts to help the firm streamline the grant process.

After three days of work, the team—the firm's engineers and the VM specialists—reached the point where they had identified all the functions of the entire grant application process. At first, they simply listed each function. Then they wrote each one out on a card. Finally, they arranged the cards on a board, as a FAST diagram, in the order in which they occurred in the grant process, where all could study them.

That is a useful technique during the study phases of existing designs and projected designs; it enables you to move the function cards around until you are sure they are in optimum order. That means that you need write each function only once, instead of numerous times, using them as building blocks while you design the FAST diagram.

In this case, once the cards were arranged in order on the board, the leader of the VM team began to question the engineers as to how long each step—function—of the process took, for the objective of this VM study was to reduce schedule time, not dollars. (Remember that the VM discipline can be applied to optimize any parameter.)

It was not long before it became apparent that the bottleneck and the chief problem lay in the many months it took the engineers in each community to write up the technical reports that were required by the grant regulations. In fact, they were taking from 90 to 180 days to write reports that should have been done easily within 30 days after the engineering work was completed if they kept good logs and/or worked at their drafts while doing the engineering work, instead of wasting time later gathering data that should have been easily at hand.

Once the problem was identified, the solution was apparent and not difficult to synthesize and implement. Obviously, something had to be done to aid the engineers in speeding up their report writing and get the reports done with reasonable facility, but this was no longer difficult to perceive. And, once the specific problem cause was identified, it was not too difficult to develop a solution.

DEFINITION OF THE PROBLEM

Note what happened in this case: Once the problem (and its cause) was properly identified and defined, possible solutions were suggested and almost obvious, defined by the identification of the problem: Some action to speed up the writing of the engineering reports was necessary. What remained was to identify and list the various options available to do this (there are several possible approaches to this) and then decide which was the best option to select and implement. These are the chief options available that are suggested by logical evaluation:

- Arrange for professional technical writers to work with the engineers and write the reports.
- Train the engineers in report writing.
- Design a standardized report form and require the engineers to begin completing the form earlier, as data accumulates.

The most practical of these choices and probably the only one that is reasonably certain to work out satisfactorily is the first one, although the idea of a standardized form for the reports is an excellent one and would probably facilitate their completion on schedule.

THE PROBLEM IS THE SOLUTION

The fact that the accurate definition of the problem contained the seeds of the solution was not a fluke. It is typical. In most cases, when the problem is truly identified or defined, it requires little additional analysis to identify the options available or to decide which of those options is the most practical and desirable one to select. Even in those cases where more than one solution appears to be completely workable and some further analysis is required to make the best choice, that is a relatively small task; the major task is done once the problem has been specifically identified.

The converse is also true: Until the solution or direct approach to solution is almost obvious, you may be almost certain that the problem has not yet been identified or defined properly. That should serve as a guide in problem analysis, to help you to avoid confusing the symptoms or the trivial issues with the true problem definition. In this way, you are guided to continue the analysis until you perceive the solution or the direct approach to it.

Confusing the symptoms with the problem is easy to do, and we are frequently not conscious that we are doing so unless we have some distinct methodology to help us make the appropriate determination. Referring again to the EPA case cited here, to the federal agency officials, the problem was that of how to get all the grant money spent in time. That was the problem as they saw it and as they turned it over to the Vermont engineering firm and the VM specialists assigned as consultants to the Vermont engineers.

On the other hand, that statement of the problem was not satisfactory for the VM consultants because it did not even hint at the cause of the delay in making the grant awards. (In the VM analysis, the first revelation was that the applications were taking too long to complete, which then led to the search for the bottleneck in the application process.) Therefore, the original "statement of the problem" was actually the statement of a symptom, not of the true problem, which demonstrated that the problem was yet to be defined. Before the consultants could solve the problem, they had to know what the problem was, so problem definition was 99 percent of the task requirement.

That also indicates that a problem definition often depends on the orientation and the special interests of the individual offering the definition. The problem viewed by those who address it by hiring someone to solve it is different than the problem viewed by those who must develop the specific solution. The interest of the EPA officials was to comply with the will of Congress and get the grant money allocated before the statutory deadline. That was all that really concerned them, so they cast their problem definition in those terms, in terms of their own need. The mission the EPA set for itself

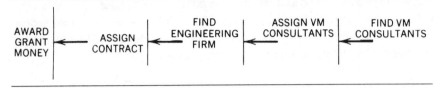

Figure 16. Principle of FAST (function analysis systems technique) diagramming.

was simply to find someone to solve the problem and turn the search for solution over as a contracted project. A FAST diagram explaining that, from EPA's viewpoint, would appear as in Figure 16. The main function was to provide engineering support to the grantees to help them accelerate the application and award processes, but the engineering firm required the VM support, so EPA had to supply both, including the VM support as a secondary function that was in direct support of the main function.

This demonstrates that someone else's "problem" is likely to be only a symptom to you. The client is likely to cast the problem definition in terms of the desired result, as EPA did (speed up the grant applications so we can get the program completed in time), but you must cast it in terms of the solution to the problem—what is required, specifically, to achieve that result.

This condition is not confined to clients who have problems that require technical analysis to develop solutions. It is equally relevant in those cases where there appears to be no question about the solution—where, for example, the client wants a number of technical or professional temporaries to work on the client's premises and help develop a training program or a marketing presentation. Frequently, such clients need help in determining their true need; it is not always what it appears to the client to be, and you should never accept the client's view of the need or problem without examining it and giving it serious study. Part of your responsibility as a proposer is to analyze the requirement as stated and render an opinion as to what the client needs.

There is always some element of risk in telling a client that he or she is wrong, of course, no matter how tactfully you say this, but you can gain a great deal of marketing leverage if you convince the client that you are about to save him or her from a disastrous mistake. It has been my personal conviction for some years, based on the experience of my own mistakes, that while you should be as diplomatic as possible, you should still be honest with a client, especially about what you believe is in the client's best interests. It is almost always possible to do so without arousing hostility if you handle the matter discreetly in your proposal.

CHAPTER 8

Writing, Communication, and Persuasion

Writing is among our most ancient arts, the proof of civilization, in fact, and despite our best efforts, it has remained far more an art than a science.

THE ROLE OF WRITING

The role of writing skills in proposal development has been deliberately downplayed in these pages until now. The reason for this was to bring sales and marketing skills to center stage, where they belong, as the most important skills in proposal development. It was a specific effort to avoid the hazard of permitting writing skill to eclipse or overshadow the role of marketing. Successful proposals are not merely "written," in the conventional sense in which that term is used, but they are developed as part of a lengthy sales/marketing process. Writing, with its many related functions, is properly the final phase of the process and not the central arena of the action.

Still, writing skills are certainly not unimportant and should not be overlooked, despite recognizing the central role of sales and marketing. Sales and marketing are necessary to the development of the all-important basic strategies and arguments of the proposal presentation, but writing implements those strategies and arguments. Because of that fundamental truth, brilliant strategies and powerful sales arguments are seriously weakened by ineffective writing, whereas relatively unimaginative strategies and pedestrian sales arguments are often made quite effective when skillfully presented in the written proposal. Now it is time to bring writing and other editorial skills center stage and grant them their due.

WHAT IS WRITING?

Do we use that word to refer strictly to the use of words on paper? Or does the word have some broader meaning or more far-ranging frame of reference? Or does that make a difference? Before we get into that question, let us consider communication itself. We have become a communication-conscious society, and we tend strongly to equate writing with communication. In fact, many of those who write and lecture on the subject of writing appear to regard *writing* and *communication* as almost interchangeable terms, or at least to consider communication to be the sole objective or purpose of writing.

Much of the difficulty in writing relates to the difficulties of communication. Massachusetts management consultant Jeffrey Geibel, for example, freely acknowledges the role of the proposal as "essentially a marketing device," but he also observes that consultants need to use proposals because "communication is critical in the marketing of an intangible. . . . people are imperfect communicators, and correct communication (understanding) is critical to the success of the consulting process and the consultant."

Geibel is, of course, quite correct in his observations. However, it is only fair to note here that if most of us are, indeed, imperfect communicators, as he puts it, that is not necessarily due to the lack of language skills in expressing ourselves. It also reflects the shortcomings of language itself as an unambiguous and unequivocal means of communication.

WHAT IS COMMUNICATION?

Like the word *writing*, *communication* is a word with many implications in today's world of jet air travel, radiotelephones, computers, and communications satellites. Therefore, it is necessary to establish what I mean when I use that term, for it is used here only with respect to proposals. For these purposes, *communication* shall mean the conveyance of specific meanings from one mind to another, and in most applications and references here, it will mean the conveying of meanings via those written presentations and related writing called "proposals."

That is a general definition, but it is not precise enough for our purposes because it does not truly define what is meant by "the conveying of meanings." In fact, its chief deficiency is that it implies a unilateral action, that communication takes place when something is conveyed from a sender to a receiver without considering how accurately or effectively that transfer of information is accomplished. It thus fails to acknowledge the bilateral nature of the process (and *communication* is a process, not merely an action or event): It is not completed until the receiver gets the message sent, and it has not taken place until and unless the receiver gets the same message as the one sent.

Therein lies the difficulty. There is ample evidence that only rarely do senders succeed in placing in the receiver's brain the identical meanings intended by the sender. This is even more the case with verbal messages than with written messages, and this is at least partially what many have in mind when stressing the need to "put it in writing" or "get it in writing." However, even the most carefully drafted of written materials rarely succeeds totally in conveying the precise meaning that the writers mean to send. Readers invariably *interpret* the words they read and hear, and each of us has our own conscious and unconscious biases that influence those interpretations.

THE RESPONSIBILITY FOR CLEAR COMMUNICATION

As a result of work by behavioral psychologist B. F. Skinner and others, modern educational theory and philosophy no longer place the total burden for learning on the learner, but compel the instructor or instructional system to bear the major part of the responsibility (unless, of course, there are special circumstances.) The modern educational theory holds that it is the instructor/instructional system that is defective and should be held responsible when the learner does not learn.

Very much the same philosophy ought to be applied to writing. It is, or ought to be, the responsibility of the writer to write clearly, unambiguously, and unequivocally, as perceived by the reader. Given a reader of at least average abilities to read and comprehend, and despite the frailties of language as a means for clear and unambiguous communication, it is the writer, not the reader, who has failed when the reader's brain records a substantially inaccurate or incomplete message.

We must recognize, therefore, that communication is not a one-way process; it is a two-way process, involving both sending and receiving and requiring success at both ends—success in formulating and sending messages "in the clear," and success in interpreting the messages as intended. But there is even more to this: It means also that writing in a way that results in readers interpreting your words as you wish them to be interpreted is not at all easy. Quite the contrary, it is very difficult. It requires you to estimate the probable biases of your readers and to understand the connotations (nuances or implications), as well as the denotations (literal meaning) of the words we contemplate using. It requires you to be sensitive to the emotional content of words, to understand, for example, the difference in connotation between *stubborn* and *determined*.

PERSUASIVENESS IN WRITING

It can be argued logically that the purpose of all writing is to persuade. (In fact, an especially effective and successful sales manager of my acquaintance many years ago insisted that whenever an exchange between two people took place, a "sale" was made, and he presented a convincing argument to support that assertion.) At the least, the writer wishes to persuade the reader to believe what he or she has written and strives to be credible. However, that generalization aside, it is the obvious and admitted primary objective of all sales presentations to persuade readers to believe and do whatever the sales presentation urges and advocates. We have, therefore, both persuasion and communication as primary proposal objectives.

There is a direct link between these two goals. Of course, it is necessary to communicate, if you are to present those motivators and arguments that, you hope, will persuade the listener or reader. Other considerations also show the close link between persuasion and communication.

Belief Versus Understanding

Disagreements are often dismissed as reflective of or due to "a lack of communication." The premise on which that diagnosis is based is that the parties did not understand each other. Of course, the opposite may be true: they may have understood each other all too well! In any case, we tend to generalize that disagreements result from some failure to communicate.

Translated freely, that "lack of communication" more often means that one party failed completely to bring the other party to agreement—failed to make a persuasive argument, that is. Many have a mistaken notion about this, too: We think that people tend to believe whatever they have come to understand. The mistaken idea that a logical explanation will bring about understanding, and through that, belief and persuasion leads to the sincere kinds of proposals that attempt to sell the proposer's services on the basis of pure logical rationale.

Alas, the approach simply does not work because the cause and effects are reversed. People come to understand whatever they have been persuaded to believe, and logic has nothing whatsoever to do with understanding unless the individual is prepared first to believe. Thus, we have those who still stubbornly maintain that humans have not traveled to the moon, but the U.S. Government has perpetrated a gigantic fraud for purposes of propaganda, and we still have those who cling to their belief that the earth is flat, as well as many others who fly in the face of massive evidence to the contrary. They can never understand what most of us do because they are unable to believe what most of us believe.

In fact, all understanding is founded in belief somewhere in the chain of logic and reason, for we cannot verify everything personally. None of us has ever seen an atom, few of us have been to many of the more exotic places in the world, and even fewer of us have been to the moon. We accept these and many other things "on faith," which means that we find the individuals and/or organizations who report these things credible, and we *believe* their reports.

Those who reject what almost all of us accept and believe are among those characterized as part of what is termed "the lunatic fringe," those individuals who are grossly and massively irrational by the logical standards most of us agree on and accept. To that extent, they are extreme examples. However, most of us are also irrational in many respects, albeit on a far less extreme scale. Most of us know very well the dictate of ordinary logic that belief arises from understanding. However, emotional forces within us tend both to demand that we understand whatever we believe, and to believe that which we prefer to believe because it satisfies some need within us. We thus have a rather profound ability to refuse to "understand" that which we prefer not to believe, as almost any argument on politics or religion will demonstrate rather quickly.

This is again testimony to the truth that we are far more creatures of our emotions than of our reason where our personal lives and desires are involved; this is the critical truth for sales and marketing. Every truly knowledgeable marketer knows that there is an easy way to persuade prospects to believe what you want them to believe: Simply tell them what they want to hear. They will always believe that, and they will require much less evidence to believe the promise they want to believe.

That is more than sardonic observation. It reflects, once again, the fundamental truth that the promise of great personal benefits is by far the one easiest to believe. That is, the motivators are invariably emotional appeals. (Of course there are exceptions: a relative handful of people are coldly logical, virtual human calculators and all but immune to emotional appeals, but their numbers are so small that it is not worthwhile to worry about them as exceptions.) The most widely used motivators are promises of success, money, prestige, love, security, protection from life's harsh realities, and other "apple pie and motherhood" sweet dreams. But do these appear redundant? Are they all addressing the same *basic* motivation— security? Of course they are. Nothing is more basic than the need to feel secure, whether security is represented to an individual by money, prestige, career success, love, avoidance of disasters, and/or other such blessing. In the end, the drive for security is *the* motivator. The difference is merely in what represents security to the individual prospect. Identify that (those) for your own set of prospects, and you have the key to your own sales/ marketing success.

Does This Apply to Proposals?

Many people find this easy to understand when applied to goods and services offered to the consumer for personal uses, but they find it difficult to believe when applied to the business world. Are managers rational, impersonal, and unemotional when they buy for someone else—for an employer, that is? Are they psychologically and emotionally totally differ- ent as executives than they are as individuals? Or do they respond to the same motivators—motivated by consideration of their personal interests— when they are making purchase decisions for their employers?

The answer to the last question is *yes*, of course. Most people in positions of authority and responsibility perceive their personal interests very much involved in any decisions or actions they take in connection with their positions. In fact, executives are frequently far more emotion-driven when acting for their employers because they perceive their prestige and security to be even more immediately at stake than when they are acting as consumers. When acting as consumers, perhaps no one else will know of any fiasco resulting from a mistaken judgment. But when acting for an employer, a mistake may have direct and potentially severe consequences to one's career. That concern can be a very powerful motivator.

Of course, an executive is motivated by the desire for gain, as well as by the fear of consequence. Therefore, the possible career benefits of doing well and becoming a local "hero" in a wise and highly satisfactory procurement are necessarily possibilities to consider very seriously.

The proposal writer should carefully consider human motivation, bearing in mind that all organizations, whether small business, huge corporations, or government agencies, are made up of people and that those people are motivated in their decision making by the same fears and desires as are others.

It is, of course, always dangerous to generalize, and there is no intention here to suggest that there is any single truth about the most effective motivations—that any single motivation is equally effective in or appropriate to all applications and all individuals. To devise successful strategies and make effective appeals, especially those that hinge on judging the best personal motivators of those making the final judgments and decisions regarding your proposal, it is absolutely essential to know something about those individuals personally, as well as about the circumstances surrounding the requirement in general. The motivator that is effective with one individual—fear of failure if an innovative approach is proposed—may fall flat with another individual who happens to want to draw attention from the corporate hierarchy by buying an innovative approach and thereby launching a dramatic initiative in the company. The ability to assess personal motivations accurately is often the basis for a proposal's success.

Credibility

Important although it is, the promise of satisfying a motivation alone is not enough. The promise is what the client wants to believe, but the client cannot accept it without some basis for believing it, for accepting the promise. Thus, the matter of credibility arises.

There are actually at least two aspects to credibility: (1) the evidence, and (2) the presentation technique. The matter of proof or evidence was discussed earlier. Although we are emotional creatures and far less rational than we prefer to believe, we are not entirely irrational. No matter how much we want to believe the promise of some much-to-be-desired benefit, we still demand at least a modicum of evidence to support our belief and give us a basis for accepting the promise. So proof, or at least evidence, is one necessary element of credibility, although not the only element.

The other aspect of credibility pertains to the presentation technique itself. Just as powerful strategies are weakened by ineffectual writing and uninspired strategies are strengthened by skillful writing, so the impact and credibility of any evidence offered depends on the skill with which it is presented. The language has its own profound psychological effect on the reader. There are many traps for the unwary in this area of concern alone. For example, hyperbole and generalization are hazards to be avoided.

Hyperbole.   There may be uses in which hyperbole aids the purposes of the writer. This is rarely the case in proposals. Here, the claim of "many thousands," when it is obvious that the actual number must be only hundreds, is a disastrous faux pas. Here the use of Hollywood-style superlatives—*magnificent, enormous, sensational,* and others of that stripe—are deadly for your purposes. Such obvious exaggeration for effect is understood by moviegoers and tolerated, often even with amusement, because it does not affect the individual greatly and because little is at stake, except the price of a ticket and an hour or two of time. On the other hand, the aura of insincerity or frivolity is the diametric opposite of the effect to be sought in a proposal, and it is not easily tolerated by executives to whom a proposal and the consulting project are serious business matters. It is therefore wise to avoid hyperbole and to be as precise as possible in offering evidence of any kind in your proposals.

Generalization.   Almost as deadly as hyperbole in its effect is the all-too-popular practice of generalization. This can stem from either of two possible weaknesses in the proposal effort and in writing technique generally: (1) Often, it is simply a technique of laziness and evasion; rather than undertake the labor of searching out the specific and even minute details, the writer resorts to generalization as a convenient expedient. (2) But sometimes, generalization is an act of desperation. The writer has no real facts and does not know where or how to seek them out, or what to do as an alternative to generalization. That is also the result of a lack of imagination, for there are many ways to cope with this.

Nouns and Verbs.   Hyperbole results from the too-enthusiastic use of superlatives—adjectives and adverbs. Restricting function descriptions to nouns and verbs enforces a discipline and compels the value analyst to make a firm commitment to a precise definition. In writing generally and in proposals particularly, an adherence to rigid economy in the use of adjectives and adverbs forces a discipline of thinking on you as a writer. That, together with a careful avoidance of generalizations and philosophical ruminations, invigorates your writing style and, more importantly, lends your writing an air of authenticity and authority lacking in writing that violates these principles. The result is a greatly enhanced quality of believability.

DON'T REINVENT THE WHEEL

With respect to what was said earlier about generalization, it is not always necessary to go to great pains to find and present detailed information. Quite the contrary, there are many ways to minimize the effort without sacrificing the results. Following are several examples to illustrate what one can do with a bit of resourcefulness and enough energy, for which the moral may well be, *don't reinvent the wheel.*

Written Procedures and Policies

In some cases, where the project requires that the consultant make many purchases as the agent of the client, the proposal request will require that the consultant include a description of his or her purchasing procedures and policies. Many large organizations have a formal purchasing manual or written procedures, which can be used in entirety or in part. The independent consultant or small consulting organization may very well not have such a document, and thus some consultants are inspired to meet this proposal requirement with vague generalizations and philosophical ruminations. (Surprisingly enough, even some rather large organizations do not have formalized procedures and written policies for these functions, other than a typed memorandum or two.)

In other cases, the proposal request may demand a copy of personnel procedures and policies, quality control directives, and/or other such formal documents. Again, the unwary proposal writer often responds, unsatisfactorily, with evasive pontifications that tend more to reveal than to conceal the lack of such formalized policies and procedures.

The sensible approach to meeting this requirement in such circumstances is to *create* the requested document spontaneously for the proposal. That document need not be a slick, bound manual, as it would be in a large corporation. It is perfectly acceptable for it to be a typed document bound with a staple or a standard report binder. Nor is it even always necessary to create such a document from scratch. You can often pick up another organization's manual or procedural/policy document and adapt it to your own situation and needs. It is wise to be alert for opportunities to acquire such resource documents for your own proposal library, where the document will be available when needed. There are also publishers who sell generic purchasing manuals, employee policy manuals, and other such publications as staples that you can easily adapt to your own needs. Your own stationer may carry such items; call and inquire.

Quantified Data

Some clients want some quantified data by which to assess your experience or other qualifications. In one case, a client seeking a technical writing consultant asked for an account of qualifications on a quantitative basis of technical documents produced—numbers of documents of each type, numbers of pages, and other such figures, rather than of years of experience. The consultant who wrote the winning proposal in this case did not have project histories recording those figures, but he did have a good recall of specific projects. He made a series of estimates, using a procedure that he believed produced results that were reasonably accurate, and he reported the resulting figures. He was also careful to report the exact figures produced by the estimating method and did not round them off, a wise precaution. (Neatly rounded off numbers tend to be suspect—such as

"97,850 pages" is far more credible, hence far more persuasive, than "100,000 pages.")

Resources

In proposing a large training project, for which the details of proposed curricula and supporting materials was a requirement, the consultant who wrote the successful proposal sent for the catalogs of textbook publishers, bought a copy of a government publication listing several thousand training films and other audiovisual training materials, and borrowed a dozen reference books from the nearby public library. Careful scanning and a large cut-and-paste operation soon produced a meticulously detailed proposed program that left almost nothing to be desired.

The client was more than impressed with the magnitude of the documentation that appeared in the proposal, which was far more voluminous and detailed than the client had expected or than competitors produced: He admitted to being "overwhelmed" and even awed by the enormous effort the consultant had apparently expended on the proposal. Ironically, because the consultant had been so resourceful, the required effort was really not very great, as compared with the impression of effort it created, and it was that very factor that permitted the consultant to include such a great volume of painstaking detail. That would simply not have been possible had he chosen to pursue all the details by the direct means of chasing down each item individually.

Again, this illustrates the principle that there is always an easier or a better way to get something done if you allow your imagination some freedom from conventional thinking and if you remember the injunction to avoid reinventing the wheel. Even if the idea or information you need is not precisely what you want, it is almost always far easier to modify it and adapt it to your needs than to start from scratch to create a copy of something already in existence. (The desktop computer has made this even more cogent an argument than ever.)

WHAT IS "BAD" WRITING?

Writing "well" has more than one meaning, depending on application and kind of writing. It certainly means something different when applied to novelists than it does when applied to scientists or philosophers writing in their respective fields. It means something else again when applied to the present application, the writing of proposals. Therefore, while some of what is said here might have some application to writing in general, that is pure coincidence, for this chapter is concerned only with what is "good writing" in proposals and/or related presentation and marketing materials.

Mechanics

I do not dwell on the mechanics of using language—grammar, spelling, punctuation, and so on. The assumption here is that you can use the English language with reasonable fluency, that you know the basics of sentence structure and other basics of using our language, that you will turn to a dictionary for guidance in using words correctly and spelling them as they should be spelled, and that I am neither qualified nor ambitious to be a grammarian, much less a tutor in the subject.

Nonetheless, there is at least one observation that should be made on the subject of language usage: What is acceptable usage in "creative" writing is not always acceptable in proposals. For example, the novelist may use sentence fragments—phrases lacking the essential sentence elements of subject, predicate, and so on, and even single words—as sentences, as well as perhaps many other violations of the usage "rules." Creative writers do these things to achieve special effects, and readers understand that. However, in the formal business atmosphere of proposal writing, such uses are not normally acceptable. Proposals should be straightforward narrative expositions, conforming to normal rules of usage.

This is not to say that there is no need to achieve special effects, such as emphasizing certain points, in proposals. However, there are ways to do this without violating accepted usage, and these ways are discussed at the proper time. "Bad" writing, as discussed here, has nothing to do with the mechanics of usage; it has to do with failures to communicate, failures to persuade, and failures generally to make an effective presentation.

Content and Organization (Not Grammar and Punctuation)

The chief fault in proposal writing that can be characterized as bad writing is not linked to usage, but to something far more serious. Even if the proposal turns out to be a little shaky in the matter of usage, a competent editor can fix that rather easily. This other problem, however, is another matter, not so easily repaired. It is the matter of essential content and organization. Editing cannot repair serious faults of content and organization, and even rewriting often cannot repair it, for the problem stems too often from the lack of substance.

The Lack of Substance. The *lack of substance* can mean any one or many more of a wide variety of faults, and it conveys to the client such impressions, whether true or not, as the following:

1.   The proposal shows *little understanding* of the problem. It appears that the consultant began to write without having first properly analyzed or truly understood what the client wants and needs.

2.   The consultant has done only *superficial research* in gathering data and organizing a plan to be proposed. It lacks the necessary detail to permit a proper evaluation.

3.   The consultant really has *insufficient expertise* in what is needed or in the claimed field of technical/professional specialization.

4.   The proposal shows *a failure to respond* to what the client has requested and offers a plan that is inappropriate and perhaps is even an off-the-shelf plan offered to every client, no matter what the client has requested.

5.   The plan has good elements, but it shows *poor organization* and perhaps even some *incoherence*; thus, it is all but impossible to understand, much less to evaluate.

6.   The proposal is spotty and inconsistent in coverage, having some excellent parts, but then having some sketchy and vague areas too, often in important matters. The impression this creates is that the consultant is expert in only some of the relevant areas, and lacking badly in others.

What all of this adds up to is serious deficiency of content. It says to the client that the proposer is not responsive, for one reason or another—does not understand the problem, is not qualified to solve the problem, was unwilling to make a serious effort to study the requirement and develop a plan to propose, is incapable of developing a plan, is reluctant to make the commitment to a serious proposal effort, cannot think well, or suffers other deficiencies.

Lack of Commitment.   Unless the client happens to be acquainted with you from some past relationship, you will be judged primarily on the impression your proposal makes. If your proposal conveys an impression of one of the foregoing deficiencies, it is unlikely that you will ever be favorably regarded by that client. Moral: If you cannot or will not make a serious commitment to the proposal and all it requires, you are much better off not to bid on the request, waiting instead for a more favorable occasion to respond.

A SIMPLE DEFINITION OF BAD WRITING

Note that the postulate of a client's opinion or reaction is based entirely on the client's perception of truth. In fact, for this discussion, *bad writing* is simply writing that fails in its purpose. Even if your proposal contains an excellent plan—perhaps even a brilliant one—it is the impression your proposal makes on the client that will influence him or her. Poor writing of itself, in the sense of awkward usage and dull rhetoric, may have a bad effect and may cast you in an unfavorable light in general terms of your professional image: The client tends to believe that a competent professional ought to be capable of expressing him- or herself clearly, if not eloquently, and the failure to do so creates a seriously adverse impression.

Entirely aside from the "image" effects of bad writing, there is the potential disaster of failing to bring the client to complete comprehension of everything your proposal says. Obviously, even the most brilliant plan and the most impeccable credentials will avail you nothing if the client does not understand and perceive them, which underscores the importance of logical and coherent organization and the other essentials of clear writing. That also includes the use of every legitimate communication device you can muster in behalf of delivering your messages with absolute precision, such as an abundantly free use of well-conceived and well-executed graphics, tables and matrices, explanatory titles, headlines, and captions, and any other *aid to understanding* that you can conceive.

WRITING IS MORE THAN WORDS

It is important to perceive in this that "writing" does not refer to the use of words alone. One of the common faults exhibited by some writers is the use of tables and matrices only when the data to be presented obviously appear to mandate being offered in tabular or matrix presentations—when tabular and matrix representations fairly force themselves upon the writer—and they often turn to graphics only as an afterthought, tacking them on to the manuscript in what is sometimes referred to as "outboard" design. (Unfortunately, this fact is quite often all too apparent to the reader.)

To use these various communication aids effectively, they must be integral to the proposal, conceived as part of the basic vehicle of communication. A later chapter presents many specific examples, which may be borrowed to use as models, but some guidelines covering their use and evaluation are presented here, after a brief discussion of organization and some methods for organizing your information effectively.

Organization

There are a number of classic patterns in which to organize information, including these basic ones:

1. General to the particular, usually in a growing pattern of focus on specific detail until the final point is made, in a kind of deductive-reasoning process, establishing the principles and then applying them to a specific case
2. Particular to the general, in a kind of inductive-reasoning process, discussing the specific data and inferring the principles or main message from that
3. Chronological, from beginning to end (present) or from end to beginning, tracing the course and process
4. Order of importance or priority, lesser to greater or vice versa

It is even possible to mix these methods, although mixing them is inadvisable if it can be avoided because an unbroken pattern of organization is simpler to write coherently and easier for the reader to follow. Mixing them successfully—without causing confusion—calls for some rather expert writing skills and careful control of the reader's orientation. This is probably a task for the experienced professional writer, and a dangerous adventure for anyone else.

Each of the methods has its pros and cons, according to the circumstances and objectives of the application. Explaining how you've arrived at a given approach is often best accomplished by a chronological presentation that describes how you evolved the ideas for your approach over some series of experiences or earlier achievements. On the other hand, sometimes it is best to trace the history of your approach by describing it and presenting the chronology in reverse, from the present to its origin. You must judge for yourself which is the more effective method.

Similar considerations apply to all other methods: You, as the writer, must judge the best method of organizing discussions. Note: Each discussion (sometimes that means each section or chapter of a proposal, but it may mean a discussion within a section) must be organized along some logical path. You need not use the same method for every discussion (and probably will not wish to do so) as long as you make clear to your reader what the pattern of presentation is to be. You must be careful to never "leave your reader behind" as you move on with your material. That means that you must observe a few absolute basics of what is taught in formal classes as "composition."

Composition Basics

You must create and maintain a unity of thought in each element—sentence, paragraph, subsection, or other. A sentence deals with one main idea, and another sentence is required to present or discuss another, different idea. Similarly, paragraphs and other elements are each about some single subject or thought.

You must keep the reader posted as to what is the subject of the paragraph, subsection, and so on. The paragraph usually opens with a topic sentence that telegraphs the subject. (Study any of these paragraphs as examples.) For a large concept, you probably require an introductory paragraph. Very large concepts, such as the topic of a book, generally need an introductory chapter, as do the topics of formal proposals of any size.

When you are through with one subject and ready to go on to another, you must begin another paragraph (or larger element) with its own topic sentence (or introductory element). In addition, you must provide a transition or "bridge," as many writers call it, which is a literary device that indicates the logical connection between the two elements, to maintain the continuity of thought. Otherwise, the reader is almost sure to become confused—disoriented, in fact—and find it difficult, if not impossible, to follow your argument.

Study the paragraphs in this book as examples, and note that there are many ways to create those bridges. Probably the best way is to prepare the reader in advance for each transition by ending each element with an introduction to the new subject to come, using some linking word or term (one that the reader will immediately recognize in the next paragraph) to make the connection. You can also do this in reverse, beginning a new paragraph with a reference in your topic sentence to the preceding one. Headlines, titles, and captions can also be used to help with this.

Headlines and Captions

Briefly, a hea*dline* is used to introduce each major new subject within a chapter or section, *titles* are used to characterize and introduce new chapters or sections, and *captions* are used to introduce figures, tables, matrices, and other such special presentation devices. (At least, that is how I define those terms here, although some people refer to figure and table captions as titles.) Their very existence aids the reader in following the continuity of thought and in perceiving the main topics. At least in theory, they also help the reader find his or her way back to specific portions of the presentation that they want to read and review again. (In fact, the array of chapter titles, headlines, and captions in the table of contents ought to offer a fair, if approximate, outline of the proposal.)

It is often painful for me to observe the missed opportunities resulting from the failure to use headlines, titles, and captions freely enough and imaginatively enough. In fact, when used unimaginatively, they do rather little to help the writer even communicate, much less persuade. Headlines, titles, and captions, offer you many special opportunities to communicate and to persuade. In addition, these devices help the reader follow the transitions of discussions from one subject to the next and should be used to help create that logical transition. However, they should not serve as the primary vehicle of transition. Headlines, titles, and captions can do much to help you create a proposal presentation of great impact and powerful persuasion.

Unfortunately, too often, writers are satisfied to ask little of their titles, headlines, and captions, which results in such unimaginative headlines as

"Introduction" and "General Background," and captions such as "Table of Characteristics." And aside from the failure to exploit the titles, headlines, and captions in some positive way, such unimaginative uses often fail even in their most basic purpose of serving as guideposts for the reader simply because the words are so uninformative that they do not register with the reader.

At the minimum, strive to use fresher words for your titles, headlines, and captions, to help gain the reader's attention and to make the reader aware of them and what they say. Find fresher words to say "introduction" and "general background." Find something more imaginative than "schedule" to introduce a milestone chart or table. Find words that not only explain and telegraph major topics and presentation aids, but also *sell* them by stressing the positive aspects—the benefits they promise the customer and the evidence that validates the promises. (A later chapter offers some specific for-instances of these.)

Tables and Matrices

Tables and matrices are basically devices for listing items that have some coherent interrelationship, making their presentation in a listing or cross-listing more efficient and more useful a presentation than a mere narrative description would provide. *Matrix* refers to a tabular presentation in which items are so related that some correlation among them exists, whereas a ta*ble* may be a simple listing, as illustrated in Figures 17 and 18.

Something more than mere identification of the table should be reflected in the table captions (called "legends"). Remember the nature of a proposal: It is a sales presentation, and every opportunity to sell should be exploited. (This is explained by specific examples in a later chapter.)

Graphic Aids

Illustrations are a must for most proposals. One of the cardinal, basic rules of selling is to make things as easy as possible for the prospect to listen receptively to your sales message. Bear in mind that the client is probably faced with a number of proposals to review, perhaps as many as 30 or 40, in fact. While there may be some psychological leverage in what appears to

EVALUATION ITEMS	POINT VALUES
Understanding of requirement	10
Approach	
Analysis	5
Viability	5
Success probability	5
Qualifications	
Staff	20
Organization	10
Management	
Project organization	15
Methods and procedures	20
Costs	10
Total:	100

Figure 17. Simple table. Criteria for evaluating proposal.

PROCUREMENT METHOD	NUMBER OF ACTIONS	TOTAL $(000)	PERCENT TOTAL
Fixed price	345	7,653	11.6
Cost plus	123	12,565	19.7
Two-step	12	1,645	3.6
Sole source	4	983	1.8
Setaside	3	765	1.3

Figure 18. Matrix-type table. Analysis of procurement methods.

be a substantial proposal, one of many pages, the client does not look forward with any great pleasure to studying many words to evaluate what you are offering. Most clients appreciate anything that relieves the necessity to read a lot, and that is precisely what a good illustration must do.

The purpose of an illustration is to convey meaning, and an illustration should be used wherever words alone are not really adequate—that is, where an illustration can convey meaning more accurately or more efficiently than can words alone. In writing a proposal, you must often present both concrete ideas and abstractions, which means that you must present both images and concepts. Words rarely convey an image as well as an illustration can because words are merely symbols, and most words must be interpreted by the reader. Many words would be required to convey the image of a piece of furniture or a communications satellite, and even then the words would not deliver as accurate an image as a single drawing or photograph would. When an accurate and precise *image* of the object must be conveyed, words simply won't do; an illustration is required. On the other hand, words suffice to convey the *idea* or concept of the chair or communications satellite, if that is all that is required.

The quality of an illustration is linked directly to and may be judged by the amount of text it displaces (makes unnecessary). The illustration that requires a great deal of textual explanation is not doing its job at all, and may not be worth having. You may judge the virtues of an illustration in that manner, by the weight of text it replaces, as well as in the absolute terms of how effectively it delivers a message or conveys a meaning.

For example, abstractions sometimes present a difficult problem in communications. The idea of a vector, for example, which is the result of two or more forces acting in different directions on an object, is almost impossible to explain properly to a lay person without an illustration, and the vector in electrical applications is more difficult to explain than is the vector in mechanical applications. (In fact, it is generally introduced first via mechanical theory for that very reason.) Thus, a graphic image of a vector would reduce the amount of text needed to define or describe it.

Analogies, Metaphors, and Other Imagery

For many abstract ideas, analogies that employ illustrations are often the only practical solution. Illustrations are not always drawings; they may be verbal illustrations, illustrations by *referents*, or by textual analogies that the reader can easily visualize. In describing the earth as shaped somewhat like an orange, round but flattened slightly at the poles, the writer takes advantage of the fact that the word orange is a familiar referent: Almost everyone in the western world knows what an orange is and how it looks, so it is safe to assume that a drawing of an orange is not required to explain the concept. Nor is it necessary then to offer a drawing of the earth, if explaining its oblate shape is all that is desired.

The use of imagery reaches its peaks in fiction and in popular nonfiction, but limits it rather strictly in proposal writing to only what is absolutely necessary to present concepts. It is far too easy, when employing imagery, to become fanciful and be carried away into hyperbole and other exaggeration cautioned against earlier.

FOCUS ON WORD CHOICE

Resort to purple prose—words found only in unabridged dictionaries (and even then often archaic terms no longer in popular usage), banalities, pompous verbal posing, and relatively unknown words used where simpler words would do—is bad writing. A study of such prose, including some of the kinds of prose that have become known as bureaucratese, often reveals an interesting fact when it is translated into simple English: Such prose often says absolutely nothing, and only the fact that it is so convoluted conceals that fact from the casual reader. Ironically, the deception is usually not even deliberate. Some writers appear able to conceal even from themselves the fact that they have nothing to say, and they offer a storm of obscure words and pontifical prose that, they manage to convince themselves, has some significance.

The causes of this are usually any of several, at least these:

- The failure to truly think out what to say—the main point or objective of the writing, or what the presentation strategy is to be
- The failure to plan ahead by outlining, preparing notes, gathering the data, and truly *thinking* about the subject before attacking the keyboard
- The failure to do adequate research, an absolute must (You cannot write a really good 5,000-word proposal by researching and gathering 5,000 words of information. You must usually have gathered 25,000 or more words of source data, from which you garner the 5,000 words you need.)
- The belief that glib writing can substitute for substance
- The fear of making clear and unequivocal statements, dreading the

possibility of being challenged and, even worse, proved to be wrong (If the writing is sufficiently ambiguous and tortuous, especially if it is such that what it actually says is by no means clear, there is less possibility of being challenged successfully. Thus, consciously or unconsciously, the writer who is lacking in confidence tends to write badly.)

The federal government, because it is a huge bureaucracy, is a frequent offender. To do something about the thousands of pages of paper on federal procurement, Congress created the Office of Federal Procurement Policy within the Office of Management and Budget. A team of people spent over five years combining, reorganizing, and rewriting some 60,000 pages of regulations, bulletins, and memoranda, creating a single unified and allegedly simplified set of procurement regulations, the Federal Acquisition Regulations. A team of people were employed in this effort, each member required to undergo a week's special training course in writing, in the interest of producing documents in clear, lay English. One resulting regulation, typical of the entire result of all that enlightened labor, repeats an earlier one that says that a contractor may not charge the government twice for the same thing, but it takes a full page of small print to say it, which is an almost verbatim repeat of the regulation that was to have been simplified. Unfortunately, that typifies the results of an expensive effort. (There seems to be no cure for bad writing.)

The late Bertrand Russell, a British theoretical physicist, mathematician, and philosopher, was one of the world's great thinkers. He was also a prolific writer, and often a sardonic one, reporting his observations with great amusement. He observed in one of his philosophical writings that it was his great good fortune that everyone knew him to be an educated man so that he had no need to impress anyone and could afford to write in the simplest of English. His many writings are a model of clear and simple English, written solely to inform the reader, with no thought of self-importance. He had risen above that need.

That is the lesson to be learned about writing simply and clearly: Keep in mind your reader and your reader's needs only. Give no thought to glorifying yourself and your image. You can't get a better image than that of communicating clearly.

THE MATTER OF "READABILITY"

Readability is closely associated with our notions of what is "good" and "bad" writing, but it also may surprise you. One surprise about readability is that most of us, even those fortunate enough to have graduate degrees, are most comfortable reading at about an 8th-grade level! (That is approximately *Reader's Digest's* level.) In fact, while almost all of us are at least high-school (12th-grade) graduates, and many of us have had four or more years of college following, many of us do not read at all well beyond that 8th-grade level. Americans generally, even the most-educated among us, are poor readers. (It was once my sad duty to advise an experienced lawyer—most reluctantly, I should add—as to what a certain clause in a contract meant.) Due to this sad fact, the 8th-grade level is the most appropriate one even for formal documents.

Early systems for measuring readability and adjusting it were rather crude and unwieldy. The computer has come to the rescue here again, with suitable software, some of which is listed in the last chapter.

THE SPECIAL PROBLEM OF LETTER PROPOSALS

The letter proposal is a special problem in several ways. The reason for a letter proposal is that the project is small, or the possibility of the prospect making an award is unknown. For example, you may be writing an informal letter proposal as follow-up marketing or perhaps simply to qualify the prospect. This tentative prospect does not justify the investment of much time and money. Yet, if the proposal is to be received seriously, it is necessary to make all the major points and present all the sales arguments here as though it were a large, formal proposal. The scale of the presentation does not change that; no presentation should be made without a serious effort to make a sale.

To complicate the problem, however, it is more difficult to be concise while still delivering all the necessary messages and making all the important points effectively. The medium imposes its own restriction. Don't be misled by the medium's brevity: It may appear to you that the letter proposal is easier to write because it is much shorter, but it is difficult to be brief and yet effective.

Do not, therefore, impose unnecessary restrictions on yourself in writing a letter proposal. I have suggested two to four pages as a typical size for a letter proposal. That is by no means a standard or a rule; a letter proposal should be as long as necessary to do the job; you may make it any length, and you may include appendices, exhibits, or other enclosures to supplement it. Moreover, you certainly may use headlines, captions, and illustrations of any kind, as in a formal proposal.

On the other hand, you sometimes find that the simple, little letter proposal you started out to write blossomed quickly into something more formidable, not truly a formal proposal, yet a bit oversize for a letter proposal. In such a case, you may find it helpful to simply add a few refinements such as a title page and table of contents, treating the presentation as a semiformal miniproposal.

What you call it is not important. What is important is simply that you make all efforts to create as effective a presentation as possible. The only rule is that you do what is necessary to win the contract.

CHAPTER 9

Special Presentation Guides and Strategies

The objective of a proposal is not truth but persuasion.

SALES STRATEGY VERSUS PRESENTATION STRATEGY

Successful presentations do not happen by chance. They are the result of successful presentation strategies implemented effectively. The proposal is itself a presentation, a *sales* presentation. Sales strategy, however, should not be confused with presentation strategy. They are not the same. The presentation strategy is conceived and employed in direct support of the sales strategy, but it is essential to distinguish between the two.

Defined as briefly as possible, the sales strategy is that concept which, you hope and expect, will persuade the client to accept your proposal and award the contract to you. The presentation strategy—or strategies, for more than one is possible and more than one may well be embodied in a proposal—is designed to give the proposal maximum impact in several respects. However, while the sales strategy may be identical with cost or technical (program) strategy, in some cases, it is unlikely that it will ever be identical with the presentation strategy. That is, you would almost certainly be deluding yourself to hope that even the most clever presentation strategy would of itself win the contract. Rather, you should expect a successful presentation strategy to help make your sales strategy effective by achieving the following for you and your proposal:

1. Focus the reader's attention on your main sales strategy
2. Capture the reader's (client's) interest
3. Generate and sustain the client's interest
4. Make it easy for the client to read and understand everything your proposal has to say
5. Inspire respect for your professional expertise
6. Make your promises and proofs believable
7. Make your appeals persuasive

Focus Attention on the Main Sales Strategy

This is the most important point because it is the basis of your entire effort. It must therefore drive the presentation strategy. If your plan is to capture the contract by virtue of a superior technical plan, for example, it is that claim on which you must focus. But you must focus on something more specific than the "superiority" of your plan: You must pin down the specific benefit of the plan that makes it superior. Will it save the client money? Reduce costs? Produce sales for the client? Solve some distressing problem? Decide what the benefit is, and explain just how your plan will accomplish this result and deliver the benefit. Make absolutely sure that the client knows *precisely* what you promise and your rationale for promising it.

The other objectives are separate and distinct objectives to be pursued, though they are not totally unrelated to each other or to your main point. Quite the contrary, some of them are closely related to each other, even to the extent that in some cases they act as constraints or defining boundaries for each other. That shows up immediately when we consider these items, as we do in the following discussions. Nonetheless, you must interpret and apply these subordinate objectives in whatever manner they can best be used to support the primary objective.

Capture Interest

You cannot focus your client's attention effectively if you do not have the client's full attention. Otherwise, the client may very well go through the mechanical motions of reading your proposal, out of an accepted moral obligation to do so, but with considerably less than full awareness of what you say in those pages. Even more significant, the client may read your proposal without paying special attention to those things to which you need to direct the client's special attention. That is, your strategy may fall flat and fail simply because it lacks the impact on the client's consciousness it must have if it is to do the job for you.

TV commercials offer many object lessons in using opening hooks to grab the prospect's attention. Movies and TV plays, for example, open with some exciting or curiosity-arousing scenes to capture the viewer's attention, and only then switch to the commercials, titles, and other less fascinating material, hoping they have now made the viewer captive.

Though there are many ways to capture a reader's attention, you would not want to resort to some of the more bizarre devices that might capture a client's attention, for you must command the client's respect for you as a professional, while your representations must also be credible. Therefore, while you must find ways to command attention, you must do so in ways that are entirely in keeping with your profession and the serious image you must maintain. For example, while it is perfectly acceptable to use simple line drawings to help present a message and/or gain attention, there is some potential hazard in using cartoons for the purpose, and you would probably be wise to refrain from doing so. That is by no means, however, the only factor of importance to consider, in connection with getting attention; there are many others.

Sustain Interest

Getting the client's attention is only a first step in getting your message across and supporting your sales strategy; you must do whatever is necessary to hold it. The relationship between the two, getting attention and holding it, is so close that it is difficult to separate the two; it is futile to get attention without sustaining genuine interest.

In fact, one of the practical arguments against the bizarre attention-getter is that, aside from the potential hazard to your image as a serious professional, getting attention through some novel device usually does nothing to help you hold the client's attention. That is especially true when the attention-getter does not arise from the content, as it should.

You can see the irrelevant attention-getter and other common mistakes made frequently in commercial advertising and sales presentations. Nor are these mistakes confined to the small organizations and the inexperienced individuals; some very large and successful organizations make these same common mistakes over and over. Here are just a few examples:

Irrelevant, Trivial, and Even Cryptic Attention-Getters. Frequently, some clever device is used to get attention, but too often the attention-getter is something that has no direct relationship to the main subject matter (or, even worse, to the prospect's interests) and so the prospect's attention is gained only momentarily and interest is not even genuinely aroused, much less sustained.

One example is one advertisement of a well-known supercorporation, which tells you that your computer "should look you straight in the eye." Only with careful reading of the body copy do you discover that this refers to the modest benefit of having the monitor mounted on a swivel, so that you can change its angle for your comfort. This is a useful feature, but hardly a major one, and it is certainly not one important enough to be the focus of the sales strategy, as this advertisement attempts to make it.

Reverse Orientations and Empty Claims. An even more serious and more common mistake is the offering of items intended to command attention that do not do so because they offer the prospect no inducement to pay even slight attention to the message. Instead of being oriented (appealing) to the interest of the prospect, they are oriented to the values of the advertiser. Typical of these are those appeals that emphasize broadly how great the advertiser is, giving these generalities as the reason to favor that advertiser with patronage.

In a specific case, a speaker advertises his services by headlining the claim that no other speaker has his credentials; he features his picture prominently but fails to give the reader even a hint of what he speaks about, much less what his speaking does for the client or even what those vaunted credentials are.

Another firm offers what it claims are "high-quality, low-cost data switches," simple switch boxes, going on to pile a few more unsupported claims on top of that, but offering not a shred of evidence to support the claim of high quality, although it does offer what appears to be a rather reasonable price for the unit.

The Deadly Sin of Cleverness.   The irresistible urge to be clever and to parade one's cleverness is the force underlying many of the disastrous approaches to presentation strategy. Puns appear to be the most tempting Loreleis that attract copy writers. For example, one presentation that is aimed at selling a sophisticated laser printer promises that "with the right tools, you can nail the competition," and then it supplies a photo of an assortment of worn hammers and other hand tools, along with an assortment of nails, to complete the pun. Still not satisfied, the writer goes on to beat the pun over the head a bit more by showing the reader how to "hit the nail on the head," etc. Finally, if the reader can find the patience to plod on and endure more of this heavy-handed humor, the reader discovers what the advertiser is selling and learns of some promised benefits, but they seem rather anticlimactic by this time.

All of these are guilty of the most common sin of sales presentations: They are so busy being clever, boastful, and self-congratulatory that they neglect their real job—selling the product or service. They forget to think in terms of the client's interests—what the client wants and what they (the advertisers) can do for the client.

Nothing else counts, as far as the client is concerned. The client is not interested in how clever you are, in being entertained, or in any of the many elaborate, but unsupported, claims you might make. Forget these.

Even the evidence of capability, dependability, honesty, and other attributes necessary to make the sale are of interest only after you have presented the one thing the client really wants to know about: What you are going to do for him or her. If the client is not interested in gaining the benefit you promise, what difference do all your other representations make? None.

One fallacy responsible for this disaster of presentation writing is the mistaken notion that claims alone are sales arguments and will be perceived by the client as promised benefits. In fact, some writers of sales copy appear to believe that the more extreme and louder the claims of excellence are, the more powerful and persuasive those claims will be. Of course, the opposite effect usually results: the more extravagant the claim, the more unquestioning credulity, even naïveté, it demands of the client. Even if the client were to be swayed by your excellence, rather than by some specific promises of benefits, you would have to prove that your claims of excellence were justified before they could help you. Obviously, the louder the claim or the more extreme the promised benefit, the greater the proof required.

Make It Readable and Clear

A cardinal principle of sales is that everything connected with the process of making a buying decision and placing the order should be made as easy as possible for the prospect. Anything the prospect finds difficult, troublesome, or inconvenient in any way discourages the sale. It is for this reason that so many sales appeals include preaddressed, postage-free response envelopes and order cards, many of which require only the recording of a credit card number, along with a name and address, to place the order. (My own mail-order office-supplies vendor asked only for the name of my bank and my account number to open my charge account, for example, and we have done business together for more than a dozen years since. I have not opened an account with a local supplier who invited me to do so, because I would be required to fill out a long and complicated form.)

Many examples used here to illustrate the principles of sales presentations were drawn from conventional advertising because they were convenient and obvious examples, but everything illustrated has equal application to proposals. However, probably nowhere is the application to proposals more significant than in the case of making the presentation easy to read and understand. A prospect might fight through a few hundred words of less-than-crystal-clear prose if the interest aroused were great enough, but asking the client to struggle through several dozen pages of stilted and difficult copy is another matter. Many clients faced with that prospect will give it up with a sigh and turn to the next proposal in the stack.

What's more, even that is only one consideration with regard to readability and clarity. There is also the matter of communication per se. Your text can be quite accurate and thorough, although difficult to read. Contrariwise, prose can also be easy to read, while failing to be clear. For the client either to be puzzled by your meanings or to misinterpret them is just as deadly to your purpose as discouraging the client's reading entirely. You can hardly sell something to the client when the client neither understands what you are selling nor grasps precisely what your arguments are.

Therefore, we are actually talking about two separate matters regarding writing per se, and they are not directly related to each other. You are well advised to keep your organization of material, usage of the language, and chosen vocabulary as simple as possible, for ease of reading. However, do not permit this to interfere with achieving comprehensive and accurate coverage—to include all necessary detail, that is, and to get the facts straight.

In this respect, you should know, if you do not already, that most of us have several personal vocabularies: We speak with one, we read with another, and we write with still another (and we think with yet another).

The size of individual vocabularies varies quite widely, from as few as 5,000–10,000 words to as many as 40,000–50,000 words. If you are one who is blessed with a large vocabulary, don't permit that blessing to become a curse by trying to use all of it in your writing. The real blessing of a large vocabulary is that it is an enormous asset to your reasoning powers: people with large vocabularies tend to be superior thinkers. Reserve most of that large reserve of words to help you reason well, and try to keep your writing vocabulary between that 10,000- and 20,000-word range. You won't be writing down to anyone, in so doing, but you will be helping yourself develop a brisk and highly readable style.

Promote and Maintain Your Professional Image

Professionalism has probably as many meanings as *consulting* does, varying according to the individual's bias. Some individuals believe that only physicians and lawyers are truly professionals, but we also make reference sometimes to "professional plumbers" and to other tradespeople as professionals. However, inasmuch as consultants normally provide their services on a custom basis, are often entrusted with the client's proprietary and confidential information, and are often given almost carte blanche freedom on the client's premises, the relationship must be based on great respect for the consultant.

Accordingly, it is essential that you develop and maintain a highly professional image, and I define that here for these purposes: As used here, the term refers to an image that goes beyond mere competence. It must be one that reflects an aura of authority in your special field, but it must reflect also dignity, integrity, dedication to your profession and to your clients, and trustworthiness in general.

Should your handling of the proposal undermine that image, it will be a threat to your prospects for success. To protect your image, and even to enhance it, you must use the language well and, at the minimum, avoid such faux pas as misspellings, ungrammatical constructions, and humorous (or serious) misuses of language. These errors convey an image of being a semieducated individual, which is hardly what you would wish.

Here are two examples of deadly unintended humor detected in proposals: One writer was attempting to explain that the proposed design for a piece of equipment that would serve a critical function would have a backup set of duplicate components. Unfortunately, although he meant to describe redundancy, he spoke of the "duplicity" of the design. Another writer wished to explain the system by which identifying numbers would be assigned to a large array of terminals. He introduced the subject with a headline that announced the subject to be discussed next as the "assignation" of the terminals.

It's a good idea to have someone edit or review your copy to detect errors and to do something about them. It's even more important to avoid trying to sound impressive through the use of language. The way to be impressive in your writing is to offer clear expositions and ample details. An abundantly detailed discussion, for example, conveys a quite definite impression of competence, for anyone can generalize and philosophize.

Make Your Presentation Believable

Offering comprehensive and accurate detail powerfully influences the credibility of your arguments, but other elements also contribute to credibility. As discussed earlier, one is the general avoidance of hyperbole and superlatives. The subdued tone of quiet confidence describes with nouns and verbs and shuns all hyperbole, and clients find that reassuring.

Frankness, such as ready admission that problems may be encountered (as compared with the "soothing syrup" of bland but unsupported promises that some proposal writers offer), is equally reassuring because it, too, reflects self-confidence.

Still another reassuring sign is either to avoid making your promises appear too extravagant or, if you believe that you can deliver truly remarkable results and wish to promise them, to be sure that your proofs do justice to the promises and are in proportion to them. Nonetheless, avoid verbal shouting if you want to be taken seriously.

Many writers have great difficulty in disciplining their writing this way; sometimes their enthusiasm is a bar to this. It is always a good idea to have a competent editor go over all your copy and excise all the extravagant prose. Instruct your editors to do just this.

Make Your Appeals Persuasive

Persuasiveness of your appeals has been an underlying theme throughout this chapter so far, and is a general objective in all those other discussions. However, it is useful to single this out and establish it as a special objective to remind yourself that all sales presentations have persuasion as their ultimate objective, and that everything in the presentation must contribute to that ultimate goal.

A FEW TIPS ON WRITING STYLE

Part of the image you should be trying to develop and nourish should be that of being thoroughly businesslike, which means alert, efficient, and direct. To encourage that image in your writing you should develop a crisp and vigorous writing style. Here are a few tips to help you do that:

- Write in active voice, rather than passive voice. This sentence is itself an example. "Proposals should be written in active voice," would express this idea in passive voice.
- Use frequent stops in long sentences—colons, semicolons, and dashes—especially for interjections. Long sentences with stops are about the same as a series of short sentences, and they are as easy to read.
- Get to the point. Ideally, telegraph your key point when you introduce the subject. At the least, march directly to the point without detours.
- Make positive statements as often as possible, and avoid overqualification of statements. Even when you are not certain of the point or cannot state something as an absolute fact, you can present it without sounding fearful and indecisive. (Whether you are or are not indecisive is not the point; whether you are *perceived* as being indecisive *is* the point.) For example, instead of hedging a statement around with many qualifications, often found in research papers in such

expressions as "The indicators tend to suggest the tentative possibility that maybe . . . ," say something such as, "The possibility indicated is . . . ," which commits you no more than the first version does, but it makes you appear far more authoritative and confident in what you are saying.

There is no doubt that to the sensitive and perceptive reader (and you must assume that the client is that kind of reader), your mental set manages to come through between the lines of what you write. Unless your writing reflects confidence in what you are saying and what you are proposing, it is unlikely that the client will have that confidence. Confidence—or the lack of it—is something you share with your reader, whether by intent or not.

The need is for balance: Confidence, promises of desirable results, clear expression, easy readability, and positive statements, balanced by reasonableness, accurate detail, and substantial evidence to support all promises and claims.

APPLYING THE IDEAS

Now let's begin to look more closely at how you can apply these ideas to the specific proposal elements. The suggested general proposal format, with brief notes explaining the main section titles and subheads, is presented in Figure 19. This is a generalized format, and must be adapted to each specific situation, for some situations may require large, formal proposals offering entire teams of specialists and their services, whereas others may be one-person projects. Still, whether you offer only your own résumé or those of a dozen associates or employees, the principles are the same: The client wishes to know your understanding of the requirement in its essence, your management philosophy and procedures, your technical/professional qualifications, your specific experience, persons to call to verify your experience and competence, and other such matters.

THE MATTER OF HEADLINES

The format shown in Figure 19 uses generic titles and headlines, rather than those that should be used in specific cases. A presentation strategy must be

SECTION I: INTRODUCTION

ABOUT THE OFFEROR	A brief introduction, with your basic qualifications; scene setting; explain that details come later
UNDERSTANDING OF THE REQUIREMENT	The requirement in essence, with obscuring trivia stripped away for a clear view of the central need or problem; sets stage for next section

SECTION II: DISCUSSION

THE REQUIREMENT	Elaboration of the understanding, bringing in of related considerations, establishment of basis for analysis
ANALYSIS	Exploration of all possibilities, surfacing of probable problems (potential "worry items"), pro and con discussions of alternatives
APPROACH	Logical conclusion of analysis, pointing to synthesis of design; identifying approach opted for and justifying decision; scene setting for next section

SECTION III: PROPOSED PROJECT

PROJECT ORGANIZATION	Description of team and/or task organization to implement approach opted for; logic of organization explained
MANAGEMENT	Principles, quality control, cost control, other controls and administration
PLANS AND PROCEDURES	Procedures, forms, standards, criteria, liaison with client
STAFF	General description of self, associates, and/or others
DELIVERABLE ITEMS	Qualitative and quantitative specifications in detail
SCHEDULES	Chart, tabular, or milestone presentations
RESUME(S)	Employees/associates who will provide services

SECTION IV: QUALIFICATIONS AND EXPERIENCE

RELEVANT CURRENT AND RECENT PROJECTS	Tabular data, brief descriptions, names, phone numbers of clients
RESOURCES	Facilities, equipment, personnel, other relevant resources
REFERENCES, TESTIMONIALS	Supplement to project histories, including certificates, letters of appreciation, other such evidence of merit

MISCELLANEOUS

FRONT MATTER	Title page, table of contents, response matrix, executive summary
APPENDICES	If/as needed

Figure 19. Each proposal section and subsection and brief definitions.

developed for each individual case, according to the merits and circumstances of each individual case, but some principles should be followed for
all cases. One of these is that to maximize the effectiveness of the
presentation strategy, everything, including titles, headlines, figure captions, and table captions, should be conceived and composed for maximum
contribution to the selling process.

The first section or chapter of a proposal is normally introductory,
introducing both the consultant and the consultant's understanding and
preliminary appraisal of the requirement. Almost everyone therefore titles
it "Introduction," "General," or other such generic title, thereby missing an
early opportunity to make an important point. To get the maximum benefit,
compose a title that reflects some important benefit, theme, or virtue of what
you are offering. Work at making this an attention-getter, while still relating
it directly to your offer. If you can tie this in to somehow support your main
strategy, so much the better.

Here are a few examples, some hypothetical, some drawn from real case
histories:

"A New Broom" (the proposer was bidding for an ongoing contract and had
gotten word that the client was dissatisfied with the incumbent and wanted to
make a change)

"A Different Kind of Service" (you have something new and different to
offer, especially when that is central to your strategy)

"A Fresh Viewpoint" (the proposer planned to offer an entirely new and far
better approach to solving the client's problems)

"Solutions Designed to Match Problems" (a proposer who wishes to stress the
custom-designed nature of his services)

The subheads, listed generically in Figure 19 for the first section as
"About the Offeror" and "Understanding of the Requirement," should
likewise be tailored to the situation. "About the Offeror" might become
"Scientific Programming Specialists: We're Small Enough to Make You
Our MIC (Most Important Client)," or whatever suits your situation and
your strategy. (The idea expressed by the example subhead is a reminder
that large consulting firms often tend to treat small contracts, especially
from small clients, rather casually. It is thus a powerful strategy not only to

overcome the possible liability of being a small consulting firm, but even to convert that into an asset. Of course, you might go the other way and say something such as "We're Large Enough to Have All the Resources to Satisfy Your Need," if you are a sizable firm and want to make that a sales argument.)

"Understanding of the Requirement" should likewise be changed to something more pungent, such as "A Closer Look at the Requirement" or "The Essence of the Requirement." However, although those are improvements over the generic subhead, even those can be further improved by composing a subhead that more directly relates to the individual proposal. If the proposal were in response to that hypothetical client with a problem of unreliable reports coming from the computer, the subhead might dramatize the requirement in its essence along the lines of "The True Requirement: Find the *Cause* of Unreliable Computer-Generated Reports." That, of course, is almost ideal for laying the groundwork to discuss the requirement in the second section of your proposal, which might then get a title following up that idea, such as "Seven Possible Causes for Unreliable Computer-Generated Reports" or "The Most Efficient Way to Track Down the Trouble" and even a subtitle, such as "A Discussion of Analytical Techniques and Troubleshooting Methods." The various headlines in your discussion section would then guide the reader through the main points and main logic of the approach and the methodology you propose there.

Of course, if you happen to have a special technique or special resources, such as a proprietary program, to help you do this job more efficiently or more effectively than anyone else is likely to be able to do it, by all means strengthen those through direct references to and indications of those in your headlines and titles.

When to Write the Headlines

The kinds of headlines just listed are actually abstracts or summaries of sales arguments. There are two ways to develop them: Probably the way most headlines are written is after the body copy is written. In recognition of this truth, my own practice is to use generic titles and headlines (some of us call those "working titles") that I do not intend to keep, planning to scrap them later, when I edit and revise my manuscript and prepare a final draft. At that time, I study the copy first to identify the most appealing benefit promised or evidence provided in each discussion. Having decided what that is, I begin to work on headlines and subheads for each discussion.

The second way is to prepare a highly detailed outline and then to convert major outline topics into headlines. This is an excellent approach if you devote the time and effort to developing a detailed outline. For this, the outlining or "idea processing" software offered today with modern word processors can be a great help.

How Long Should a Headline Be?

Some of those headlines and titles can become fairly long, even two or more lines, as some of the examples used here demonstrate. That should not stay your hand. First of all, there is nothing wrong with lengthy titles and headlines, popular belief to the contrary. Book titles, which themselves serve as headlines when well conceived, furnish many examples of lengthy titles that did not hamper the sale of the books and probably contributed to their success. Here are titles of several highly successful books, some of them even best sellers:

How to Prosper in the Coming Bad Years
How to Form Your Own Corporation without a Lawyer for under $50.00
How to Succeed as an Independent Consultant
How to Write, Publish, and Market Your Book
How I Turn Ordinary Complaints into Thousands of Dollars

The supposed rule about keeping titles and headlines short is not even conventional wisdom; it is pure mythology, perpetrated and perpetuated by individuals expressing their personal biases. The almost unlimited number of successful "exceptions" reveals that rather clearly. The idea that the title or headline must be short to be effective is nonsense, in any case.

Even if there were any validity to the idea that titles and headlines must be short and "punchy," the goal of making them so would have to be subject to a rule of practicality. The title or headline that fails to do what you want it to do is worthless, no matter how short and punchy it is. So if you cannot devise a short title or headline that suits your needs, you've little choice left, logically, except to use a longer one.

The simple fact is that if your headline or title captures the client's attention by appealing to his or her own interest—that is, if the client *perceives* that it is in his or her own interest to read what you have to say—wild horses will not stop him or her from reading your headline and as much body copy as you care to offer. For that and for no other reason, those books cited here as examples were and remain successful, some of them for many years. Only if the client ceases to identify his or her personal interest in what you say will he or she stop reading and go on to something else. It's as simple—and as complex—as that. Go back and study the several examples of titles listed here and see if they do not appeal directly to the self-interests of many potential readers.

How to Develop Titles and Headlines

There is only one really sensible rule for judging how long titles, headlines, and copy generally must be: The titles, headlines, and copy must be exactly long enough to do the job, and not one comma or letter longer. Of course, that leaves us with the problem of determining just what that means: How long is "long enough to do the job"?

The answer is clearly implied in one of the many observations about the editing process. Someone quite familiar with the processes and problems of writing and its related functions has stated that editing is most typically a function of reducing the bulk of a writer's copy, probably eliminating about one third of the average manuscript.

Like most generalizations, this one has too many exceptions for it to qualify as anything resembling a rule or a principle, but it does reflect (1) the common problem of excessive verbosity on the part of many writers and (2) the fundamental truth that even the most skilled writers usually over-write (sometimes deliberately) in their first drafts and then tighten their manuscripts in revision through boiling out a great deal of nonessential material and/or finding more efficient ways to express their ideas.

The second idea is especially appropriate to writing advertising and sales materials, such as proposals, including titles and headlines. The best practice, for most of us, is to write a first draft that says everything you can think of that is relevant, using as many words as you wish. In that draft, you concern yourself primarily with including everything that contributes to the client's understanding of what you propose and to persuasive arguments for your proposal. It is more urgent, in this draft, to see to it that you have not left out anything important than it is to be eloquent or efficient in your language.

Once you have satisfied yourself that you have included all the necessary and relevant information, you can begin the self-editing process to edit out extraneous material, tighten expressions, and polish your language generally.

With titles and headlines, the process often has to be altered somewhat because quite often the headline or title you select proves to be entirely inappropriate to what you have written. Therefore, you must maintain an open mind about titles and headlines and be prepared to edit and revise them ruthlessly, or even to scrap them entirely and make a fresh beginning at coining an effective combination of words.

Once you have formulated the headlines and subheads for each discussion, you may want to work on titles for sections and captions or titles for illustrations and tables, working these over until you have polished them for maximum effect and minimum number of words.

THREE BASIC KINDS OF PRESENTATION STRATEGY

The strategic objective we have been discussing here has been that of getting attention, and we have been examining one general strategy that is always available to you in pursuit of this: Devising titles and headlines that command attention through appealing to the client's self-interest and, whenever possible, dramatizing the message. However, there are also other ways to get attention and capture interest. There are at least three basic approaches to attracting attention, each of which represents a different kind of presentation strategy:

- The copy itself: what your proposal says and how it says it
- Cosmetic effects and special elements of the proposal
- Special devices related to, but not integral parts of, your proposal

THE PROPOSAL COPY

More About Titles and Headlines

Titles and headlines are a major element of presentation strategy when used well. To get maximum benefits from their use, you must give a great deal of thought to composing them, and you must use them liberally. They dramatize and emphasize important points in your presentation generally and in your sales arguments especially.

Titles and headlines can do even more than enhance your presentation strategy: They can reinforce your sales strategy. They can guide the client through your proposal and lighten the burden of reading by serving as guideposts so that the main messages come through, even if the client does not read every word with deep consciousness. (A rule of advertising is to sell in the headline, which then renders the importance of body copy far less critical.)

In recognition of this sales benefit of headings, it is important that you have a title, headline, subhead, or caption for every important point in your proposal. Titles and major headlines should draw attention to all major points you want to make, but they can also be used to summarize lesser points. All key points should be covered in headings, following the philosophy that even if the client were to read only the titles and headlines, he or she would have gotten most of the main messages and understood the main thrust of your proposal. (That consideration alone justifies the titles, headlines, and the effort to develop them.)

Test the entire array of your titles and headlines (they should be in your table of contents) by scanning them to verify that they accomplish three things:

1. They provide a reasonably detailed outline/abstract of your proposal.
2. They present and point out every important point in your proposal.
3. They offer a good sales argument for your proposal by providing promises and proofs.

Section I: The Introduction

Objective of Section I

The introduction is brief, and yet it is important. If you are submitting a requested proposal, as distinct from an unsolicited proposal, you can expect the client to read it as a necessity. But if you want the client to read with interest, you must do something *immediately*—in the introduction—to capture that interest. Capturing the client's attention and interest should be your main objective here.

About the Offeror (First Subsection)

One way to hook the reader is to introduce the most attractive, novel, and/or dramatic element of your proposal immediately. Ordinarily, you use the "About the Offeror" opening discussion to furnish your business name, a few words to qualify and explain your interest and qualifications, summarize your credentials briefly, and advise the client that all of these are described in greater detail later. That much is routine. But we are looking for nonroutine matter here.

These summary explanations should be dramatized here for their greatest effect. If you happen to have something impressive or novel to say about any of these things, by all means do so here. Even more important, search out the most impressive, novel, dramatic, or appealing promise/evidence/fact in your proposal and introduce it here on page 1, even before introducing yourself.

Obviously you can't do this until you have written your proposal and decided precisely what to offer and how you would do the job. Therefore, the introduction is written *last*—when you know exactly what it is that you are introducing. If you are the type of writer who needs to work with a "lead," as many writers do, you will probably need to draft a working introduction. You should expect to scrap it later when you write the final introduction and introduce that interest-capturing jewel you have extracted, usually the item that is at the heart of your program strategy. Here are a few examples of such items:

- A promise of extraordinary results, with only a hint of why and how you can offer this and the promise of details to follow shortly
- A promise of remarkably low costs or speedy results, with the aforementioned hints and promise
- Hints or even brief identification of a serious problem (worry item) and the promise of a soon-to-come explanation of how it will be solved
- Some extraordinary resource available or searched out especially for the project, such as a well-known authority persuaded to serve on the project or the pledged assistance of some prestigious organization

The strategy underlying the preceding tactics is fairly obvious. Most are teasers, arousing the client's curiosity, as well as interest, through promising that full revelation will be made in later pages. All bear some direct suggestion that the client will benefit directly from the proposed program.

It is usually possible and certainly desirable to work that hook or some broad hint of it into the section title and/or subsection headline that precedes the initial text of this first section.

Understanding of the Requirement (Second Subsection)

This, too, should be brief, but it is an outstanding opportunity to capture client interest early. Always remember that the client may not be expert in the work required, and presumably is not because he or she is seeking help. Therefore, the client not only may very well be intensely interested in your view of the problem, but may also be greatly influenced by it. At the least, most clients read your feedback analysis of the requirement as a first indicator of your capability. The "understanding" portion of your proposal's first section is therefore an opportunity (a) to help the client gain a better understanding of the true problem, and (b) to score points as you get down to cases (down to the true *essence* of the requirement).

Keep this discussion short because it should identify and focus entirely on the core issue of the requirement. (Otherwise, you may blur the focus and obscure the client's view of your main point.) Show here that you are not distracted by peripheral issues but are capable of keeping your eye firmly on the ball.

Also, this subsection should introduce something to help hook the client—build interest—even more firmly. First, make it abundantly clear that you are deliberately focusing here on only the essential or core problem, and you will analyze and discuss the requirement overall more discursively in pages to come. If at all possible, raise a worry item here (or expand on one raised in the first subsection), and promise to have a great deal more to say about it soon. Or, as an alternative to that, suggest some technical boon or special asset you will provide, again with the promise of fuller discussion soon.

The purpose is, of course, to build suspense and desire to learn more about these questions you raise. Accordingly, for maximum impact, you must link these to something important to the client, and the most important thing at this point is the overall success or failure of the entire project.

Therefore, don't waste time and energy on items that affect relatively trivial matters, but seek out those that bear directly on and seriously affect overall success and failure.

Section II: Discussion

Objective of Section II

Section II is a major element in the entire sales effort. Here is where you must do the bulk of your selling, for while it is ostensibly the technical discussion that explains your understanding and approach to satisfying the requirement, it is also your principal sales argument. If you fail to convince the client here that yours is the most desirable plan or set of services, it is unlikely that you will be able to do so elsewhere in the proposal or by other means than the proposal, no matter how well you reinforce your arguments with other proposal sections and/or other related sales activity.

The understanding summarized in the first section bridges directly into this section, where you unfold your program strategy, after first elaborating on your understanding, to explore the requirement more fully. Here, you must continue and expand the discussion, especially those elements about which you have raised questions or made promises. You present your analysis in detail, with your rationales ("thinking out loud") so that the client can fully understand the logic of the process and develop a belief in the worry items you project, your technical approach, and the results you promise.

Analysis

It is in this section that you employ a competitive strategy by (1) demonstrating greater insight into the problems and needs of the client, (2) revealing greater wisdom in responding to those needs and problems, and (3) unveiling your special methods for being less costly, faster, more reliable, or otherwise better than others in some way. Here, too, is where you try to persuade the client to make specific comparisons of your offer with that of others. The ways already suggested for doing this are relatively subtle, however, and they depend on the chance that the client will make specific, point-by-point comparisons, in addition to the inevitable general comparison.

Subtlety is totally out of place in most sales presentations; you need to be direct without being crude. One way to do this in a proposal is to make an actual statement of the qualifications you believe necessary for success in satisfying the client's requirement. This, if it is persuasive, almost compels the client to make a point-by-point comparison that is usually an effective competitive strategy when handled well.

Maximizing Impact

To introduce this idea of listing specific qualifications required to handle the assignment successfully, you must somehow demonstrate the logic (prove the validity) of your analysis. This is best done in some striking manner that focuses sharply on that logical progression of ideas that build to a climax presented as your approach to the project.

Approach

The approach you propose is a key element because many clients study this as an indicator of the practicability of your proposal. It is thus essential that you define your approach quite clearly and justify it as the logical outcome of your analysis. It helps, also, to dramatize this so that the reader cannot miss it.

An excellent way to dramatize this and draw attention to it is by giving it special treatment, such as by making it a figure, with suitable introduction, rather than including it in the main text. Figure 20 suggests a format for doing this, using as an example the requirement of the U.S. Postal Service calling for materials for on-the-job training (OJT) of maintenance technicians for bulk-mail plants.

Note the head data and, especially, the "Most Critical Task" item. In this case, as in many others, there is a task that is not only critical to success of the project, but is not well recognized. In this case, it was not readily apparent that the consultant would be required to identify the maintenance requirements and design the maintenance programs (electrical/electronic and mechanical) before designing the training programs themselves. The client had furnished no information on course content, evidently completely overlooking the need for this, and this changed the nature of the qualifications required. The request had been issued apparently with the thought that consultants specializing in training design and development would be the chief respondents.

Basic Requirement: Develop on-the-job materials for bulk-mail maintenance technicians to be trained for work in 21 bulk-mail centers.

Most Critical Task: Design and develop maintenance data and maintenance program for each option.

Most Important Secondary Problem: High turnover (attrition) rate of technicians leaving Postal Service and going on to other employment after heavy Postal Service investment in individual's training.

- -

Special Problem: Much of the equipment is new, virtually prototype, with no maintenance history on which to base development of curriculum and weighting of course content.

- -

Important Design Objectives and Approaches to Them

1. Design maintenance program especially for bulk-mail equipment: Research, compile list of and technical data on all bulk-mail equipment; analyze and project estimated maintenance needs. (Devise and perform failure-probability analyses.)
2. Structure training to minimize turnover of trained technicians: Avoid overtraining, to minimize turnover of technicians. (Confine course content to Postal Service equipment and provide technical coverage only to depth/extent required for Postal service maintenance.)

- -

General Qualifications Required

1. Technical knowledge/experience in electrical/electronic and mechanical equipment and typical maintenance needs and practices.
2. Experience in design/development of sophisticated maintenance systems for electrical/electronic and mechanical equipment.
3. Capability for gaining access to and using technical data on Postal Service bulk-mail equipment.
4. Capability for development of maintenance-needs on quantitative, as well as qualitative, basis, drawn from research.
5. Capability for translating of data into comprehensive and suitably weighted training specification.
6. Knowledge/experience in training-systems design generally, including development of all documentation necessary, and in on-the-job systems especially.

Figure 20.   Major strategies implemented in a single presentation.

This consideration raised a question as to the consultant qualifications necessary, as the figure shows. It argues and presents evidence supporting the position that competence in training-system development is not enough, and that the consultant must have technical/professional qualifications in understanding electrical/electronic and mechanical technology and systems, and in the design and development of maintenance programs for such equipment and systems. (It is difficult enough to write a training program in a highly technical subject when the writers are not personally expert in the subject. In this case, the writers had to also *design* the maintenance program in which the learners were to be trained. That requirement could easily be inferred but was not plainly apparent in the request. It was reasonable to assume that the client had not really considered the requirement in this light.)

To design this for maximum impact, you must have some idea of (a) who you are competing against, (b) your competitors' strengths, (c) the client's perception of truth, and (d) what you must assume that the client knows. However, remember also that you are really only dealing with those strengths, weaknesses, and qualifications about each proposer that the *client* knows about, generally based on what each proposal says. Therefore, if your competitors fail to grasp all these points and thus fail to describe and list all those special qualifications (a common shortcoming in many, many proposals), they might as well not have them at all, for the client will assume that they do not have such capabilities. Even if the competitors are able to say, "Me, too," in later follow-up presentations, they are in seriously weakened positions, resulting in your having an advantage.

This kind of presentation is in itself a major competitive strategy when you believe that the client has overlooked some important point that you can take advantage of, as in this case and in many others. (Remember the point made much earlier that it is often possible to persuade the client to accept arguments that are actually just your own modification of the requirement?)

Figure 20, then, turns out to be a summary of the most important points of the client's request, of the proposed approach, and of the main strategies, all presented in a small package—almost an abstract of the proposal, focusing on key issues and points. It can only be developed as you build up your proposal generally, and most of it reflects the substance of the Section II discussions and presentations, although it can be used on a much wider basis, as a result of its scope.

This tabular figure is such a powerful tool that it can be used effectively in many and possibly even more important ways than in support of your Section II discussions. You might even do well to introduce this figure quite early in your proposal and use it as an attention-getter and an interest-arousing hook on its own. It is quite suitable as a basis for frequent references throughout the proposal, and it can thus become a major tool for exploiting all your strategies. It can even be the chief basis for your entire presentation, along with the functional flowchart, as an effective means for aiding the client in following your arguments and understanding the logic of your approach to satisfying the requirement. An effective way to use such graphic summaries and overviews is to expand them into large charts suitable for viewing in a meeting room (e.g., 3 x 4 feet) and using those charts in either (or both) of two ways:

1. Supply the charts to the client by including them with your proposal, calling them "exhibits" or "enclosures." (This has been highly effective in getting special attention and impressing clients favorably.)

2. Use them as the basis for verbal presentations, following up the proposal submittal.

Section III: Proposed Project

Objective of Section III

In some respects, this is the essence of your response, the proposal per se, for this is where you commit yourself to specific actions and "end-items" (products) to be delivered to the client. The main objective here is to deliver the proof of your offer: what you propose to *do*, in absolutely specific terms. Previous sections of your proposal have theorized, philosophized, and argued. This section must be a detailed specification of what you pledge yourself to do and what you commit yourself to deliver. This is the essence of the contract you offer to sign. There is some flexibility in what it ought to include, but I recommend that it include all the following items: (a) management specification, (b) résumés, and (c) graphic elements.

Management Discussion

Management is often a prime concern with clients, who tend to recognize that technical capability and competence are not enough when a project is not capably managed. Though a great deal is written and lectured about management every day, much of it is relatively vague and philosophical. Clients about to entrust important work to an outside contractor want to know specifically what management will be provided. Specificity and detail are the key elements here, and that applies to all elements of management, including organization, controls, deliverable items, and schedules, especially two elements that many proposal writers neglect: quality control and specific procedures that will be used to ensure proper control of all operations.

Here again, you can gain an advantage over competitors by the mere fact of being entirely specific. Many proposal writers are defensive, so they do whatever they can to avoid specific commitment, especially in the matter of thinking out and planning specific management plans.

Also, résumés may be offered here or in the next section, but wherever they are offered, the almost inevitable question of format arises.

Résumé Formats

In the question of résumé formats, many proposal writers have the deplorable tendency to confuse the résumé requirements of a proposal with those of a job-seeking résumé, and to make at least two basic mistakes in the presentation of résumés in the proposal. One is to structure the résumé as one would for a job application, and the other is to use a boilerplated or standard résumé for all proposals, without regard to the specific needs of each requirement and each proposal seeking a contract. If you are to invest the time and money in a proposal, which is usually a significant investment, it is foolish to try to save an insignificant part of your investment by using a standardized résumé. The résumés should be customized to each proposal, using a format along the lines of Figure 21.

The format suggested there is such that it is possible to revise résumés rather easily for each new proposal, especially if you are using a word processor. The logic of the format is rather obvious, of course, tailored to the individual proposal and the requirement to which it responds.

Priority in presenting information in a résumé should always be given to accomplishments first (patents, awards, outstanding achievements of any kind, as long as they are somehow relevant to the requirement), to experience second (previous positions, most relevant and important ones first), and then to education and educational achievements (degrees, honors, awards).

Name

Normal position

(e.g., President, Systems Analyst)

Proposed position

(e.g., Project Director)

Summary introduction: General qualifications in narrative format—most relevant achievements; experience; education; special training, including current employment; in order of importance/relevance to project without regard to chronology. (Keep brief for maximum focus and impact.)

Experience details: Chronology of positions/functions/assignments in current and previous employment. (Precise dates not required; approximate time periods satisfactory.)

Education, other details.

Figure 21.   Suggested format for resumes in proposals.

The customization of the résumé to each proposal is thus primarily in the position proposed and the introductory paragraph. The remaining data, which is entirely amplifying detail, can usually be kept unchanged. This makes it fairly easy to customize résumés for each new proposal, especially if you use a word processor, the magic of which greatly simplifies copying a file and revising it quickly.

Graphic Elements.

Graphics are as helpful here as they are elsewhere. If the requirement specifies a staff of several people, you must have an organization chart of some kind, as in Figure 22. Schedule commitments may be made by a tabular schedule, as in Figure 23, but it is often more useful if presented as part of a milestone chart, as in Figure 24, because this kind of schedule presentation aids the client in visualizing the interdependence of the various events.

Another presentation that belongs in this section of many proposals is a tabulated estimate of tasks, assignments, and hours, as illustrated by Figure 25.

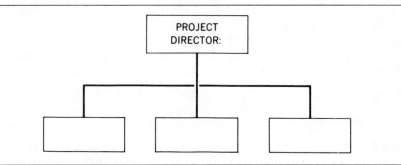

Figure 22. Typical organization chart.

There are several reasons for including such a chart or table in this section:

1. It reduces the risk in proposing because it compels you to plan in detail, rather than in broad terms, and it thus makes you calculate effort and costs realistically. (It's quite easy, otherwise, to persuade yourself to take the easy way out by ballparking your estimates, with the attendant hazard of badly under- or overestimating the effort required and the cost of the project. Instead, force yourself to the discipline of some detailed planning.) This gives you confidence in your estimates.

ITEM	WORKING DAYS AFTER AWARD
Preliminary meeting	1
Report of initial analysis	10
Client review, comments	20
Submission of revised plan	30
Work begins	35
Draft of final report	90
Client review, comments	120
Revision, submission of revised report	150
Client signoff	180

Figure 23. Tabular schedule of events.

Working days after award →

	20	40	60	80	100	120	140	160	180

First meeting ....■

Report initial analysis ....■

Client review, comments ....■

Submit revised plan ....■

Work begins ....■

Draft of final report ....■

Client review, comments ....■

Submit revised final report ....■

Client signoff ....■

Figure 24. Milestone chart as schedule.

TASKS, ASSIGNMENTS, AND EFFORT REQUIRED

	Staffing		
Tasks	**Project Manager**	**Second Investigator**	**Totals**
Totals			

Figure 25. Suggested format for presentation of task/labor estimates.

2. It is excellent evidence of your mastery of the requirement and what is needed to satisfy it because this represents planning detail, which is itself evidence of capability for designing and managing the work. It thus gives the client the same confidence in your estimates that you feel. In general, moreover, an abundance of detail in a proposal is almost always highly favorably impressive.

3. It supports cost estimates, demonstrating their validity.

4. It contributes to your competitor strategy as a silent but eloquent commentary on the proposal of any competitor who is less frank and less thorough.

It is wise to be equally thorough in all other areas of this section. For example, try to present as much detail in your qualitative and quantitative descriptions or estimates of deliverable items. If you are going to develop a manual or report of some kind as the final product of the service you render, describe it in some detail: estimated number of pages, illustrations, and tables; as detailed an outline of content as you can forecast; number of copies to be provided; and other relevant data. If there are to be interim products, formal presentations, seminars, or other items developed, do the same for these.

Section IV: Qualifications and Experience

Main Objective of Section IV

The main goal of this section is to demonstrate your competence and dependability as a consulting service entity. Even if you are an independent consultant, functioning alone—"Peter Smith & Associates," for example— you must manage to discriminate between this presentation and your personal résumé, thinking of yourself as an organization, rather than as an individual practitioner.

For one thing, the client wants the reassurance of knowing that your services have been and are acceptable to others, that you are capable of carrying out the proposed program in both technical/professional knowledge and abilities and in the practical sense of having the resources to do so: relevant experience/accomplishments, physical facilities, staffing resources, and anything else required.

Some clients become concerned that the consultant may be straining his or her resources to cope with the requirement, and that therefore even a relatively small problem or small miscalculation could cause the program to abort. Thus, one objective in writing this section is to point out that you have adequate resources for the program, so that you can fall back on a reserve of whatever is needed, as a kind of insurance.

In previous sections, you have worked at selling the client on and building client's confidence in your plans and your personal credentials. Now you must sell the client on and build client confidence in the capabilities and reliability of the professional entity you represent, whether that is you alone as an independent practitioner or you as a smaller part of a larger business entity. You should provide such information as the following examples.

Relevant Current/Recent Projects

Whether the client requests it or not, a presentation of current and recent relevant projects and clients is useful. Of course, many projects are confidential, and many make you privy to confidential and proprietary information. Many of your clients may not wish to have even the mere fact of some of their projects revealed without their express permission. It is therefore wise to request that permission before identifying clients or revealing information about current and recent projects.

Within whatever constraints that may impose—that is, to the extent that those constraints permit you to—this is the kind of information a subsection on relevant projects ought to include

- Name, size, type of project
- Relevant details
- Client
- Brief contract history: degree of success, adherence to schedule and budget, other indicators of success
- Contact person (individual who can verify data), with telephone number

The project descriptors should be presented in order of importance and relevance to proposal. Therefore, like the résumés, this table should not be completely boilerplated, although many of the individual project descriptors may be, so that the table can be easily modified for each new use. They are probably most efficiently presented in a tabular format, but a new table should be organized to suit each proposal. Again, if the descriptors are written up as elements of one or more computer/word processor files, reorganizing them into a new table for each proposal is relatively simple.

Proposing Organization

Clients are usually interested in the specific organizational unit offering the proposal. If you are part of a department or group within your company, explain this and show it with some kind of organization chart. Show, also, where and how your work group fits into the organization, especially to reflect the degree of independent control the proposed project is likely to enjoy in the organization. Show the client that the project is important enough to you to give it some priority of staffing by assigning a senior person to head it and direct the work. (See also the paragraphs following the heading, "Corporate Organization.")

Facilities and Resources

There are various kinds of facilities and resources in most organizations. Following are some kinds of descriptions that are appropriate to demonstrate your total capability to carry out the work proposed:

Physical Facilities.   Office space, office equipment, computers, laboratory resources, warehouse space, or other—this can be a simple tabular listing, which may be supported by drawings and/or photographs

Software Resources.   Library, files, computer programs, or other such facilities

Additional Staff.   Other staff persons who could be made available to support the project, if needed

It is also appropriate to list and explain access to additional facilities and resources, beyond those that are integral parts of your own organization, so that you can provide additional insurance against the program becoming hampered in any way. Those might include résumés of associates available to you, laboratory facilities you have made preliminary arrangements with, or other organizations who have agreed to back you up, if necessary.

References and Testimonials

The names of current and recent clients appear in your table of relevant current and recent projects, if you have been able to list a few. In addition, it is always useful to present a list of references generally (again, with permission of those listed) and especially useful to include such testimonials as laudatory letters of appreciation and complimentary remarks in forms rating your seminar and other presentations.

It is usually not difficult to get such letters after you have been in business for a time, but clients rarely think to send them on their own initiative. On the other hand, many clients will cheerfully furnish such letters if you request them, and you can gather an impressive set of such testimonials in a short while.

Corporate Organization

If your work group is made up of more than a single subdivision within a corporate entity, it is appropriate in this section to explain this, to illustrate it with a corporate organization chart, and to show where the proposing entity fits into the overall structure. Again, bear in mind that no client wishes to see his or her project treated casually. Clients want to see evidence that their projects are taken seriously.

Miscellaneous

There are several other areas in the typical proposal, all of which should be at least introduced here, although they are discussed in more detail later and are still miscellaneous matters at this point. Some of these fall into the general classification called "front matter," which means that they customarily appear before the first page of text; others are appended or loosely attached to the back of the proposal.

Response Matrix

Without a doubt, the most important and most useful piece of front matter in a formal proposal (which is a response to a formal RFP—request for proposals) is a device I refer to as a "response matrix." Some discussion helps to explain the usefulness of this item.

It was pointed out earlier that clients usually do not have an easy time evaluating proposals on a comparative or even on an absolute basis because each proposer employs a different format and a different philosophy of presentation and response to the request. The response matrix helps the client evaluate proposals by offering within the proposal a guide to each item the client wishes to see covered.

The response matrix is developed along the general lines of Figure 26, which presents a suggested format and a few sample entries. This guides the client's review so that you get credit for responding to all requirements, including some that may not have been explicit, but that you deduced from your own study of the client's needs, as stated and as you inferred them from your analyses.

This matrix is useful for all proposals, but it is especially valuable when proposing to government agencies, for they make actual numerical evaluations of your proposal's technical merit. Experience has amply demonstrated that this type of presentation almost invariably maximizes the technical scores achieved by the proposals in which they are used.

The items are rather easy to gather if you have made up the checklists at

REQUEST FOR PROPOSAL	PROPOSAL RESPONSE	CLIENT COMMENTS
pp. 3, 4: Understanding of the requirement	pp. 1–3	
p. 12: Current/recent experience	pp. 1, 5, 15–18	
p. 14: Facilities and resources	pp. 19–22	

Figure 26. Format for response matrix.

the beginning, as suggested, for they contain the items that go into this matrix. That, in fact, is one of the several reasons for the checklists.

In making up your matrix, be sure that you direct the client's attention to your various graphics devices, as well as to textual passages, for the use of the matrix also helps you bring more impact to your presentations in this way—that is, by directing the client to the specific places in your proposal where you make your best and clearest arguments.

The blank right-hand column is for the client's convenience, so that he or she may verify and check off your responses and make notations, as well.

Executive Summary

A number of years ago, when I wrote proposals at Philco's Communications and Weapons division in Philadelphia, a standard section of our proposals bore the title "Why Philco Should Be Awarded This Contract." This plainly stated the objective of this section: It was a section in which we summed up the principal selling points of the proposal and asked the client to focus sharply on our main arguments. Today, that practice and intent is reflected in most formal proposals in a portion of the front matter titled "Executive Summary."

Nominally, that bit of text is intended as an abstract of the proposal, and yet it is not so titled. Instead, its title suggests that this is intended for those top-level executives who would not normally read the entire proposal— really have no need to spend time poring over details that are usually of interest to only the technical/professional staff specialists and technical managers. (Of course, the technical people also read the executive summary.)

The executive summary should summarize the proposal, of course, but it must focus primarily on the benefits and proofs—the reasons for favoring the proposer with the contract. This is its purpose, and it should appear in each proposal, whether the client has requested such a summary or not.

Appendices and Exhibits

An appendix is a place to present information that you expect to interest some, but not all, readers of your proposal. It's the way to avoid burdening readers with details they do not wish to wade through, without denying that information to those who will find it useful and who do want to see it. That includes such things as additional résumés (some proposal writers put all résumés in an appendix), drawings, papers from technical journals, reprints of articles, and other such matter.

In some cases, particularly when it is impractical to provide more than one copy of the item (and many proposal requests require multiple copies of the proposal), the term "exhibit" is employed, and the item is not an integral part of the proposal but is an exhibit of the proposal. (However, some people use the label "exhibit" to identify such items as illustrations in the proposal.)

ONE OTHER DEVICE: STORYBOARDING

There are a number of other devices and ways to strengthen your presentation. These are largely ways which are, in fact, not truly new or novel as editorial and publications devices, but are not used as often as they should be in proposals because proposal writers are usually not familiar with them. In fact, some organizations use what they call a *storyboard* approach to proposal writing, which makes use of some of these devices.

Storyboards

The term *storyboard* springs from the audiovisual and movie industries, where it is used as a planning and presentation tool. In its simplest form, it consists of a series of simple sketches and accompanying text, somewhat like a cartoon strip. These are organized into logical sequences.

Adapted to proposal writing, the storyboard becomes a bold headline or title at the head of a page, followed by a "blurb" or "gloss," followed by amplifying text. The goal is to present a new topic, in this format, on every page. But even if that is not always possible to start a new topic on every page, as it often is not, it is possible to start every new topic on a new page, along with its headline and blurb.

Blurbs and Glosses

The *gloss* is a rather time-honored device, found even today in many formal textbooks, where it appears as a marginal note in small print, summarizing or explaining the text alongside which it appears.

A *blurb* is just a bit different. It is a brief statement, such as the summary of an article or some intriguing element of an article, which appears under the title of the article in a periodical. (Significantly, the term is also applied to brief advertising messages.)

Technique

In the storyboard technique, the blurb appears under the bold headline at the top of the page, and the blurb has as its purpose summing up the important substance of the page, almost as an explanatory subtitle or abstract of the page. However, its purpose is to sell, and it is used to make the greatest contribution possible to that function, so it is generally used to emphasize or dramatize a selling point that should dominate that page or topic.

Used together to exploit them fully, all these many devices, tactics, and techniques can double your chances for success. Even if you have a truly outstanding offer to make, you need to do these things to get a fair reading and fair consideration of your offer.

CHAPTER 10

GRAPHICS

Graphic aids—illustrations—are more than a convenience; they are a necessity. The consultant who tries to write a successful proposal without using adequate graphic aids is working under a self-imposed handicap that is likely to prove crippling, if not fatal.

WHY GRAPHICS ARE A MUST ITEM IN PROPOSAL WRITING

The Three Basic Sales Problems/Objectives

Many proposal writers tend to use too many words and too few graphics. The purpose of a proposal is persuasion, of course; it is a sales presentation. That means inducing someone—a client—to decide that he or she wants something that you sell. However, the sales problem is not always simple, nor is it always the same problem. It may be any of three basic sales situations and problems, as summarized here:

1. In many cases, particularly where you are submitting an informal and/or unsolicited proposal (which usually means a noncompetitive one), you are probably simply trying to persuade the client to want the kind of service you offer because you are the only one offering it to this client.

2. On the other hand, if the client has already decided to buy the kind of service you offer, your marketing problem and main objective of your proposal is to induce the client to buy that service from you, rather than from someone else.

3.   In some cases, you may have the double task of persuading the client both to buy the service and to buy it from you in particular. (Some sales presentations succeed in accomplishing only the first of these tasks, and thereby create a sale for a competitor!)

Understanding Must Precede Persuasion

Whichever is your sales mission, you must somehow induce the client to understand your arguments, specifically the promise(s) you make and the evidence (sales arguments) you provide to support and validate your promises. Further, you must do so in such a way that it does not place an intolerable burden on the client to study your proposal, to understand your proposed program, and to grasp all your sales arguments. To so burden a client is, in effect, asking the client to sell himself or herself, which rarely works. The client expects you to do the selling, which underscores a fundamental sales principle (enunciated earlier): Always make it as easy as possible for the client to buy what you're selling. That means easy to understand your point, easy to agree with your arguments, and easy to place the order. To enable your client's ease of understanding, keep your entire proposition simple and straightforward.

Words Versus Graphics in Communication

Words are the principal and most common means for communicating among ourselves as a matter of pure necessity. Over the centuries, humans developed more and more sophisticated and efficient means to transmit words to each other, in terms of both mass communications (printing and movable type) and communications over long distances (telephone, telegraph, radio, and TV).

Still, there is evidence that the earliest nonvocal communication was via graphics. Throughout the world, we find artifacts attesting to this, from crude prehistoric drawings on the walls of ancient caves to sundry forms of art (paintings and sculptures of every kind), created by every civilization and society we know of.

It is significant also that movies, and subsequently TV, were immediate successes, and that worldwide TV transmission and reception were among the earliest and most popular applications of satellite communications systems. Moreover, the use of computer systems for the generation of graphics also proliferated rapidly, with the translation of spreadsheet data into graphic representations (e.g., charts and graphs) the primary goal of many sophisticated software programs.

Why Graphics?

Illustrations of all kinds, but especially graphic illustrations, facilitate and improve communications for more than one reason:

Pure Efficiency. In many cases, a good illustration is simply more *efficient* than words are in getting a message across: A simple drawing, when conceived and executed properly, gets an idea across to a reader with barely more than a glance, and it usually requires less physical space than equivalent text would require.

Less Effort Required. The illustration presents the desired image directly, eliminating the need for the reader to try to translate the written text into images or concepts that can be visualized. Thus, less effort is required of the reader to absorb a concept or image presented graphically than is the case when the reader must read and translate words. (Once again, the principle of making things as easy as possible for the client.)

Greater Accuracy. Even with the greatest effort exerted by readers, words are rarely translated or interpreted so exactly by readers that they create the precise image you want. That is because words are merely symbols, and they require the reader to search for a *referent*, so that the ways in which readers translate language depends largely on their own vocabularies and personal referents. We all tend inevitably to introduce our personal memories and biases into our interpretations of what we read. Thus, it is not surprising that each reader's interpretation of the meaning of any given textual passage is somewhat different than anyone else's interpretation. A drawing or photograph of an object, on the other hand, tends to be seen largely in the same way by every reader.

Various Degrees of Complexity

All of the foregoing is true for even the simplest communication needs, such as helping the reader to visualize the appearance of an object. Those principles are even more applicable to more complex cases of communication, such as those cases where it is necessary to assist the reader in perceiving and understanding an abstraction or a complex relationship (such as a flow process). You cannot expect the reader to find it easy to grasp technological or technical abstractions, such as the concept of phase relationships in an electrical or electronic circuit, or the theorem of Pythagoras unless you offer some graphic devices to facilitate understanding.

Further, it is not only in technological subjects that the problems of conveying abstractions and complex relationships arise. The problems are the same in many presentations that are not technological in any sense. Presenting and explaining business problems, societal relationships, professional functions, political processes, and many other subjects can be equally complex and challenging to present in easily understood explanations. Moreover, it is often necessary to use graphics to create explanations that are easily understood by laypersons.

Using graphic devices is not always a case of simply aiding both the writer in making the presentation and the reader in following the explanations. In some cases, it is simply not possible to make a sensible presentation by words alone, so graphic aids become absolutely necessary, rather than merely convenient. After a discussion of principles for using graphics, this chapter considers all these cases and the many ways to cope successfully with the presentation problems of each case.

A FEW UNDERLYING PRINCIPLES ABOUT GRAPHICS

The Sales/Marketing Consideration

What is said here about the logic and practices of using graphics properly applies to all writing and publishing. However, remember also that these ideas become even more important to you when they are applied to the preparation of proposals. That is, the reader of a book or report might have to struggle through difficult text passages that could and should have been made easier through graphic aids, but because the reader is intrinsically interested in the subject, the reader will persist. (Just as you now continue to invest your time in reading this book despite other demands for your time.)

However, because the proposal is a sales presentation, the client reading a proposal is under no compulsion to do so and is likely to discard the difficult-to-follow proposal in favor of a more readable one. Therefore, in addition to every other guideline, principle, rule, and/or caution offered to help you judge where, when, why, and how to opt for a graphic aid, always consider also the possible contribution an effective graphic aid may make to sales persuasion—to winning the contract.

Relative Costs

Graphics used in proposals—drawings and photographs, normally—are relatively expensive. It is possible today to create many, if not all, your own drawings at professional or near-professional quality by turning to the many ready-made artist's aids that anyone can use. Any well-stocked art-supplies emporium, and even many large stationers can supply such items as templates, paste-down lettering and rules, stencils, and other such items; even the professional artists use these today. Moreover there is the possibility of generating thoroughly acceptable drawings with your own personal computer and suitable graphics software. Even without special graphics software, with a little imagination, you can use your word processor to generate many useful drawings. (Some examples are shown later in this chapter.) Nonetheless, even when you generate the drawings yourself creating a drawing can be costly in time, if not in dollars. When special art departments are used to generate highly professional finished drawings, a definite dollar expense is involved.

Consequently, it is understandable that the complaint is sometimes raised in publications groups that graphic illustrations, especially detailed drawings that are generated for one-time use, are too expensive to be used in any case where the use is not an absolute necessity. The argument is that a "page of illustration" costs several times more than a page of straight text.

This reflects a lack of understanding about the economics of using graphics—properly. This lack deters the use of graphics, leading to the impoverishment of product quality (such as the quality of your proposal). What the originators of such objections do not take into account is that the comparison is faulty: The cost of a "page of illustration" should not be compared with the cost of a single page of straight text, but with the cost of several, perhaps many, pages of text. Unless the illustration eliminates and makes unnecessary at least several pages of text, the illustration is a poor one, which fails in its mission and should not have been created.

Why Many Graphics Fail

There are three common reasons for the failure of a graphic illustration. Only one of these causes reflects on the illustration per se: This occurs when the illustration is poorly conceived and simply does not do the job it ought to do. The other two cases occur when an illustration is unnecessary and used where no illustration would be helpful, or when an illustration is used by a writer who fails to take advantage of the illustration and insists on adding unnecessary language to explain what the illustration already makes quite clear. This third frailty defeats the basic objective in using the illustration. The unnecessary text is a needless expense and a needless added burden to both the writer and the reader.

Relevant Rules and Principles Inferred

All these types of failure point to more than one basic rule or principle, the first and most general of which is that a graphic illustration is not or should not be a supplement to textual presentation but is itself as primary and independent a means of communication as are the words. Each depends somewhat on the other, of course, but the interdependence is incidental, and each medium must also stand on its own. To do that, each must be used where it is the right medium to meet the need.

That means that as a writer of proposals, you must think and plan in terms of *what* you want to communicate before you consider *how* you will do so. First of all, bear in mind that everything you must communicate is either concrete or abstract information. More basic, perhaps, is the consideration of whether you are trying to communicate an image or an idea. We think in both images and words, and even when we are trying to understand and digest abstract ideas or concepts, we tend to conjure up images that analogize the concepts. Obviously, when the reference is to some common object or idea that is familiar to everyone, it is rarely necessary or profitable to employ a graphic illustration; the reader will furnish that mentally. The judgment of need for an illustration should be based entirely on what is to be communicated and how that is most effectively and/or efficiently accomplished.

Remember in this connection that *efficiency* has a somewhat different meaning here than it might in another writing application because this discussion relates to sales presentations. Therefore, *efficiency* refers here to more than efficiency in communicating information; it refers to effectiveness in persuading the client to your arguments. In many cases, a graphic aid will be more persuasive than words, even when it might not communicate information any better than words would, and so it adds efficiency in achieving the primary objective of the proposal. Therefore, also consider the impact of graphics in terms of persuasiveness, as compared with the persuasiveness of words alone.

GENERAL TYPES OF GRAPHICS

There are many types of graphics, and they vary widely in costs, time required for their execution, the skill required to create them, applications for which they are most suitable, and other parameters by which they may be compared with each other. A first broad discrimination might be made between photographs and drawings.

Photographs

Photographs have rather limited use in proposals, generally, although there are exceptions. In the case of a project that required the proposer to offer a warehouse site with ready access to a seaport and all facilities necessary to dockside operations at such a port, at least one proposer offered photographs, including an overall aerial photo of the proposed site, with appropriate "callouts" (arrows and labels surprinted on the photos) indicating the various facilities.

One great advantage in using photographs, rather than simple drawings, in such a case as this, is the much greater credibility of photographs. In fact, in such a case as this, where the question of suitable facilities bears on the client's final decision, drawings purporting to show the facilities are claims, whereas photographs are evidence. Even elaborate and costly "artist's conception" types of drawings (often developed by architects to depict the final building planned) reflect what the proposer promises, while photographs invite the client to view with his or her own eyes, obviously a far more persuasive alternative.

This example shows that in some special cases, a photograph is certainly the most effective and probably the least costly way to get the information across to the client. In general, however, photographs may be used to show clients your own facilities and equipment, where that is relevant—offices, library, data processing system, and/or whatever else is evidence of your ability to serve the client's needs well.

Photographs are usually less costly for this application if you have them prepared in printed form in sufficient quantity simply to bind them into all your proposals or, as a practical alternative, to include them in a standard capabilities brochure, which you use as part of the "qualifications" section of your custom proposals.

General Types of Drawings

For proposal purposes, drawings to be considered are almost always of the general type known as *line drawings*. That general category includes all types of graphs, charts, and other pictorials that do not include subtle shadings, as do photographs and renderings in oils, water colors, charcoal, and other such artistic interpretations. (Although some shadings are achieved even in line drawings, they are achieved via mechanical means or special ready-made materials that anyone can use.)

It is rather difficult to draw up a complete list of types of line drawings, for there are many classes and subclasses, according to both the characteristics of the drawings and the applications to which they are put. Even the following list does not convey a complete profile of all the possible types of line drawings, but it does serve to establish that there is a broad range of types from which to choose the type that is most suitable for a given application:

- Pictorials
- Networks

- Bar charts
- Pie charts

- Flowcharts
- Clip art
- Logic trees
- Matrixes
- Graphs

- Plots
- Milestone charts
- Organization charts
- Block diagrams
- Cartoons

Even within these types, many broad subdivisions are possible. Note, also, that this list includes matrixes, which are more like tables than drawings, but they are functionally in the same class as line drawings. The following discussions include examples of types of line drawings, although a more complete set of samples and examples is offered in an appendix as reference material for your use later in preparing proposals.

Pictorials and Diagrams.   A simple pictorial is shown in Figure 27, which depicts a simple local area network in a ring configuration. This network is also presented and explained in the simple diagram of Figure 28.

These illustrate quite clearly the difference between the two methods of graphic presentation. Both offer the same information, but obviously the pictorial drawing is somewhat more effective in demonstrating the system in more than one respect: First of all the pictorial is far more effective than

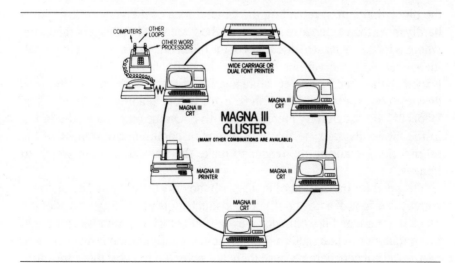

Figure 27.   Pictorial representation of local area network in a ring. Courtesy of A.B. Dick Corporation.

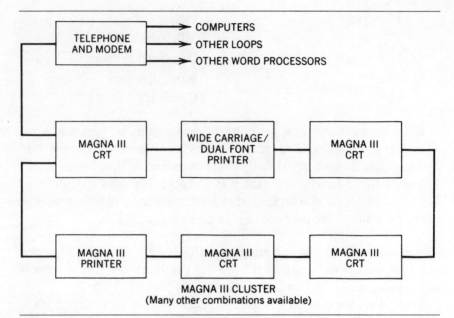

Figure 28. Block diagram of the local network shown in Figure 27.

the block diagram in reflecting the general idea of the system. It requires hardly more than a glance to understand the system, at least in general terms, whereas it takes at least a little study of the block diagram to grasp the overall idea, even with the various labels and identifiers. That is the key to the principal difference: a reader can recognize instantly such familiar items as desktop computers and telephones, even before reading the labels. The labels are almost entirely merely supportive. On the other hand, the labels in the block diagram are the only means of communicating most of the information, requiring the reader to make the translation from words to images.

The need for translation of labels isn't the only difference. The pictorial conveys the idea of a ring configuration much more efficiently than does the block diagram, and it would do so even if the block diagram was arranged in a circular or ovular pattern. The particular configuration is an important part of the concept here because there are several other possible configurations for local area networks.

Further, because the reader of the pictorial is not required to translate the words of the block diagram into the images of the equipment (but is shown a good representation of the equipment as it actually appears), the writer far more effectively controls the communication. That is perhaps the most cogent argument for the use of pictorials whenever and wherever practicable: They offer you far greater control of what the reader sees and "hears" in reading your proposal.

Unfortunately, pictorial drawings tend to be more expensive than many other illustrations because they usually require the services of professional illustrators. (Exceptions to this, are explored later.) They also tend to require more lead time to prepare. For both reasons, it is usually impracticable to use them indiscriminately, so their use should probably be confined to the most important messages you wish to deliver to the client, and perhaps just to broad and general overviews of complex projects. They often prove especially useful in this application, for they are often the key to brushing aside the trivia and the distracters, and focusing, at least for the moment, on the real essence of the problem.

On the other hand, even disregarding cost entirely, pictorials are not always the most effective graphic illustrations to use. For some applications, other graphic representations, such as networks, more effectively help the client to grasp the concept easily.

Networks   (These are also known in their various manifestations as "CPM," for critical path method, and "PERT," for programmed evaluation and review technique.) Networks are especially useful for showing serial and parallel relationships, interdependencies, alternate paths, and numerous other absolute and relative characteristics of the assorted elements. An illustration such as Figure 29 can demonstrate that there are several paths to the ultimate goal or objective of the project, and it facilitates demonstrating to the client the validity of premises underlying a discussion of possible alternatives.

In Figure 29, item 1 represents the starting point of the project, and item 16 is the objective. The ideal path from the start to the objective is the shortest one, a straight line from 1 to 16. However, because it is rare that any project goes that smoothly, you have anticipated the possible forced detours of the project or, better yet, planned the various alternatives that you will have ready, in the event these problems materialize.

Thus, this figure helps you explain what is necessarily a rather sophisticated and fairly complex project plan, while it also demonstrates the high

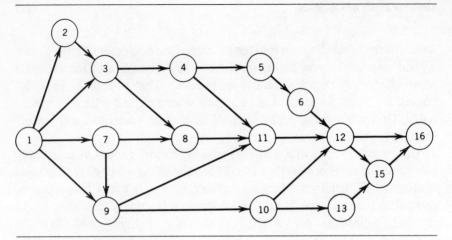

Figure 29. A simple network.

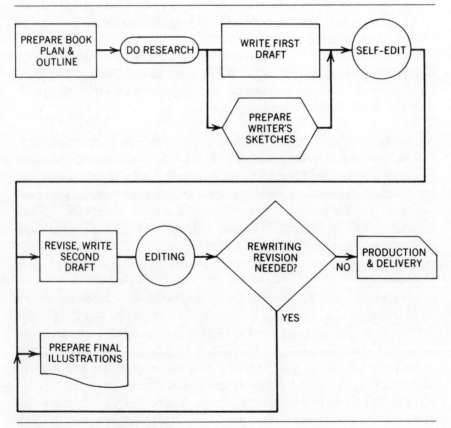

Figure 30. A simple flowchart.

caliber and thoroughness of your planning and preparation. In drawings such as this, you can label each of the numbered elements, or you can simply prepare a set of notes—a legend, in fact—explaining each numbered element.

Flowcharts. In a simpler presentation, an illustration such as Figure 30 may be used. The boxes in which the various steps and functions are explained can be any shape—rectangular, circular, or other, as illustrated in Figure 31. Many people use an assortment of shapes in such illustrations, to make the illustration interesting and pleasing in general appearance, as well as informative. In some applications, such as computer program flowcharts and logic diagrams, the shapes of the boxes have individual and distinct meanings—specific shapes are used for specific applications. If any of your readers have backgrounds in logic, in programming, in courseware

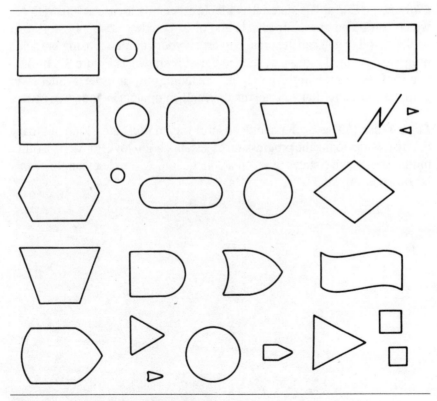

Figure 31. Standard drawing templates.

design, or in other technical fields, determine the symbols that have specialized meanings, and use those only to signify those meanings.

These figures were drawn with standard drawing templates, which are readily available in art supply shops and at many well-stocked stationers. Templates have been designed for an enormous variety of applications in all kinds of professions—all the engineering fields, architecture, mathematics fields, and many others. You can choose from literally dozens of different kinds, many of them in a number of sizes, too.

Stick-on Drawing Aids. Templates are only one kind of drawing aid. Many other drawing aids are available, including boxes, arrows, borders, symbols, and other such devices. Many of these are offered in paste-down (self-adhesive) or transfer (decal) forms. The wide variety of aids applies to many fields.

Clip Art. "Clip art" is material available especially for use as illustrations, which can be purchased in sheets and/or in booklets at supply stores. In addition, today you can generate clip art on your computer, using graphics programs. A small sample of such material is shown as Figure 32. In fact, many of these drawing capabilities, including clip art, are available in graphics programs that you can run on small computers in your own office.

Logic Trees. These offer another useful way to illustrate a kind of binary or Aristotelian logic: the progression of yes–no, high–low, go–stop, or other mutually exclusive states to reach a conclusion. A simple example of this is shown in Figure 33.

Figure 32. A sample of computer-generated clip art. (Courtesy of Prosoft®.)

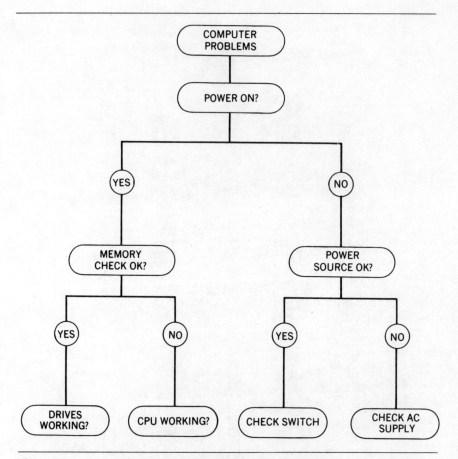

Figure 33. A simple logic tree. CPU, central processing unit.

CHAPTER 11

The Executive Summary (and Other Matter)

Used properly, the executive summary often proves to be the most important element in the proposal. At the least, it would be a serious error to underestimate its importance and so fail to utilize it effectively. Also, other elements of front matter require attention.

FRONT MATTER

In any formal publication, certain elements appear before page 1—before the presentation begins, that is. At a minimum, there are usually a title page and a table of contents. There are often other elements, as well: prefaces, forewords, abstracts, and notices of various kinds. Formal proposals are no exception to this. They also generally include in their front matter elements not normally found in most other formal publications.

The title page and table of contents are de rigueur, found in just about every formal publication of every kind, including formal proposals. Other elements normally found in formal proposals include an abstract, an executive summary, a foreword or preface, and in some cases other special elements, such as the very useful one I have referred to as a response matrix. That and the executive summary are probably the most important elements of front matter in proposals.

WHAT IS AN EXECUTIVE SUMMARY?

Many things are not quite what they appear to be, and to some extent, that may be said for the executive summary. As mentioned in an earlier chapter, the term *executive summary* suggests that it is a kind of abstract of the entire proposal, offered to help executives absorb the main thrust of a proposal with a brief reading. That is true in a general sense, but there is more to it than that. In the hands of an astute marketer, an executive summary is far more than an abstract.

In principle, the executive summary is particularly appropriate in proposals that are highly technical. In fact, it was the growing complexity of technical detail presented in major proposals, along with the massive and unwieldy size of many proposals (literally thousands of pages and several volumes, for many large contracts) that inspired the idea of the executive summary and all but mandates its continued use.

The rationale underlying the idea is simply that in many cases, it is impractical for executives on the client's staff to read or attempt to read entire proposals. They will not normally read the main text of the proposal for more than one reason: (a) The executives may not be in a position to appreciate and appraise the technical detail, (b) even if they are, it is an inappropriate and inefficient use of their time to read the entire proposal. The typical executive needs only to get a general overview and thus a broad appreciation of each proposal. There are usually specialists on staff whose duties include studying proposals in depth, including the technical detail, and making their evaluations and recommendations to management.

As mentioned previously, though the executive summary is addressed to management, experience shows clearly that almost invariably everyone who reads the proposal reads the executive summary, and reads it first. It serves the useful purpose, from the reader's viewpoint, of providing an advance orientation and thus a road map to help the reader grasp the proposal overall.

The executive summary is therefore an element that everyone reads, ordinarily. That should suggest to anyone responsible for proposal preparation some uses to make of the executive summary. From the proposer's viewpoint, it offers many potential benefits.

THE USES OF AN EXECUTIVE SUMMARY

Recall that Philco, some years ago, regularly included in each proposal a final section titled "WHY PHILCO SHOULD BE AWARDED THIS CONTRACT" (see Chapter 9). This section of Philco's proposals recapitulated and summed up all the major sales appeals and arguments that had appeared in the earlier pages of the proposal. This organization was not the least bit coy about their desire for the contract and their conviction that they were by far the best-qualified proposer for the job. They took pains to assure the client that they did, indeed, sincerely want to win the contract and did believe that it was in the client's best interests to make the award to them. (Marketing is no place for subtlety or modesty, and proposals are no place for shrinking violets!)

It is still perfectly proper to include in your proposal some element that makes that desire and conviction plainly apparent to the client by stressing it and drawing special attention to it. Today, the convenient and popular mechanism for doing so is almost always that executive summary. The inclusion of such an element in proposals has almost become a de facto standard. It appears in the front matter of the proposal, rather than as a final section, and it is probably more effective there.

The executive summary thus becomes a major sales tool, perhaps the most important one in your proposal. It becomes the opening argument of that sales presentation you offer a client as a proposal, and in so doing, it provides certain distinct strengths that can prove decisive:

1. You get an unusually good opportunity to get attention and arouse interest immediately—even before the client comes to page 1.
2. You gain the benefit of being able to establish that important favorable first impression.
3. You can condition the mind of the client—position yourself and your offer advantageously.
4. You can focus the client's attention on the key points and, in so doing, greatly increase the impact of those key points when the client reads and recognizes them again in the main text.

For these reasons, it is important that you do not underestimate the importance of the executive summary. Expend enough effort on it to use it to your greatest advantage.

WHAT TO CALL AN EXECUTIVE SUMMARY

For discussion purposes, I use the generic and descriptive term *executive summary* here. On the one hand, you want to persuade the client to read this section as a time-saver that will offer a quick appreciation of the entire proposal. On the other hand, you want to take advantage of all opportunities to persuade the client to your cause, to *sell*.

Therefore, there is considerable advantage in employing the principle enunciated earlier of making all the titles, headlines, and captions sell for you by stressing the benefits and proofs you offer. On the one hand, the title "Executive Summary" is important because many clients expect (and some even demand) such a section of your proposal to be offered, and they will look for it by that name. The client may well be dismayed if he or she cannot find a portion of text so named—That is, the client may fail to recognize an executive summary if not identified clearly as such. On the other hand, you want a title for this element that helps sell your proposal, while also persuading the client to read this curtain raiser of your proposal. One way around this dilemma is to use a subtitle, such as the following:

Executive Summary:
Advantages Offered by [*your name*]

The subtitle should follow the philosophy of making titles work on behalf of the sales effort. Following are some suggestions for such subtitles, offered here as idea starters. (You probably can come up with better ones.)

Summary of Leading Features
Summary of Benefits
Why _____ [you] Should Be Awarded This Contract
What _____ [you] Proposes to Do for You
The Benefits of _____ [your] Proposed Program

A FEW RELEVANT PRINCIPLES

Because the client will expect the executive summary to provide an overview and virtual abstract of the proposal, it is important that you provide that in writing your executive summary. However, your goal is to accomplish that while still achieving your marketing goal of making the executive summary an important principal selling tool. Therefore, every item listed in the executive summary must be couched in positive terms, as a sales argument. In fact, it is helpful to think of the executive summary as being a miniature proposal in and of itself, with the following objectives:

1. Introduce yourself briefly in highly positive words, words that demonstrate the advantages you offer.
2. Focus on the most critical or important aspect(s) of the requirement (your main strategy) and demonstrate that you have the necessary 20/20 insight.
3. Sum up, in clearly focused and to-the-point delivery, the benefits and proofs—the sales appeals and arguments.

A CASE HISTORY AS AN EXAMPLE

Nothing makes all of this quite as clear as an actual example from a case history. The successful proposal of North Atlantic Industries, Inc., for a large and important Navy procurement of a computerlike item of equipment owed at least part of its success to an excellent executive summary. A description of their executive summary, along with an outline that includes the actual headlines they used, is presented here to help illustrate these principles and practices:

THE PROPOSER: SUPPLIER OF THE AN/USH-26(V)
North Atlantic Industries (NAI) pointed out another Navy program, which they were carrying out successfully; mentioned some outstanding achievements in that program; and demonstrated the relevance of that experience and accomplishment to the proposed program. They pointed out, for example, the

excellent performance and demonstrated reliability of the cited equipment, and a Navy award for excellence in quality.

SUPPLIER'S COMMITMENT

NAI stressed the importance of the procurement, pointing out key elements, compared favorably and point-by-point the needs of the program with what NAI had to offer, and pledged their total commitment to the goals of the program. They observed that the program had an importance larger than might be suggested by its relatively modest size, also pointing out that the program would be relatively small to a large corporation, but it was large and important to them, as a small company. [*This was to stress the advantages of using a smaller company as the contractor, of course.*]

BASIC PREMISES

Here, NAI drew four points, analyzing the requirement and pointing out the four critical considerations they perceived as what ought to be the areas of concern in developing a design, with due regard to the present state of the art and what could be reasonably anticipated in probable future developments, given recent experience in the fields of interest.

A LOGICAL CONCLUSION

From the preceding, NAI presented, as a logical conclusion, the indicated primary requirements of any practical design, specifying that these were carefully considered in drawing up the NAI design.

A LOGICAL SOLUTION

Here, NAI set forth its specific design objectives, derived from and chosen as the logical outcome of the preceding technical arguments. [*This was to prove the integrity and authenticity of the technical analyses.*]

AN ADVANCED DESIGN

NAI provided here some additional data on the proposed design, pointing out that it was truly an advanced design, as promised, and it was both suitable to the requirement and responsive to the capabilities of current technology.

TOTAL COMPLIANCE

NAI affirmed here that they were in total compliance with the RFP in their response, as they will be in their performance.

EXCEEDING REQUIREMENTS

NAI listed nine individual and specific items in which they pledged that they would not only meet all requirements, but would actually exceed them— deliver more than is required, providing the client many special and additional benefits.

SPECIAL FEATURE
This promised feature overcomes to a large extent one of the drawbacks—relatively slow access—inherent in using tape for storage purposes.

SOME EXAMPLES OF ENHANCEMENTS
NAI described possible enhancements to the design—options the client could elect to include—and listed nine specific items under this headline.

TECHNICAL SUPPORT SERVICES
NAI summarized the required support services and how their organization could and would respond to these.

GEOGRAPHICAL ADVANTAGE
NAI indicated an advantage in their locale (Long Island, New York), which is a center of relevant industries and resources.

UPGRADABILITY
This paragraph showed how both the system and the individual units proposed could be "upgraded" quite easily, in the field.

MANAGEMENT
The proposer summarized its several levels of management—technical/project, general/administrative, and corporate—as they would relate to the program.

WHY NORTH ATLANTIC INDUSTRIES SHOULD BE AWARDED THE CONTRACT
[*This headline should have a familiar ring. You may remember that it was once the title used for an entire proposal section. As used here, it introduced*] several paragraphs [*that*] reinforced briefly all the arguments that had gone before. Then was presented the final argument that NAI should be awarded the contract because what was proposed was what the client needs—that is, the proposed design is exactly right for the requirement.

HOW LONG SHOULD AN EXECUTIVE SUMMARY BE?

An executive summary, by its nature (i.e., as a *summary*), should be short. In the case history abbreviated here, the summary met this criterion: Despite the length of the actual explanation and the use of 14 headlines, this entire presentation was not more than about 2,500 words: 9 double-spaced pages in a proposal of nearly 250 pages.

No specific rules govern the ideal length of an executive summary.

However, aside from the fact that its very name dictates that it must be short in relation to what it summarizes, a lengthy executive summary defeats its own purpose. It cannot, for example, succeed in focusing the client's attention on key issues and critical points if it rambles on about many other matters or fails to get directly to the point for each item covered. It is therefore largely a matter of individual judgment, but some guidance may help you to form judgments in developing effective executive summaries:

1. The executive summary cited here as a case history represented approximately 3.6 percent of the total proposal. That is a reasonable percentage, although it is desirable to make it even more concise, if possible. Two to three pages of executive summary for every hundred pages of main proposal is a good rule of thumb for sizable proposals.

2. Do not misinterpret this as an absolute yardstick by which to measure all executive summaries; it is not that. A commonsense rule for length is this: Make the executive summary long enough to present all those points you believe to be decisive, but no longer than that. That is, do not short-change your presentation because of any perceived hard-and-fast rule of maximum allowable size. Far better for it to be a bit longer than it ought logically to be, and present everything important, than to be brief and fail to present important items. Never lose sight of the purpose of the executive summary: It is designed ostensibly to present a brief overview of your proposal, but your chief objective is actually to make a sharply focused and hard-hitting sales presentation by summing up your most cogent arguments. It therefore must be brief, but also complete, to get that job done.

HOW TO WRITE "TIGHT" EXECUTIVE SUMMARIES

Rewriting Is Far More Important Than Writing

Concise and effective executive summaries are never written; they are rewritten. That is a rule for all writing, in fact: The experienced writer does not expect to get his or her best work down on paper (or on a floppy disk) in the first draft. The first draft should be written in complete freedom, getting thoughts on paper or computer disk. In subsequent drafts—and even the best writers often find it necessary to revise through several subsequent drafts—the writer works a steady improvement in a number of ways:

- Cut excess verbiage.
- Organize effectively.
- Employ a dynamic style.

Rewriting (and Editing) Means Cutting Copy Down

As noted earlier, at least one experienced editor asserted that the essence of editing, and certainly the first task of editing in most cases, is to boil down the copy, which is almost invariably overwritten. Many and perhaps even most writers are too verbose, and the editor can often delete as much as one third of the copy without losing anything important. Recognizing this as an almost unvarying truth, many professional writers simply do not worry about verbosity when they are writing a first draft. In fact, they make a concerted effort to get *all* the ideas down on disk or paper, with the full expectation that they will then review what they have, choose the best and most relevant material, and eliminate the extraneous material and excess verbiage themselves, even before the editor sees the copy.

This is especially true of—and probably the best approach for—writing an executive summary. First, go through the proposal and transcribe all the "goodies"—promises, benefits, proofs, credentials, and whatever else appears to help. Then go through this and begin to sort, determining which are the most important items and which are merely clutter and should be dropped from the summary.

This process takes a lot of self-discipline. There is an almost instinctive tendency to be "polypharmacological"—to put everything into the prescription in the hope that the larger the number of ingredients, the greater the possibility that one of them will work. But it is a self-defeating idea because too many items dilute the overall effect and weaken the presentation. Force yourself to discriminate between important and unimportant items, and scrap the latter. Unless yours is an exceptionally large proposal, try to restrict the number of items to no more than 10. Then start organizing the items into a logical sequence and work especially at selecting the most powerful ones for the first three in the list.

Organizing the Executive Summary

The logical sequence for your executive summary is not necessarily the same as that used in the case history cited here. You will have to decide what sequence is best for implementing your strategy. Logically, you should lead with whatever is your main strength. In the case of NAI, one of their major strengths was the record of performance they had already established with the client on a previous contract, and they decided to lead with that. Your own case should be decided on its own merits. For example, your main strength might be one of these (or one of many other things, of course):

Special capabilities and/or experience/accomplishments
Special resources
Features of your plan
Technical advantages offered
Insights into the requirement
Cost-reduction ideas

Whatever your decision, build your approach around that major item, use it as your lead, and build your case on it.

The Next Stage: Achieving a Dynamic Style

That first stage addressed reducing the number of items to those of greatest importance. It was necessary to gather up all the items first, of course, and then make judgments as to which to keep and which to discard as not important enough for the executive summary. With that done, it is time to address the second stage of condensation of the summary. That is an editorial kind of stage: No items will be eliminated—presumably, you have by now dropped all items that were not truly essential—but the presentation will be tightened up and made more vigorous by dropping unnecessary words and simplifying expression generally. It is usually acceptable to use special space- and time-saving devices, too, such as telegraphic style (eliminate articles, such as "the" and "a"; use briefest verb forms, such as "run" for "running"). Also, use bullets for listings, and otherwise get meanings across with greatest possible economies of presentation.

The purpose of all this effort to keep the executive summary as short as possible is not only to conserve the reader's time, but also to achieve a much more dynamic style. These measures add a lot of vigor to the style, increasing the impact of the words. Compare the following two items, for example, portions of an executive summary. The first was written in simple but conventional style, and it represents the final stage of drafting and polishing the copy before reducing it to the telegraphic, punchy style of the final version:

[ORIGINAL VERSION]

Medical Management, Inc. (MMI), offers to provide a detailed medical management plan that includes a complete set of step-by-step procedures; a complete (8-hour) training seminar for as many of your staff as you wish for us to train; complete documentation in the form of procedural, policy, and training manuals; and special consultation services at no charge for 90 days following installation of the MMI system.

MMI offers extra options, at nominal additional costs: (1) MMI will make this a turnkey program—will ourselves install the system: operate it for 90 days and debug it; train your staff; and then turn over the trouble-free and smooth-running system to your own staff. (2) MMI will remain on call for one year, as needed to help solve problems, deal effectively with new and unanticipated problems, and/or answer questions and provide additional training for your staff. (3) MMI will operate your system for a full year, while providing training and customizing all procedures, policies, and documentation for your own organization.

[REVISED, FINAL VERSION]

Medical Management, Inc. (MMI), proposes a detailed and specific program:
- Complete step-by-step procedures
- 8-hour training seminar for all staff
- Policy, procedural, and training manuals
- 90 days free consultation

Also, these options available for nominal additional costs:
- Turnkey program: we operate, debug, train and turn over after 90 days
- MMI on call, for full year, as consultant, troubleshooter
- MMI operates system for full year

Note that the final version is far less verbose, without missing any of the important points, but it is far more vigorous, making each point sharply and guiding the reader's attention to focus on the benefit, not becoming distracted by irrelevant adjectives and adverbs. The client has no difficulty in grasping immediately the specifics of your offer—and your proposal is an offer, not a plea.

EXECUTIVE SUMMARY IN A LETTER PROPOSAL

A small program usually calls for a letter proposal rather than a formal one. A letter proposal is rarely more than two to four pages, even with a program outline. Obviously, such a brief and informal proposal will not include a formal executive summary, such as that discussed and shown here. Nevertheless, the letter is still a proposal, and it is, as such, also a sales presentation.

For that reason, the philosophy of the executive summary still applies, although it may appear as a simple narrative paragraph or two. It is also perfectly proper to make a "laundry list" type of presentation, as in the examples just used, when a number of items are to be featured. Whichever the case, the summary should be as close to the opening of the letter as possible, or even as the opening itself, as in the following examples of each style:

Because Marketing Consultants, Inc. (MCI), has stored in our computer and other files over 200,000 of our proprietary marketing materials, we are able to assemble a custom-designed system for you almost overnight and at unprecedented low cost. Though we will make recommendations, you have the opportunity to review these materials and make choices of your own.

On the other hand, it is possible to adapt the listed-item and telegraphic style where there are numerous points you wish to stress:

Marketing Consultants, Inc. (MCI), offers clients unique services:

- Widest choice of materials & styles in industry—GUARANTEED.
- System completely custom designed for you—GUARANTEED.
- Turnaround (delivery) in less than one week—GUARANTEED.
- Lowest cost anywhere—GUARANTEED.

MCI can do this for you because our library has over 200,000 proprietary designs and marketing materials in our computer and other files. We recommend, but you have the right to choose.

OTHER FRONT MATTER

Sequence of Front Matter

The following sequence is recommended for the front matter:

1. Copy of letter of transmittal (inside cover)
2. Title page
3. Executive summary
4. Preface or foreword, if used
5. Note introducing response matrix
6. Response matrix
7. Table of contents

Title Page

Unless you are preparing a truly large formal proposal and going to the considerable expense often associated with the preparation of such large proposals, your letterhead is likely to serve well as the basis for the title page of your proposal. Figure 34 is an example of such a title page.

The example includes reference to an RFP—request for proposals. Where such a formal request does not exist, for whatever reason, reference is simply not made—that is, the two lines beginning "in response to" are simply deleted.

The notice of proprietary information is likewise not always appropriate. Where it is, however, such a notice should be printed on the title page, and the actual material cited should be identified as confidential and/or proprietary on those pages, by suitable notations there. If you are submitting a formal proposal to a government agency, the RFP will normally suggest the wording for this proprietary notice, but it will be along the general lines shown in the figure.

HRH COMMUNICATIONS, INC.
P.O. Box 1731   Wheaton, MD 20902
Fax: (301) 649-5745   Voice: (301) 649-2499

PROPOSAL

Offered to Hardesty & Hardesty, Inc.

in response to RFP HH-86-001

dated June 22, 1989

NOTICE:

Information contained in pages 33-37, 45, 49, and

76-82 is confidential and proprietary to HRH

Communications, Inc. and should not be disclosed

to anyone not a recipient or reviewer of this

proposal. However, in the event of award, this

information may be disclosed to and will be used

in behalf of and according to the interests of

Hardesty & Hardesty, Inc.

July 15, 1986

Figure 34.   Typical title page of a formal proposal.

The copyright notice is a good idea for all cases, as further protection for your confidential and proprietary information, as well as for your proposal itself. Many people are imitative, especially when they observe a success. Some of them are likely to plagiarize your exact wording if they manage to get copies of your successful proposals, which happens frequently these days. You are entitled to copyright your proposal, and you need to do nothing more than what is shown here to secure to yourself a common law copyright. (It is only necessary to have that copyright registered with the Copyright Office of the U.S. Library of Congress if you get involved in litigation concerning your copyright, and you can register it at that time, if it ever becomes necessary.)

Table of Contents

The table of contents of a publication lists, as a minimum, the titles of chapters or sections and the page numbers. Some writers choose to list for each chapter all the major headlines, thus offering almost an abstract of each chapter, probably an exceptionally good idea for a proposal presentation. (See the table of contents for this book as general example.)

Among other refinements possible for the table of contents, although not universally practiced, are the inclusion of additional sections in the table of contents headed by such titles as "List of Figures" (or "Illustrations"), "List of Tables," and "Foreword," or "Preface."

Unlike books, proposals do not often carry prefaces or forewords, although there is no good reason why they should not do so, except that the executive summary serves at least part of the purpose generally served by a preface or foreword. However, other purposes can be served by such introductory remarks. For one thing, in the large consulting organization, the CEO (chief executive officer) may use this to address the client with assurances of his personal concern and his pledge of conscientious effort. (This is otherwise conveyed in the letter of transmittal, but it is almost certainly more effective in a foreword or preface.) Also, a preface or foreward may be used to carry any other special message or preliminary remarks deemed suitable and helpful.

Response Matrix

The item I call a "response matrix" is an especially important and useful element of the front matter. It's a device to help ensure that you respond to all matters of concern. Even more important, however, it helps the client verify that you have done so—that your proposal is completely responsive.

The matrix is derived from the RFP and, more specifically, from those checklists you made earlier in analyzing the requirement and what the client wished you to respond to. It is usually several pages long for any proposal of size. Figure 35 is part of a single sheet from one such matrix. Note the column titles: "Specification" refers to the RFP and what it specifically calls for. "Compliance with Specification" calls for a "yes" or "no." "Exceeds

MATRIX TABLE SHOWING COMPLIANCE WITH ELEX-T-551

Specification		Compliance?	Exceeds?	Proposal Reference		Title/ Remarks
Par.	Title/Subj.			Par./ Graphic	Page No.	
3.5.8	Printer copy	YES	—	2.3,1, 2.3,2	2–14, 2–46	
3.5.9	TEMPEST	YES	—	3.1	3–1	
3.5.10	ELEC. DESIGN	YES	YES	2.3, 4	2–14	
3.5.11	THERMAL DESIGN	YES	—	2.5, 6, 8, 9	2–16, 2–17	
3.5.12	TEST MEASURE.	YES	—	2.13	2–18	
3.5.13	TEST PROVISIONS	YES	YES	2.15	2–20	
3.5.14	CLASS A TEST	YES	—	2.15	2–21	
3.5.17	CLASS B TEST	YES	YES	2.16	2–22	

Figure 35.   Sheet XIV from a many-page response matrix.

Specification" also calls for "yes" or "no." "Proposal Reference" refers to the page numbers in the proposal (and the paragraph numbers where paragraphs are numbered, as they were in this case). "Title/Remarks," in the rightmost column, is left blank, for the use of the client in checking off the compliance with all specifications.

Of course, this form should be modified and adapted to your own needs, which are likely to be less formalized than this one was. For example, you may not have numbered paragraphs, and you may even not have a formal specification to refer to. You may wish to substitute other column titles, such as "Need" for "Specification."

The matrix is an important element, and it should be developed carefully and introduced with a brief explanation that it is provided to assist the reader in locating specific responses to required information, as well as to ensure that the author of the proposal has made all necessary responses.

LETTER OF TRANSMITTAL

Informal or letter proposals are complete in and of themselves, usually. Formal proposals usually have three elements:

1. Technical proposal (may be more than one volume)
2. Cost proposal (often required to be a separate document)
3. Letter of transmittal

The letter of transmittal is a courtesy, but it is also more than that. Many consultants believe that the letter of transmittal is of great importance; although others think it is mere formality and of little significance in making an award. The truth falls between those extremes, of course, as truth usually does.

The importance of a letter of transmittal— or the lack of importance— is at least partly the consequence of its treatment. Obviously, if you treat it as a pure formality, that is all it will be. However, you can compel it to assume greater importance if you design it to be more important.

The matters that a letter of transmittal ought to cover are these, at a minimum:

1. Confirm that the proposal is a response to some specific RFP (hereby

identified), an informal request, submitted as agreed to earlier, or citing whatever circumstances led to the proposal.

2. Make brief mention of the requirement to which it responds and the chief characteristics or features of the proposal (but especially of any major feature).

3. Confirm that you are authorized to make the offer, and that it is a firm offer.

4. State the period of time for which the offer made in your proposal is firm.

5. Offer to provide any additional information desired, in any form desired, including in writing and in face-to-face discussions, with or without formal presentations.

The letter of transmittal is addressed to the client or to whomever issued the RFP, such as the client's purchasing agent. (In the case of proposals to the government, it is normally addressed to the contracting officer.)

It is a common practice of many consultants to bind a copy of the letter of transmittal inside the cover of each copy of the proposal, so that every reader of the proposal can read the letter also.

THE COST PROPOSAL

Everything discussed in this chapter has, so far, been front matter. The remaining two items (the cost proposal and the appendices) are not front matter, but they require only brief discussion and can be fitted here as well as anywhere else. The cost proposal is occasionally required to be a separate proposal. The reason for making the cost proposal a separate item is to withhold from evaluators all knowledge of costs. This is done to encourage evaluators to make their evaluations of technical proposals uninfluenced by cost considerations.

Government agencies almost invariably require separate cost proposals, and they usually provide forms on which to list costs and explain how the proposer has arrived at the bottom-line figure. Usually, the cost proposal is only a few pages, at most, although there can be exceptions to this also.

APPENDICES

The appendix is a simple item—a place to include material that will be of interest to some readers, but not to all. That might include additional résumés, drawings, professional papers cited in the body of the proposal, sample materials, or other items qualifying to be appended, but not included in the main text.

CHAPTER 12

Common Problems and Ideas for Solutions

"When life hands you a lemon, make lemonade." Despite the triteness of the expression, the idea is valid and can be made to work in almost all cases.

SOME QUESTIONS ABOUT SMALL, NEW, AND/OR INEXPERIENCED PROPOSERS

The problems you encounter in writing proposals are probably much more common than you think. Following are a few typical ones, to illustrate this. In fact, these examples report on questions I get again and again from attendees at my proposal-writing seminars and from many readers of my earlier book, *How to Succeed as an Independent Consultant* (John Wiley & Sons, Inc., 1983 and 1988).

> I am a very small business, and I can't list a half-dozen qualified specialists as staff employees for those projects that need a half-dozen or more professionals. How can I handle that?

There are several variants of that question. Some of the questioners are independent consultants, having no employees. Some are partnerships without other employees. Some are even part-time consultants. But all address the same question: Will it be disastrous to admit that they do not now have all the staff necessary, or will it be disastrous to propose that they will hire employees or use associates to perform on the contract?

There are a number of analogous problems, all related to a common problem of being small or new, and therefore perceiving great difficulty in putting up a show of strength in the matters of resources, experience, and other qualifications. Several other questions reflect those kinds of concerns:

I am just starting out, and I really have no experience to describe or other clients to list. How do I answer a requirement to list current and recent projects? Or: I have only a little experience. Or: I have a little experience, but sometimes it is not the right kind for the project, although I know that I can do the job.

I work at home. Do I need a downtown office in a building so that I look as though I am a real professional? Is having my office at home unprofessional? What do I do if the client wants to see my facilities for handling the job? I can arrange to use a friend's office address as a kind of "front." Would that be a good idea or a bad one?

How do I avoid using long and difficult words, as you advise, when I am in a field that communicates in such jargon? Won't clients think I am unqualified or inexperienced if I don't use the right jargon or "buzz words"?

Should I be incorporated to make myself look more important in my proposals? Doesn't being a corporation add prestige?

Does it help to have an important-sounding name, such as International Marketing Associates, Inc., instead of John Smith, Consultant or John Smith and Associates?

Other questions reflect the questioner's inexperience with proposals and often with some of the practical problems of producing multipage bound documents. Several questions reflect that inexperience, fear, and uncertainty:

Should I have my proposals typeset and printed, with printed covers and professional artwork?

What about that statement in some government requests that warns readers against submitting elaborate proposals? What does that mean exactly?

I find that I am usually making wild guesses at the price estimate. Is there any kind of rule or guideline for estimating costs? Is it important to be the low bidder?

I find that there is usually not enough information in the RFP. What is the best way to get more information?

Sometimes the client limits the number of pages I may use, and I have trouble with that. Any ideas about handling this?

Does it help to have the proposal typeset, printed, and bound formally?

How can I reproduce very large drawings without going to more expense than I can afford?

All these questions have been answered in the general discussions of earlier chapters, but it is not likely that you will have total recall. In any case, it will surely be helpful to focus on the most commonly experienced problems and provide suggestions for coping successfully with them. Let's take these up, one by one, as well as several other problems that are likely to trouble you now or in the future, and you will see that the picture is not as bleak as you might fear.

THE (APPARENT) PROBLEMS OF SMALLNESS

If you are an independent consultant or have a small consulting organization, it's common to see your small size as a handicap instead of recognizing the ways in which being small offers advantages. Smallness *does* offer advantages, even in the marketing of your services. You can take advantage of being small when you write your proposals. However, before you can solve the problem, you must understand it. First, examine the reasons you see smallness as a drawback and then consider generally some of the benefits of smallness.

If you perceive the image of smallness as a weakness in your competitive position as a consultant, you manifest insecurity. This insecurity is born entirely out of fear, fear of what appears to be the overwhelming advantage of your large and (apparently) well-established and entrenched competitors.

Cost Advantages and Disadvantages

The humans employed by your large competitors are no less fallible than you and, in all probability, no more talented or experienced generally as individuals. Their advantages are primarily in having some kind of "track record"—experience and other resources to draw on. In some cases, they can offer a cost advantage as a result of size. (The cliché here is "economies of scale.") Where that is the case, it is almost always because there is an optimum size for an organization; at that optimum size they can operate most efficiently, which usually means at lowest overhead rates.

On the other hand, the direct rates—principally, the direct cost of all labor, before overhead enters the cost picture—tend to run considerably higher in larger organizations than in small ones, especially in the case of independent consultants where the principles often furnish the bulk of the labor themselves. That cost difference tends to counterbalance any overhead advantage the large organization might have, so that as a small organization, you can usually be cost competitive.

In fact, if you are an independent practitioner, you can afford to make some sacrifices, such as working overtime without charging yourself for it, as one means of competing. This is a special advantage when you are in an early stage and need special advantages to get started and begin to build your own track record.

The Importance of Costs

In ordinary circumstances, the very fact that a prospective client requests proposals, rather than quotations or bids, indicates that cost is not the first or most important consideration, but competence, reliability, and other such factors are. However, if cost is not always the most important consideration, it is never unimportant. Moreover, when two or more proposers are judged about equally attractive in all other respects, cost is likely to suddenly become the decisive factor. So do try to be as cost competitive as you can be without taking unacceptable risks.

Probably the most important message with regard to costs is *don't be greedy*. Yielding to the temptation to win a few extra dollars of profit costs many proposers assignments that they could otherwise have won. Do price to cover all costs and produce a reasonable profit; not only are you entitled to that, but you must have it to survive. However, be satisfied with that unless you are willing to lose many bids you might have otherwise won.

On the other hand, waste no time or tears lamenting the bids you lost when you priced properly. You lost a bid that would have cost you money, and you should have no regrets about that.

A FEW WAYS TO HANDLE THE SMALLNESS ISSUE

One of the major advantages of smallness in marketing via proposals is being able to point out tactfully to clients that what is a small and not very important project to a large corporation is a very important project to you. (Philosophically, this is the "Small enough to serve you properly, but big enough to get the job done efficiently" argument.) Therefore, while the large organization would quite likely use other than its most experienced and most qualified specialists on the projects, you would give the project your full and undivided attention and see to it personally that every detail is attended to properly.

That argument, properly handled, can be a telling blow on your own behalf. And "properly handled" means getting the point across effectively to the client while being tactful. That means avoiding giving the appearance of making a direct attack on competitors. (You can compare yourself favorably with your competitors, but it is always a bad tactic to openly "knock" competitors and best never to mention them by name.)

An excellent way of making this statement diplomatically is to point out that there is an optimum size for handling the project in question and to make the technical arguments for this view. Explain the potential hazard of a relatively small project becoming lost among large projects. That is the point at which you explain that this cannot happen with you because your operating philosophy is to focus on small, highly specialized projects. When you put the argument this way, the client will get the point quickly enough.

You can also use the successful approach made popular a few years ago by the car rental firm Avis: "We're Number 2, so we try harder."

Your concern about smallness may go well beyond the image of your size. You may be concerned about that more specific problem of pursuing a contract that requires a half-dozen consultant professionals, while you have only yourself or only one or two others on staff or even as associates. Nonetheless, you can still make lemonade of this problem, to actually finesse the problem by seizing it and making a strength of the weakness. Let's first try to get a more insightful look at this problem than appears on the surface.

DEFINING AND REDEFINING THE STAFFING PROBLEM

Two Very Hot Problems

Some problems can't be solved directly, instead, the harm caused by the problem can be avoided without removing the cause. Consider the case of our space program, in which reentry was an early problem that appeared insurmountable to some. There was (and is yet, at least so far as is known today) no practicable way for a space vehicle to reenter the earth's atmosphere at any but extremely high speed. That means almost unimaginably great friction, with the resulting heat great enough to melt and even vaporize any metal or alloy we know of, not to mention what such heat would do to the interior of the vehicle and its occupants.

Because we did not know of any way to avoid this problem of speed, friction, and heat, our choice was to give up the program or to find a way to succeed in spite of the problem. That is, we had to accept the great heat as a condition to live with if the program were to continue.

Once we accepted that, we changed the nature of the problem: Instead of being a problem in how to avoid the heat, it became a problem in finding a way to shield the vehicle and its interior from the heat. That quest resulted in the *ablative* heat shield—a ceramic shell on the surface of the reentry vehicle (ceramic tiles on the space shuttle) deliberately designed to burn off during reentry.

Charles Kettering faced a similar problem in designing an automobile self-starter. He knew, as every automotive engineer did, that any starter motor large enough to crank an automobile engine would overheat if it were not as large as the engine. Making it that large was impractical, but he had already decided that he must and would create a workable self-starter. He therefore changed the problem from one of trying to design a practicable self-starter that would not overheat to a problem of how to design a practicable self-starter that could endure overheating without being destroyed by it, which he did so successfully.

The Insoluble Redefined

Remember the earlier admonition that a true problem definition itself points to the solution or to more than one possible solution? That means that if the problem is insoluble as defined, it must be redefined. Redefining the problem means first accepting any condition that is unavoidable, even if it appears to be a barrier to solution. Then create a new definition that accepts the unavoidable condition but points to a solution that is workable despite the given condition! If you go back and reread the two examples of how to solve the "insoluble" with this in mind, you will see how problems were solved by first redefining them and then attacking the solution that the new (and true) definition pointed to. Now, apply this idea to some of the proposal problems:

In the case of not having enough key people on staff or as associates to handle the proposed project properly, there are several possible ways to approach this, each way based on redefinition of the problem. The original problem is conceived as being one of appearing to be totally unqualified for the project as a result of being disastrously understaffed. The fact of not having the necessary staff on board is the unavoidable condition that must be accepted.

The redefinition is simple enough: The problem must be redefined to become one of how to appear well qualified in spite of not having the necessary staff on board. Aside from "hanging paper"—an act, practiced by unscrupulous proposers, of misleading the client by offering résumés of people you don't even know and haven't talked to, pretending that they are on staff or associates—you appear to have only these alternatives: (a) Proposing to hire new people after award or (b) proposing to seek out other consultants to act as subcontractors or associates, offering résumés and letters of agreement from such people to verify that they are professional associates and will work on the project with you. Either of these, however, might still be regarded as an expedient, to compensate for a weakness in staffing capability. Something less defensive in appearance is needed to solve the problem satisfactorily. Otherwise, these expedients appear to be just that, and they appear also to be apologies for not being fully qualified, a suicidal approach to marketing.

Defensiveness is always a tactical mistake, for it is an admission of weakness, and you can win only by attacking from strength. You must take the bull by the horns and say, in effect, "Here is what I am going to do for you," as you finesse the problem. One way has worked well in turning this apparent weakness into a strength: State boldly that the special nature of the requirement indicates to you a need for certain specialists. You have therefore sought out the most notable and outstanding such specialists in the field and obtained their agreement to work with you on this worthy program. Of course, you must do more than make that kind of general statement. You must prove your case with suitable technical arguments and appropriate résumés, and you should indeed have an understanding with those specialists you name as staff members.

In general, in all such situations, never appear to be apologetic and defensive, and never lie about real conditions. In this case, you need never admit that there is only you or you and one or two others, for you never address the matter of the size of your permanent, in-house staff at all. Instead, you bore in aggressively with résumés of these highly specialized new associates and their letters of agreement to work on the project with you. If the question of your staff and its size does come up at any time, you can easily say that you handle all projects with hand-picked associates because a significant feature of your consulting is exactly that: seeking out and employing on behalf of your clients the precisely right specialists. In fact, you can make that kind of positive argument in your proposal, if you wish to make an issue of it there and establish it as a basic premise on which you base your entire approach to satisfying the requirement. That would be a direct attack, and probably a novel approach.

QUESTIONS OF EXPERIENCE

Two kinds of experience are in question when writing a proposal: (1) the direct and personal experience of any whose résumés are offered, and (2) the experience of the proposing organization. If you are an independent consultant working alone, there is a certain ambivalence about this. On the one hand, the client wants to know about your experience and achievements as an independent consultant serving clients under contract. On the other hand, all your "organization" experience is your personal experience. Practically, they are the same. Technically and philosophically, they are not. Serving your employer's clients, with your employer bearing the ultimate responsibility, is not the same as winning the assignment on your own and being totally responsible in all respects for the work. So if you are only recently established as an independent consultant, you are in short supply of qualifying organizational experience.

Many consultants get around this problem by careful wording that does not specifically claim individual experience as organization experience, but encourages the reader to so interpret it. That expedient works for many who are skillful enough and careful enough in writing to bring the idea to reality.

A second approach, which I am convinced is more effective and which should be used whenever practicable, is to meet the issue squarely, head on. Argue the case of fresh ideas, an open mind uncluttered by conventional ideas, technology transfer resulting from your diverse earlier experience, and other such bold tactics, as they fit your own experience. If your earlier experience included association with some prestigious firm, university, or other impressive reference, by all means capitalize fully on it.

Again, avoid at all costs any appearance of defensiveness, apologia, or other self-deprecation. Those are defeatist tactics, and defeat is the result of such tactics. The same philosophy applies to those cases where you are in pursuit of a contract to do something a bit out of your usual field, but something you are sure you can handle well, despite your inability to point to directly related experience. In such cases, it is important to dwell at length and in detail on your specific program designs and plans. Demonstrate whatever basis (e.g., technology transfer) on which you have built your program strategy. Show, in as much detail as possible, exactly what the strategy is and why it is not only appropriate, but also advantageous to the client.

Remember in all cases that the client's number one concern is what he or she thinks is in his or her own interest. The more whatever you offer appears to be in the client's interest, the less proof of anything else you need to offer. Always seek the argument that indicates that what you propose is best for the client's direct interest.

In this milieu, nothing is good or bad in absolute terms, but only good or bad in terms of the client's interest. It is therefore bad for the client's interest to have the project put "on the back burner" or assigned to junior personnel by the large consulting organization, as it is good for the client to have the project get the full, personal attention of a fully qualified professional.

HOW "PROFESSIONAL" DO YOU HAVE TO BE?

When I gave up my own costly suite of offices in downtown Washington in favor of a comfortable office and conference room in my own home, I did so with some trepidation. The move was very much in my own interests in many ways, but I feared its psychological effects on some of my clients. Particularly, I had misgivings about how one particular client would react to this move. This was a prominent and prestigious corporation with approximately 20 companies, very well known in the business and financial worlds, and I was dealing with people very near the top of the corporation. So it was with some hesitancy that I announced the change to the corporate vice president with whom I had most of my direct dealings.

To my relief and pleasant surprise, the reaction was along the line, "Cutting overhead, eh? Great idea. Smart move." They approved!

In the years since, I have worked with people from this corporation and others in my own home conference room, although the nature of my consulting work is such that I do not often have need to receive clients in my own office. Having my office and conference room in my home, in a quiet residential neighborhood near a shopping center has never proved a disadvantage or, as far as I can tell, caused me any loss of respect by my clients.

I do not believe that it is necessary to be located in an office building, as far as it concerns your credibility, image, or prestige as a consultant. There may be very good reasons for renting space in an office building, but image and prestige would be the wrong kind of reasons to do so. Nor should you ever fake it by using someone else's office. To do so is not only deceit that will harm your image—who will trust you after discovering your subterfuge (and it will eventually be discovered)—but it is also totally unnecessary.

On the other hand, if you have your office at home or in a suburban business district and must meet and confer with a client in town, it is perfectly legitimate to make temporary arrangements. However, don't deceive the client; be candid about it, and you'll suffer no harm for it. In fact, most clients will be appreciative of your action in making things more convenient for them.

ON INCORPORATING

Incorporating yourself today is extremely easy to do. In most states, you can do so for $40 or $50 by filling out a simple form or two. (In Maryland, the form is a single page, and the fee when I incorporated there was $40 plus $6 for a certified copy of the approved form.) It is so easy to do, in fact, that for that reason alone, no special prestige is attached to being a corporation. There are good reasons for many consultants to be incorporated, but gaining prestige is not one of them. It will not make your proposal more impressive, and it should never be done for that reason.

Very much the same philosophy applies to the name you choose for yourself. One executive I know who reviews capability brochures and proposals quite often has remarked more than once, "The bigger the name, the smaller the company," whenever he encounters a lengthy company name in his reading. He smiles when he murmurs this because he is amused by the effort to be impressive via the route of a lengthy and pompous name.

The same philosophy applies to the personal titles you bestow on yourself and others. Of course, you are the president and chairman of the board of your own corporation, but you gain nothing but perhaps an amused smile by making a major issue of it in your proposal.

The following names of a few of the most prominent and successful consulting companies are probably the best answer to the question of how helpful is a lengthy and "impressive" name:

Ernst & Co.
Price Waterhouse
Arthur Young & Co.
Booz Allen & Hamilton, Inc.
Coopers & Lybrand

HOW ELABORATE THE PROPOSAL?

Proposals ought to be "professional"—neat, clean, grammatical, spelled correctly, well organized. They may be typeset, but composition by electric typewriter or computer printer is quite acceptable. They may be printed in an offset print shop, but duplication by office copier is quite acceptable. They can be bound in printed covers, but binding in a patent report binder is quite acceptable.

Those admonitions about "excessively elaborate" proposals refer to a day when the Department of Defense was spending billions recklessly (although that does not appear to have changed very much) and defense contractors were going to such extremes as binding multivolume proposals in morocco leather with specially built cases to hold the several volumes, and some of the illustrations were of the ultracostly process-color type, à la *National Geographic* magazine. *That* is considered to be "excessively elaborate." That, however, certainly is no bar to typesetting, printing, and binding according to normal commercial standards, if you wish to go to that expense or happen to be equipped to do such things in-house, as many companies are.

PRODUCTION PROBLEMS

Until now, we have been discussing tactical problems, problems of proposal content and appearance. The question of what is excessively elaborate in a proposal is a production matter, and you may encounter a few production problems.

Production refers to all the details of making up the physical proposal, in whatever is the required number of copies, for delivery to the client. At the low end of the scale, where only a single copy is required and, especially, where that is an informal letter proposal, you need make only a single file copy for yourself and probably require only the simplest kind of graphics, if you need graphics at all. (It is likely that you will not, in such cases.)

On the other hand, as the proposal becomes more formal and larger, the practical production requirements change considerably, and related problems may arise. This is especially the case if you are an independent consultant with typically limited resources.

Reproduction

Today, with the ease of using modern office copying machines and the high quality of the work most of them produce, it has become common practice to "print" the required number of copies in this way. In fact, even photographs may be reproduced with fairly good quality on many modern office copiers.

In terms of cost, it is usually less expensive to reproduce proposals by office copier than it is to print them because proposals are usually produced in only a handful of copies. (The economies in offset printing are not realized until the number of copies begins to mount into hundreds.)

Photos

If you wish to include photos in your proposal, you may be able to make reasonably good copies on an office copier. If not, or if you aren't satisfied with the admittedly less than perfect xerographic reproduction of a photograph, you can have a printer screen your photos to prepare them for printing and can then print up enough copies for your needs, or you can bind the actual glossies into your proposal. Frequently, if you are duplicating only a few copies of your proposal, it is least costly to bind the actual photos because glossy prints of photographs are relatively inexpensive today. (However, if your original is a printed copy of an original photograph and it is sharp and clear, you can probably copy that quite well on an office copier because it is already a reproduction of a screened photograph.)

Line Drawings

As noted already, you can prepare most and possibly all your own graphics with the aid of templates, paste-down symbols and type, and other modern artist's aids, and you can achieve nearly professional quality in doing so. Or, if you prefer, you can hire someone to prepare your graphics, either a freelance illustrator or a local graphic arts shop.

One problem that arises is that of large drawings. If you do develop functional flowcharts and other such drawings, they can easily grow to sizes well beyond that of a single page. The usual practice for using such drawings is to make foldouts of them—lengthy drawings folded down to page size, with a binding edge left free so that the reader can extend the drawing to its full size. Such drawings can easily become several feet long, which poses a special kind of problem: How can it be reproduced inexpensively, as it must be when you must deliver more than one copy of your proposal? (In any case, even when you need deliver only one copy, you still need a file copy for yourself.)

The alternatives are (1) have a printer print several copies for you; (2)

reproduce the drawing in sections, on an office copier, and paste the sections together to make complete drawings; and (3) use another process, such as ozalid copying.

Printed Copies.   The first alternative is one sometimes used by large corporations turning out major proposals that require a large number of copies. It's an expensive alternative because a large printing press is required, and a large negative and plate must be made. Moreover, it is not always easy to get the job done quickly, this way, and that alone is often a bar to using this method, given the tight, often "impossible" schedules that are typical of proposal requirements. The second alternative is tedious, time-consuming, and not too pleasing aesthetically.

Ozalid Processing.   The third alternative is often the most practical approach. *Ozalid* is a process used by most large blueprint shops. Most shops of this type can make copies of a large drawing economically and quickly. The process is such that it can copy anything drawn on a transparent or translucent medium, such as vellum or mylar. If possible, have your original drawing on such a medium. Otherwise, a negative of the original must be made first. (Most large blueprint shops are equipped to handle that for you, however.)

Binding.   The question of where to bind foldout drawings in a proposal arises. Conventional practice regarding placement of graphics in publications of this type is to have the illustration follow the first text reference to it as quickly as possible, which in this case normally means on the next page. For foldouts, however, this can create another kind of a problem: You may wish to make numerous references to the drawing, and it becomes quite awkward for the reader to flip pages back and forth, folding and unfolding the illustration.

A way around this problem is to bind all such drawings at the back of the proposal. This permits the reader to leave the drawing folded out for easy repeated reference.

PAGE-LIMITED PROPOSALS

It has become a fairly common practice of government and some other proposal requesters to ease the burden of reviewing and evaluating large formal proposals by limiting their size. Without such controls, the sizes can vary wildly, from a few dozen pages to thousands of pages. The client, in such cases, makes a judgment as to a proper size—the number of pages in which a proposer ought to be able to make his or her presentation—and mandates that as a limit.

When an RFP mandates a page limit, it usually specifies minimum type size (usually 10 point, expressed as 12 pitch for a typewriter or printer), spacing (whether the pages are to be single- or double-spaced), and the size of margins. Frequently, such RFPs except certain elements of the proposal from the limitation. It is not unusual, for example, for the RFP to except résumés, some front matter, and sometimes appendices from the restriction. On the other hand, the RFP may fail to state specifically whether there are any exceptions. Or it may warn that appendices and exhibits are included in the limitation and will not be reviewed or taken into account in the evaluation if they exceed the page limit.

Most often, this is a general and overall limitation, but not always. In one recent case, the RFP limited the proposal on an element-by-element basis, calling out maximum page counts for the executive summary, the résumés, the discussion, and the other major elements.

This is a problem to many proposal writers, but it is also a problem to your competitors and therefore offers you a special and additional opportunity to excel. In fact, such a limitation can be made to work to your advantage by compelling you to do what you should do anyway in writing a proposal: Be concise. It therefore ought not to be a major problem, nor should it require any subterfuge to overcome. For one thing, experience has shown that the clients' estimates of what is necessary to make an adequate presentation are usually quite sound. For another, it is in your own interest to keep your proposal as "tight" as possible, which would be the result of good writing and editing practices, in any case. Two major points should be made here, both of which are guidelines to follow when responding to any proposal request, whether page limited or not:

1. Use graphics effectively, and you will eliminate many pages of text by that measure alone. Be conscious of this possibility in reviewing and editing your drafts, judging where the presentation could be made more efficient with a graphic illustration. Then generate those illustrations to reduce verbiage.

2. Don't attempt to limit your writing in the first draft; get all the details down. Then edit it down to size. That alone should, in the typical case, boil out about one third of the text as extraneous, redundant, covering trivia, or otherwise easily dispensed with. (If you still have too much, reduce the copy by eliminating the least important material that is not specifically required by the client.) Properly, you should not *write* a proposal to satisfy a page limitation; you should *edit* the proposal to comply with that limitation.

In my own experience, these measures have proved to be effective in every case, achieving compliance with the size limitation without compromising the effectiveness of the presentation.

PACKAGING

Packaging refers to physical and cosmetic characteristics of the proposal package you will deliver. Usually, there are at least three elements in the "package": the technical proposal, the cost proposal, and the letter of transmittal.

Even in those cases where the client does not mandate that the cost proposal be physically separate from the technical proposal, it is a good idea to separate them to encourage review and evaluation of your technical proposal as objectively as possible.

The original letter of transmittal is normally in a separate business envelope, accompanying the package of technical and cost proposals.

Binding may be done in many ways, of which these three are probably the most popular and most commonly used:

- Side stitching—stapling the sheets and cover together
- Three-hole binder, either a hard ring binder or a report binder
- Spiral binder, using plastic "spines"

Spiral binding requires special equipment to punch 18 or 19 rectangular holes in the sheets and install the plastic spines. (The number of holes depends on what model of binding equipment you use.) Such binding offers the advantage of the proposal lying flat, when opened, and the client may appreciate that convenience.

Three-ring binding offers this same advantage, when a hard 3-ring binder is used, rather than one of the stationery-store report binders, with its metal clips. However, repeated handling of a document in a 3-ring binder almost always means that some of the pages become detached.

It is possible to buy hard binders to accommodate those 18- or 19-hole sheets, thereby combining some of the better features of each alternative. There are also some other types of jiffy binders that are easy to use, without any special equipment or special preparation, and they are usually suitable if your proposal is small.

CHAPTER 13

Miscellaneous Useful Information for Proposal Writing

Other consultants' views, ways to overcome some inherent handicaps to proposal writing, ways to find more proposal opportunities, and several references may help you to write your proposals more easily and effectively.

QUESTIONNAIRE RESULTS

In researching and preparing to write the first edition of this book, I sent out a brief questionnaire to a large number of consultants, most of them small companies and/or independent practitioners. My purpose was to unearth common problems in proposal writing, to be able to report factually to you on what other consultants do and how they feel about proposal writing, to validate my own opinions and experience in this field, and to validate (or amend) my own judgment as to what information and guidance should be included in these pages. The questionnaire petitioned the consultants' responses to a series of questions, some calling for factual reporting, some for opinion or speculation, and others for identification of concerns and perceived problems. Additionally, respondents were invited to make any comments they wished to and to send copies of proposals or related materials they use. (Figure 36 is a reproduction of the questionnaire.)

I mailed many questionnaires directly to consultants known to me, but many more responded to a copy of the questionnaire included in an issue of the *Consulting Opportunities Journal,* a bimonthly newsletter published by Steve Lanning, whose generosity made it possible to reach his readers with this questionnaire, many of whom I would not have otherwise reached. Many of the responses reported here are therefore from readers of that newsletter.

In preparing to write the second edition of this book, I went back to a number of those originally polled, as well as to others, to determine whether any purpose would be served by instituting a new questionnaire and survey. I found little changed, so I have chosen to reproduce the original questionnaire and results, adding a few notes and comments.

THE ORIGINAL SURVEY

(Reproduced from the first edition, with minor additions and updating.)

A tabulation of results, by percentages, is included here for the factual items reported in each category, with accompanying explanations, observations, and remarks, as necessary and appropriate. As almost always occurs in surveys of this type, there is a large element of "opinionaire" to the survey so there are a few anomalies. My purpose here is to provide whatever guidance you can gain from this admittedly limited survey of the consulting field.

Respondent Specialties

Before presenting those figures, it is useful to look at some of the various consulting specialties represented here because consulting is remarkably diverse both as a profession and as an industry. This diversity accounts for many of what may appear to be anomalies in the results of this survey.

The survey did not require respondents to identify themselves, but a large majority—slightly more than 87%—did so, although not all furnished enough information to indicate clearly their consulting specialties. Following is a list of some of the specialties that were identified (many consultants function in more than one of these fields):

QUESTIONNAIRE

USE OF PROPOSAL IN MARKETING

[ ] Never   [ ] Rarely   [ ] Frequent   [ ] Always   [ ] Only when requested

[ ] Whether requested or not   [ ] Other: _____

HOW OFTEN REQUESTED

[ ] Usually   [ ] Occasionally   [ ] Rarely   [ ] Other: _____

SUCCESS WITH PROPOSALS

[ ] Over 75%   [ ] 50–75%   [ ] 25–50%   [ ] Under 25%   [ ] Other: _____

TYPE OF PROPOSAL USED AND FREQUENCY

Informal/letter:_____% of time   Formal:_____% of time _____

PROPOSAL PRACTICES

[ ] All original material   [ ] Parts boilerplated   [ ] All boilerplate

[ ] Quotation plus standard brochures and letter

[ ] Other: _____

SECTIONS/MATERIALS NORMALLY INCLUDED IN PROPOSALS

[ ] Statement of problem/need   [ ] Technical discussion   [ ] Resume(s)

[ ] Qualifications   [ ] Descriptions of deliverables   [ ] Schedules

[ ] Facilities & resources   [ ] Price   [ ] Letter of transmittal

[ ] Other: _____

PROPOSAL PROBLEMS, NEEDS, COMMENTS

_____

_____

_____

_____

(Add comments, as necessary [use other side for more room]; attach/enclose samples of your proposals and/or brochures, other materials, if possible.)

Figure 36.   Questionnaire form.

Lecture	Sales
Management	Computer programming
Financial services	Direct mail
Training	Organizational development
Marketing	Proposal development
Digital systems	Polling and surveying
Engineering	Apparel
Conference management	Direct response marketing
Seminar production	Theatrical productions
TV productions	Small business management
Personal grooming	Modeling/models agency
Advertising	Business/personal image management
Medical-secretary training	Health-care-cost containment
Telephone usage	Mailing-list management
Communications	Commercial real estate

The tabulated results of the questionnaire are indicated immediately following each category of response.

Use of Proposals in Marketing

Rarely:	6.45%
Frequent:	51.6%
Always:	32.23%
Only when requested:	9.67%
Whether requested or not:	22.58%
Other:	6.45%

Note, first, that no one checked off "never," and less than 7 percent indicated any rate of use less than "frequent." However, there is one apparent anomaly: It might seem reasonable to expect that anyone checking off "Whether requested or not" would also check off "Always." That is not the case: Many of those who checked off this item also checked "Frequently." Apparently, persons who offer unsolicited proposals at times still find that proposals are not always a key element of their marketing effort.

Those checking off "Other" used this as an occasion to make a remark to explain that they used something as an alternative to a proposal. (Nido Qubein, for example, prefers to use what he calls "action plans," which result from a paid-for needs analysis.)

How Often Requested

Usually:	35.48%
Occasionally:	48.38%
Rarely:	12.9%
Other:	3.23%

Success with Proposals

Over 75%:	33.33%
50–75%:	26.66%
25–50%:	26.66%
Under 25%:	13.33%

Type of Proposal Used and Frequency

Of all respondents, 45 percent reported using informal and letter proposals more than one half of the time, with most reporting such usage as approaching 100 percent, and with a few actually reaching that figure. In contrast, 32 percent reported the reverse orientation, using formal proposals most often. The remainder tended to about an equal or near-equal division of formal to informal proposals.

Proposal Practices

Some respondents checked off more than one item in this category, and the results are shown by frequency of appearance, with no attempt to make correlations:

All original material:	42%
Parts boilerplated:	55%
All boilerplate:	3%
Quotations plus brochures:	42%
Other:	13%

"Other" included qualifying or explanatory remarks, such as "On major applications, full-scale business plan," "Depends on level of relationship with client," and "Letter."

Sections/Materials Normally Included in Proposals

Respondents were expected to check off several items in this category, and responses are reported by frequency of occurrence, with no attempt to make correlations:

Statement of problem/need:	97%
Technical discussion:	45%
Résumés:	55%
Qualifications:	58%
Descriptions of deliverables:	74%
Schedules:	77%
Facilities & resources:	58%
Price:	90%
Letter of transmittal:	52%
Other:	10%

"Other" was used to make qualifying remarks or to explain a practice that is peculiar to some given field. Tom Hill, of Drubner Industrials in Waterbury, Connecticut, a commercial real estate specialist, notes in this block that his proposals normally include maps and zoning regulations. Another used this block to explain that he sends clients a statement of contract terms, while still another remarks that his prior checkoffs are provisional and depend on client needs and the specific situation of the moment. JJ [sic] Lauderbaugh, a California image and grooming consult-ant, advises that she sometimes includes audio- and/or videotapes, which is understandable enough in her case. She also notes that her clients some-times require a form of their own to be filled out, which she complies with, of course, even if she has already prepared a proposal.

Proposal Problems, Needs, and Comments

Among the comments invited are many of special interest. A few are quoted here:

Dr. William Cohen, Professor of Marketing at California State University, a marketing consultant, a former federal government contracting officer, and author of a number of business books of his own, observed "If you've done your preproposal marketing correctly, your audience should find no surprises in your proposal . . . but you must never, never forget that the proposal is a sales document."

Francine Berger, a speaker, seminar leader, trainer, consultant, developer of in-house speakers' bureaus for corporations, and president of her own firm, Speechworks, of Stony Brook, New York, added this to her response:

> I hate to write [proposals]—much rather discuss the specifics face-to-face or by phone—then write a little follow-up letter to confirm. Also, whenever I deal with the president, they usually say "Go ahead" and don't need one or want one. In dealing with middle managers of traditional bureaucratic companies, they do need one.

An anonymous respondent opined that a proposal is, in its "best sense," a confirmation of work that has been verbally approved, except when it represents a competitive bid, and probability of success then is only 10 percent.

Still another respondent stated flatly that proposals are very costly to prepare and should be undertaken only when the probability of success is quite high. He cited [Peter] Drucker on "cost of transactions" to support his view.

Still another viewpoint, one with a great deal of validity, was expressed, "Proposals do not often 'get the job' but often get the opportunity to discuss and negotiate in person." In fact, it is a legitimate viewpoint that the immediate objective of a proposal ought to be to induce the client to invite you to discuss what you propose.

Dave Hamilton, Commercial Operations Manager of the Tulsa division of Quadrex Corporation, reflected his insights into marketing and proposal quality with the valid observation that one "must continually review/rewrite for 'selling statements' inclusion, benefits analysis and promotion," pointing out that too often the proposal is a "straight technical dissertation."

Finally, Strategies Management Consulting, of Modesto, California, pointed out that their clients are all small businesses and that for their practice, the usual proposal is a one-page document that is also the agreement between consultant and client when signed by both, but it may be supplemented by oral presentations and attachments to proposals. The sample document they enclosed demonstrated that even one-page proposal-agreement furnishes a definition of the project or service to be provided, the schedule data, the estimated time and fees required, and the terms.

Many of these viewpoints are worth considering, depending on your specialty, of course.

Perhaps more significant than those added comments are some results reported by Howard Shenson, a trainer of consultants and publisher of *The Professional Consultant & Seminar Business Report*, a monthly newsletter. (See listing under "Periodicals" in reference section.) Shenson conducts frequent surveys of his own, and found the average consultant billing rate for 1988 to be about $929 per day, and the average annual pretax income for consultants to be $91,102. This is a small increase over the previous year. The daily billing rate is up about 2.9 percent, and the average annual pretax income up about 0.26 percent. Projected over four years, 1985–1988, however, the average daily billing rate has increased by about 21.3 percent (5.3 percent annual average), and the annual pre–tax income increased by about 19.8 percent (5 percent annual average).

THE PROPOSAL AND RESOURCE LIBRARY

The Value of Resources

For most consultants, two problems in proposal writing are common. One is that it is always an ad hoc activity—something improvised as an interruption to regular daily activities and requiring a special, nonroutine effort. Important though proposal writing is as a marketing and business necessity, it is difficult for most of us not to regard it as an unwelcome disruption of our daily routine, an activity for which we never seem to be prepared.

The second problem is that there is never enough time to do the job: Proposals are almost invariably written in haste against a pressing and all-but-impossible schedule, and the need seems always to fall at a time when we are busy and trying to get some important project completed. Consequently, even when we finally get the proposal writing job done, we often have the feeling that we didn't do as well as we should have and would have, had we had just a bit more time.

Large corporations who do almost all custom work and must rely on proposals for all or nearly all their business often establish permanent proposal-writing departments, suitably equipped and staffed with professionals who are specialists in the art. Smaller organizations cannot do this, as a practical measure. Nonetheless, small firms can do something similar to offset at least some of the difficulties resulting from these two common problems: create a special proposal-development resource, a proposal library.

Unless you write or plan to write a proposal only once in a great while—in which case, you probably would not be reading this book—you are tying your own hands unnecessarily if you do not have a proposal library. The efficiency and effectiveness of your proposal efforts will be greatly increased by the existence of a well-stocked and well-thought-out proposal library. It will give you an organized basis for all your proposal work, give you more time to devote to the task, and make it considerably less an impromptu or an improvised effort. Even more important, it will enable you to steadily improve the quality and the success incidence of your proposals.

Obviously, a first requisite for that library is a collection of reference books pertaining directly to your own career field and/or those technical/professional activities in which you specialize. As a consultant, however, you are in the somewhat ambiguous position of all consultants, compelled to be the master of both your technical/professional specialties and of the technical and business skills and resources required for your consulting services. Included among the required resources for consulting-business skills are reference and other materials that normally constitute a proposal library.

The term *library* is used here in a rather special sense, referring to far more than a collection of books, although it certainly includes those. But a properly stocked and well-organized library also includes many other kinds of on-the-shelf resources to make it easier to write proposals and to make it possible to write better—more effective—proposals. It can do this in several ways: by speeding up the process, an important consideration in most proposal efforts, through organizing useful materials and making them readily accessible; by placing the special materials—those of proven outstanding merit—conveniently at hand; and by providing ready access to those materials that will contribute to the bid/no-bid analysis and decision making and to the evolution of a suitable approach and strategy.

Classes of Resources

To these ends, your proposal library ought to include at least these general classes of resources:

Reference books
Relevant periodicals
Special reports relevant to your field, to consulting, and to proposals
Your own past proposals
Stocks of your own brochures and other promotional literature
Copies of competitors' proposals
Copies of competitors' brochures and other promotional literature
Swipe files

To do the subject full justice requires individual discussions of these classes of materials and the media or forms in which they should be stored and made available for use.

Reference Books

At least three groupings of reference books can be put to good use in your proposal library. One is, of course, those already referred to as those dealing with your technical/professional specialties. A second group is that rather small collection of books that deal specifically with proposal writing and a much larger collection of books about sales and marketing, as they bear on proposal writing. A third and possibly the largest grouping is that of general reference books that will spare you a great deal of research time by their ready availability. The following are some of the general types. (Some specific suggestions appear later in this chapter.)

- Books dealing with consulting skills generally
- Catalogs relevant to your field

- Directories, general and specialized
- Relevant how-to manuals
- Proceedings of relevant conferences and symposia

Periodicals

Variety of Periodicals

An estimated 30,000 different newsletters are published in the United States (some people estimate a much greater number), in addition to a large number of other periodicals—magazines, journals, tabloids, and other publications. Few of us fully appreciate the huge number of such publications because a relative handful of these appear on the newsstands or are otherwise clearly visible. Even the most completely stocked newsstand, for example, does not carry on its shelves most of the periodicals published as "trade journals," dealing with and of interest only to those engaged in such specialized fields as direct mail and business conferences. Even more prominent by their absence are the many periodicals published by associations and corporations of many kinds, both profit and nonprofit, for their members, their clients, and anyone else with a special interest in the field. There are literally thousands of these specialized trade periodicals, from simple newsletters, through tabloids, to slick magazines with "four-color" (full photographic process) art known to the writing trade as "house organs" and by other names.

Controlled-Circulation Periodicals

Many of these, especially the trade publications, are distributed free of charge to "qualified" applicants, as "controlled circulation" publications. The qualification is to be part of or have direct business interests in the industry addressed, such that you are a reasonable customer prospect for those whose advertising appears in the periodical.

That resulting ability to address the publication almost entirely and exclusively to those who are good prospects for the publisher's advertisers makes it worthwhile for the publishers to give free subscriptions to those so qualifying. With the circulation figures verified by an audit agency, as is the case with controlled-circulation periodicals, the publisher is able to command premium advertising rates, making the venture worthwhile. (Those who do not qualify for free subscriptions are usually permitted to purchase subscriptions if they wish to.)

Several directories list these publications. (A few are listed later in this chapter, in the reference lists of publications.) Some of these directories are rather expensive, but it is not necessary to buy them, for most well-stocked libraries have reference copies available for your use, and librarians are quite helpful in guiding you to such public library resources.

The usual requirement for a free subscription to those periodicals that are distributed without charge may be merely an application on business stationery and/or a business card. However, it is an increasing practice of such publications to require the applicant to fill out a brief questionnaire, generally consisting entirely of checkoff items, requiring requalification every year.

Past Proposals

You should have a complete inventory of your own past proposals, especially those that were successful. They are useful in more than one way: Reviewing them may uncover a previous proposal that has many points of similarity with your current effort and so can save you time in all phases of the effort, from research to final writing. You may also be able to save yourself time and expense by reusing some of the graphics and other materials from earlier efforts. Keep a tight rein on these; the loss of even one file copy of your past proposals may be a disaster. Though "loss" may even mean merely mislaying it, it is nevertheless a true loss, at least for the moment. You should probably never dead-file old proposals generally, and certainly not old successful proposals.

Brochures and Promotional Literature

As confirmed by the results of my questionnaire-survey, many consultants use standard brochures and other sales literature as parts of their proposals. This enables them to develop and submit more proposals than they would otherwise be able to handle. Even if you do not incorporate the actual brochures and other materials—sales letters, reprints of articles by and/or about you, your own newsletters and reports, and other such material—they are often handy time-savers for the creation (paste-up) of rough drafts. Also, many, especially reprints of articles but not confined to those, are useful as enclosures—appendices and exhibits—to your proposals.

Competitors' Material

From time to time you get opportunities to acquire copies of competitors' proposals. One way to do so, if your competitors do business with the federal government, is by requesting copies of winning proposals under the Freedom of Information Act. Copies can also come into your hands by other means, too, such as via new employees who are eager to contribute what they can to your success.

Competitors' general literature—brochures and other items—are relatively easy to acquire, especially at trade fairs, national conventions, conferences, and other such conclaves.

Such material is valuable through all phases of proposal development, from the initial bid/no-bid analysis and decision making to the development of written arguments.

Swipe Files

Anything and everything in your proposal library is potentially useful to actually borrow ("swipe") and use in your new proposal. For most situations, it is only after spending much time to review many things in your library that you uncover such useful materials and decide whether they can be used without or almost without change—readily modified for a new use, that is. On the other hand, there are usually certain items that fit so well into most of your proposals that you find them reusable again and again, with little or no change necessary to adapt them to the new uses. Examples include milestone charts, schedules, labor-loading matrices, tabular/text descriptions of past projects, lists of resources, and other such items.

It should not be necessary to spend a lot of time tracking down such universally useful materials. Because they will be used again and again, they ought to be made readily accessible. To achieve this, it is necessary only to make master copies of such material and to store them in special files, suitably indexed for quick search and location.

Filing Methods

Typical libraries include books arrayed on shelves, periodicals arrayed in some suitable stand or file, and other materials on shelves and/or in filing cabinets, along with suitable indexes or catalogs to make search and retrieval possible. However, things have changed quite a bit in the past few years, and one change that is affecting libraries as much as it's affecting consulting and proposal writing in general is the advent of the personal computer, which is now rapidly becoming as commonplace in the office as the typewriter was. Aside from its benefits as a replacement for the typewriter, when armed with a suitable word processor or database program, it offers enormous benefits as a filing system, with unparalleled search and retrieve efficiency, far beyond that of manual systems.

If you have such a system, you will find it advantageous to have as many files installed on your disks (whether floppies or hard disks) as possible. That applies to many, if not all, of your text files, many of which you may very well have originally created via word processing. You may, for example, already have all or many of your past proposals, articles, reports, and other data on magnetic disks. If you are familiar with computer operation, you are already well aware of the ease and speed of summoning up files and examining them on-screen, as compared with our older, manual methods for search and retrieval of filed documents.

There is no point in keeping paper files of what you have already magnetically filed on disks, although it is wise to always have two copies of anything important, so that for safety your library copy is "backed up" with an archived copy. (Data on disk is durable, normally, but can be destroyed easily. Backup copies are a sensible precaution against such casual losses of disk files.)

Swipe files should likewise be on disks. You can create these easily by copying from your various proposal and other files any materials you expect to be able to use frequently and repeatedly. Then set up special files for these materials, along with suitable indexes. (Many catalog and indexing software programs are available, which will help you create suitable indexes to facilitate searches and retrievals.)

One of the many advantages of doing this is that you need not keep any copies of the original, paper or otherwise, because you can easily and swiftly make a copy of anything in your disk files. In fact, you should never alter or modify the original copy in your files when adapting it to a new use. Make an exact copy, which is quite easy to do, of course, and make your changes to that copy. (What's more, if you run into difficulties or make mistakes that are troublesome to correct, don't even spend the time to fix them; just make a new copy and start over.) Also, always consider when you modify a copy of master file to create something new whether it might not be worthwhile to add that new item to your swipe files as another original or, perhaps, whether the new material is such an improvement over the old one that you might wish to replace your original with a new original. In this manner, your files grow not only in their abundance, but also in their inherent quality, with resulting benefits in your future proposal efforts.

FEDERAL GOVERNMENT BUSINESS OPPORTUNITIES

If you wish to pursue government business, you should subscribe to the U.S. government publication *Commerce Business Daily* (*CBD*), which is published every business day, listing requirements for various agencies in synoptic form and advising you where to write or call for the RFP and full package of information. The publication may be ordered from the Superintendent of Documents, Government Printing Office, Washington, DC, 20402. However, the publication is also available as "CBD ONLINE" (via computer and modem, with dial-up telephone connections) from the following services:

Data Resources, Inc.
2400 Hartwell Avenue
Lexington, MA 02173
617 863-5100
301 589-8875

Dialog Information Services, Inc.
3460 Hillview Avenue
Palo Alto, CA 94304
800 227-1927

United Communications Group
4550 Montgomery Avenue
Bethesda, MD 20814
800 638-7728

Figure 37 lists some of the typical consulting requirements of government agencies. In fact, these are probably the most far-ranging kinds of requirements to be found anywhere in the world. There are few products or services the U.S. federal government does not buy, and mostly these must be custom services, designed especially for the federal agencies' specific needs. Therefore, many consulting services are required, although they're listed under a variety of headings in the periodical.

Unfortunately, the *CBD* does not list all government requirements. In fact, it lists only about 10 to 15 percent of the requirements, and at least 35 percent of government requirements (nearly $200 billion annually at the time of this writing) are filled via open competition among all those interested. The other resources for uncovering RFPs include filing the federal government Form 129, Application for Bidders List, which is available from the offices of Small Business Administration, the General Services Administration, the Department of Commerce, and any government contracting or procurement office. Most of these can be found in the nearest federal office building, and you can usually find them listed in the local telephone directory under "U.S., Government of."

There are several other ways to get information and to learn more about both the federal procurement system in general and the specific business opportunities in the multibillion dollar market it reprsents. You may also visit the nearest Government Printing Office bookstore, where you will find government publications discussing how to do business with the government. You can also write to the Department of Defense, the Small Business Administration, the General Services Administration, the Department of Commerce, and other federal agencies to ask for information. These requests will usually produce a variety of brochures and manuals that will help and that will cost you nothing but the postage stamp for your letter of inquiry. There is, in fact, quite an enormous array of useful literature available via such sources as these, and you can compile a substantial library from these sources alone.

STATE AND LOCAL GOVERNMENTS

What is true about doing business with the federal government is also largely true about doing business with the thousands of state and local

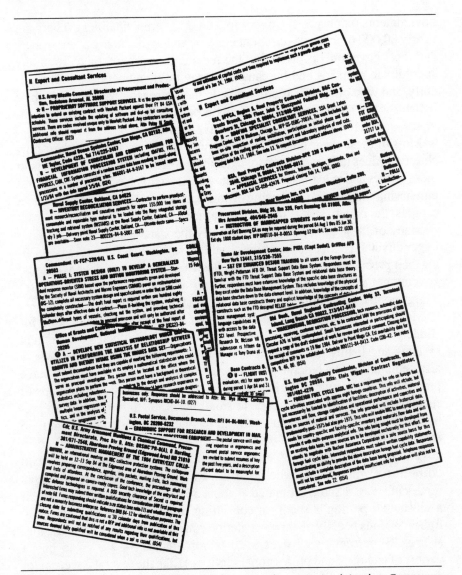

Figure 37. A few government consulting needs synopsized in the *Commerce Business Daily.*

governments (county, city, township, and other municipalities). There are nearly 80,000 of these government entities, and within many of these state and local governments, as within the federal government, there are many subordinate agencies and bureaus who may buy your services independently, and who often solicit proposals. In the aggregate there are perhaps a half million or more prospective clients as part of the government establishments, and that is probably a conservative figure.

Most of these governmental entities urge contractors to visit their purchasing offices to become personally acquainted with the various buyers in these offices and to learn at first hand how the systems function. The central purchasing offices and purchasing officials are generally located in the state capitals, the county seats, and the city or town halls.

Many of these governments, especially the state governments and the larger city and county governments, publish substantial literature describing their procurement systems and policies, as well as lists of dozens of local government agencies, bureaus, and establishments, so that these too offer a large contribution to your store of information resources.

Most of these have their own counterpart of the federal Application for Bidders List, in addition to their literature describing their procurement systems and listing information useful to prospective contractors. Many also, emulating the federal government socioeconomic programs, have programs of their own, offering loans, loan guarantees, and other kinds of special assistance and preference to small business, to minority entrepreneurs, to women entrepreneurs, and to handicapped individuals who are employers in or employed by small businesses. Many state and local governments offer some preference to local suppliers, although all agree to do business with anyone who qualifies. In all, these many governments represent a vast market, estimated at about $612 billion annually, of which a substantial portion is spent for consulting services of many kinds. (The figure depends heavily on how you define consulting, but it is probable that at least 20 percent—well over $120 billion annually—is used to buy a variety of technical and professional services.) Like the federal government agencies, state and local governments and their agencies tend to perceive many of their needs as unique, which therefore inevitably require specialized custom (consulting) services.

On the other hand, state and local governments do not have an equivalent of the federal government's *CBD* in which to announce their requirements and solicit inquiries and expressions of interest from consultants. Maryland, however, does announce at least some of its requirements in the official *Maryland Register*, the state's equivalent of the federal government's *Federal Register*, and occasionally a local government has some official publication they can use for this purpose.

For the most part, state and local governments seeking consulting services use their bidders' lists but they also rely primarily on local newspapers to announce their requirements, synopsizing them in classified advertising columns under the heading "Bids and Proposals." State and local laws generally mandate that requirements be so advertised in whatever is the leading daily newspaper in the locality of the procurement office. (For example, the city of Washington, DC and most surrounding Maryland and Virginia counties and municipalities advertise their requirements in the *Washington Post.*)

Too, again emulating the example of the federal government, state and local governments have their own small-purchase laws, and they permit procurements defined as small purchases in their procurement regulations to be made under limited competition and, for the smallest classes of such procurements, often without competition. Therefore, many of the smaller projects are never advertised at all, handled instead through direct negotiation, usually following submittal of an informal letter proposal and/or an unsolicited proposal, formal or informal.

SELECTED GOVERNMENT OFFICES

A few key federal government offices, central or headquarters offices of the agencies, in most cases, are listed here. (Local offices of these agencies are generally listed in local telephone directories. If not, a call or letter to the agency will bring you information on where to find the nearest local office of the agency.) A simple inquiry by mail and a request for information, general or specific, will generally bring you necessary forms, such as the Form 129, Application for Bidders List, as well as much useful literature to add to your library. The literature will guide you in finding opportunities to pursue government business and information that will be helpful in writing proposals.

Included here is the address of the Federal Procurement Data Center, which compiles detailed data on federal procurement and releases periodic reports that are extremely useful to the serious marketer as marketing research tools. Also included is the address of the main bookstore (and plant) of the Government Printing Office (GPO). The GPO is a rich source of books, brochures, pamphlets, and other helpful information that can constitute a valuable resource when researching data for a proposal, and it would almost surely be useful to know of and visit the GPO bookstore nearest you. The GPO can, of course, furnish a list of their bookstores.

Department of Agriculture
14th Street & Independence Avenue, SW
Washington, DC 20250

Department of Commerce
14th & Constitution Avenues, NW
Washington, DC 20230

Department of Defense
The Pentagon
Washington, DC 20301

Department of Education
400 Maryland Avenue, SW
Washington, DC 20202

Department of Health and Human Services
330 Independence Avenue, SW
Washington, DC 20201

Department of Housing and Urban Development
451 7th Street, SW
Washington, DC 20410

Department of the Interior
18th & C Streets, NW
Washington, DC 20240

Department of Justice
10th Street & Constitution Avenue, NW
Washington, DC 20530

Department of Labor
200 Constitution Avenue, NW
Washington, DC 20210

Department of State
2201 C Street, NW
Washington, DC 20520

Department of Transportation
400 7th Street, SW
Washington, DC 20590

Federal Procurement Data Center
4040 N. Fairfax Drive, Suite 900
Arlington, VA 22203

Small Business Administration
1441 L Street, NW
Washington, DC 20416

General Services Administration
18th & F Streets, NW
Washington, DC 20405

Government Printing Office
Main Bookstore
North Capitol & H Streets, NW
Washington, DC 20402

RECOMMENDED PUBLICATIONS

The following is a partial list of publications I believe will be helpful additions to your proposal library, and I stress both *partial* and *recommended* because a great deal depends on your special interests and needs, especially with regard to periodicals. There are, in fact, few publications that bear directly on the subject of proposal writing, but there are some that cover relevant subjects, such as marketing, writing, editing, and publications processes.

Books

Careful Writer, The, by Theodore Bernstein, Atheneum, 1965

Elements of Style, The, by William Strunk and E. B. White, Macmillan, 1972

How to Create a Winning Proposal, by Jill Ammon-Wexler and Catherine Carmel, Mercury Communications Corp., 1976

How to Make Money With Your Micro, second edition, by Herman Holtz, John Wiley & Sons, 1984, 1989

How to Succeed as an Independent Consultant, second edition, by Herman Holtz, John Wiley & Sons, 1983, 1988

Persuasive Writing, by Herman Holtz, McGraw-Hill, 1983

Thinking with a Pencil, by Henning Helms, Barnes & Noble, 1964

Words into Type (3rd ed.), by Henning Helms, Prentice-Hall, 1974

Word Processing for Business Publications, by Herman Holtz, McGraw-Hill, Byte Books, 1985

Writing for Results in Business, Government, the Sciences and the Professions, by David Ewing, John Wiley & Sons, 1979

Periodicals

Consultant's Voice, The, American Association of Professional Consultants, 9140 Ward Parkway, Kansas City, MO 64114

Consulting Opportunities Journal, Consultants National Resource Center, P.O. Box 430, Clear Spring, MD 21722

Marketing Professional Services, 11800 NE 160 Street, Bothell, WA 98011

Professional Consultant & Seminar Business Report, The, Howard L. Shenson, 20750 Ventura Boulevard, Woodland Hills, CA 91364

Professional Marketing Report, P.O. Box 14302, Albuquerque, NM 87191

SOME SUGGESTED STANDARD FORMATS

You can save a lot of time by standardizing the formats of items you use in all or nearly all your proposals. Some of the kinds of items exemplifying and suggested for this have been presented earlier in these pages. There also appeared a few items designed to guide and help you in requirements analysis and development of approaches and strategies. The following is a list of such items, and the list is then followed by examples of additional items designed to help you. It would probably be useful to compile a set of copies of these in a master file to be used in each proposal effort. If you are working with a computer, these can be entered as computer or word-processor files, for even greater flexibility.

You may (a) use these items in your proposals with or without change,

(b) choose one from among several where alternatives were offered, or (c) modify and adapt them to your own needs, as you prefer.

Items That Have Appeared in Previous Pages

First steps in devising strategy	Figure 1
Proposal format	Figures 2 and 19
Exercise sheet: consulting specialties	Figure 3
Bid/no-bid analysis reporting form	Figure 4
RFP requirements checklists	Figures 5 and 6
Functional flowcharts	Figures 7–10 and 30
Value management (FAST) diagrams	Figures 13 through 16
Typical organization chart	Figure 21
Schedule, as table and as milestone chart	Figures 22 and 23
Résumé format	Figure 24
Format for task/labor estimates	Figure 25
Format for and sample of response matrix	Figures 26 and 35
Block diagram	Figure 27
Pictorial diagram	Figure 28
Simple network	Figure 29
Standard drawing templates	Figure 31
Sample of computer-generated clip art	Figure 32
Logic tree	Figure 33
Sample title page	Figure 34

A Few Additional Offerings

Modular Recent-Project Presentation Format

To provide efficiency and flexibility in furnishing references and information on your current and past performances, you ought to modularize your project descriptions so that they can be fitted into the general format suggested here, while being reorganized (most relevant projects first) readily for each new proposal. Figure 38 illustrates this.

CURRENT AND RECENT PROJECTS	
PROJECT TITLE OR FUNCTIONAL NAME	**CLIENT ORGANIZATION**
Summary description, highlights, size (dollars, man hours, time, or other measure), record of performance with regard to schedule and budget, most impressive accomplishments	Contact: Name, address, telephone number of purchasing agent or other individual(s) responsible for monitoring project and able to furnish information
(Next project description)	

Figure 38.   A modular format for describing other project experience.

Cost Summaries

Small projects are usually quoted with either a fixed price for the job or a consulting rate with, usually, an estimate of consulting time (hours, days, weeks, or other time unit) required. However, where the project is to be a large one, it is not unusual, especially in the case of government agencies, for the client to ask for some details on how the cost estimate was established. Government agencies, especially those of the federal government, usually provide a standard form for this. But even in those cases where clients do not provide such a form or prescribe the format, they ask for essentially the same information. In general, Figure 39 shows a form that serves the purpose quite well.

This form is predicated on the assumptions (a) that no significant amount of materials is required (those businesses with heavy materials costs tend to have separate overhead rates for materials), (b) that the accounting system does use a general and administrative (G&A) indirect expense pool to accommodate certain types of indirect costs, and (c) that the overhead rate includes fringe benefits. Of course, if your own accounting system does not conform to this—does not include a G&A rate and/or you list fringe benefits as an item separate from the overhead pool—you must modify this form to reflect that. If your fee is a flat figure and not a percentage, change that also.

Direct labor:

_____ _____ @ $ ____ = $ _____
(functional title)   (hours)   (rate)   (subtotal)

_____ _____ @ $ ____ = $ _____ $ _____
                                                      (dir. labor total)

Labor overhead:

$ _____ @ _____ % = $ _____
(direct labor)   (overhead rate)   (overhead total)

Other direct costs:

_____ $ _____
(itemize)

_____ $ _____ $ _____
                                                      (ODC total)

General & administrative cost: _____ % $ _____
                                 (rate)

Fee or profit: _____ % $ _____

Grand total: $ _____

Figure 39. A general form for breaking down cost estimates.

By the way, G&A is a rate that is applied to all costs that appear above it on this form. The same is true for the fee or profit rate.

This is to be used only when the client demands it and you are willing to reveal your various cost centers and burden rates to the client. In most cases, the government will require it for any project running more than a few thousand dollars—perhaps $25,000, which is the small-purchase rate today. Commercial clients are less likely to demand this, but those who do government work and subcontract to consultants tend to emulate government methods, and sometimes are even required by their government contracts to subcontract according to federal procurement methods. Often, even purely commercial organizations tend to impose this requirement for large contracts.

If it happens that you do not know precisely what your overhead rate is—and it is not uncommon for circumstances to create that uncertainty—the usual practice is to estimate it as a "provisional" rate, subject to subsequent audit and adjustment. But that audit and adjustment is generally applied only to contracts of at least $100,000, if then.

Experience and Qualifications (Résumés) Summary

For many projects, the individual qualifications of the proposed staff are of primary concern to the client. Figure 40 offers an efficient means for organizing individual experience and qualifications into a single, concentrated summary, a matrix, in fact.

The cells of the matrix are developed according to the individual requirement. Each "item," for example, will be a given discipline, special skill, educational major, or specific experience, such as data processing, budget control, training, writing, or other. The set of items should, of course, represent all the qualifications required, and the candidate names proposed must represent the professional and key staff offered for the project.

Sample Selling Headlines and Captions

The point was made earlier that in proposal writing, every opportunity to drive home a sales message—make positive and persuasive arguments—must be exploited, and that the titles, headlines, and captions are too often

PRO-POSED (Name)	EDUCATION (Degree/Univ.)	AREAS OF TRAINING/EXPERIENCE				
		(Item)	(Item)	(Item)	(Item)	(Item)

Figure 40.   Format of qualifications and experience summary matrix.

BEFORE	AFTER
Costs	Cost Consciousness
Cost Considerations	Proposed Ways to Cut Costs
Schedule	Objectives That Will Be Met
Milestone Chart	Milestones Marking Success
Functional Flowchart	How the Problems Will Be Solved
Qualifications and Experience	Proof That _____ Can Do the Job
Qualifications Matrix	An Array of Capabilities
Understanding of the Requirement	The Essence of the Problem
Discussion	Specific Steps to Success
Proposed Program	Delivering on Our Promises
Our Facilities and Resources	Resources Placed in Your Service

Figure 41. Examples of selling titles, headlines, and captions.

neglected. To illustrate this more clearly, Figure 41 shows a few before-and-after examples.

Note, however, that these are generalized and generic, and they can be further sharpened and made even more positive by expressing them in the specific terms of the requirement. For example, instead of "Proposed Ways to Cut Costs," a specific proposal to develop or revise a computer program might title this, "A Tighter Program to Cut Operating Costs." Or, if the schedule is a tight one and there is some evident concern on the client's part about capability for meeting the deadline, the schedule item might be phrased, "How [your name] Will Deliver [the end-item or service] by March 15." The idea is, of course, to concentrate on the client's worry items and in so doing make references to and reinforce those worry items, the benefits you promise to deliver, and the proofs that you can and will deliver on those promises. Those titles, headlines, and captions should be an unending series of reminders of the most important elements of your strategy and theme.

SOME FINAL WORDS: GUIDELINES TO CURE "BAD WRITING" AND MAXIMIZE CREDIBILITY

1. Don't start writing a draft too soon. Avoid this common writing mistake. Too many proposals don't make it beyond the initial reading because the proposal reveals that the writer began to write before he or she fully understood the requirement, and never did bother to perfect his or her knowledge of what the client wanted.

Spend at least as much time in studying, analyzing, planning, researching, taking notes, and otherwise *preparing* to write a draft as in writing. It will be time well invested and will save you enough false starts and rewriting to more than compensate for the time it takes. Your ability to do all the other things listed here depends on your first doing what is urged on you here.

2.   Don't allow yourself to wander aimlessly. (Many proposals are like river rafts: They drift from one place to another, with no apparent destination. Draw up specific objectives—all the major points you must make in your proposal. Know in advance exactly where you want to go. Otherwise, you are not likely to get to where you ought to be.

3.   Don't write down vague ideas about how you will reach or achieve each objective. Draw up your subordinate objectives: Know in advance your itinerary—the route you plan to take to get there and the milestones (subordinate objectives) you must reach along the way.

4.   Don't try to work from plans in your head, or even from a generalized philosophy. Develop an outline in which all major points and objectives are specified—not an outline of what you will talk about in your proposal, but an outline of what you will say in your proposal.

5.   Don't expect to write a perfect first draft. Expert writers become expert writers because they know that first drafts are rarely as good as second, third, and later drafts are. Expect to do some self-editing and rewriting.

Examine everything you have written, in your self-editing, and judge whether each sentence, paragraph, and other element achieves its objectives. Determine whether it not only can be understood, but also cannot be misunderstood—that is, it is not only clear, but also unambiguous. (If it can be misunderstood, it will be. You may rely on that.)

6.   Don't be elegant, subtle, clever, or humorous in your writing style. All such characteristics are misplaced in proposals, which are read by busy people who probably do not enjoy reading at all, much less analyzing what they have read to see if they understand it correctly. (In fact, if what you have written evokes a chuckle from the reader, that is probably ominous.) Focus

only on meaning. Think about your reader and no one else, not even yourself.

7. Offer as much detail as possible in the areas you believe to be most important in influencing the client. Anyone can generalize and philosophize, and being able to do so suggests that you are glib, but it does not prove that you are in complete command of the subject or that you possess the necessary capabilities. The ability to plan and describe in details—to specify—on the other hand, indicates a complete command of the subject and both a technical and a managerial competence. It makes such a proposal much more credible than one that provides glib general assurances.

8. Be sure to have a clear-cut strategy for meeting the client's needs, rather than a vague idea or hope that the client will see you as superior to everyone else. Without such a clearly understood strategy underlying your proposal, it is difficult for your proposal to have a positive tone; it almost inevitably comes across as a defensive plaint. Also, without a clear strategy, properly implemented, you are not even partially in command of the situation.

9. Be sure that your proposal has a theme. The theme should be linked closely to the strategy, and it should, in effect, reinforce the strategy on almost every page of your proposal. (If, for example, your strategy is based on low cost, your theme might well be along the lines of "Efficiency and Cost Consciousness," and this could even be a running head or foot appearing on each page to remind the client of your promise.)

10. Finally, be sure that you have been absolutely explicit, both quantitatively and qualitatively, about what you promise to deliver, and communicate distinctly what you have to offer without making it appear to be a plea.

COMPUTER SOFTWARE

Among the programs listed here are both commercial programs and shareware. Shareware is software developed by individuals and offered on a try-before-you-buy basis. Some shareware is quite excellent, some not so excellent. For some kinds of software applications, there is far more shareware than there are commercial programs available. Communications software is one such application, and readability measurement and control is another. Shareware is available on most electronic bulletin boards, at computer clubs, and by mail. (See advertising in *Computer Shopper* and other computer magazines.)

Key Redefiners

Key redefiners, programs that enable you to change the function of any of your keys and to store information that you can recall with a single keystroke, are enormous aids to speed and efficiency. In concert with William F. Buckley, Jr., "I can hardly imagine life without SmartKey," which is the dean of such programs, in my opinion, although there are others.

SmartKey™, Software Research Technologies
ProKey™, RoseSoft, Inc.
Word Processors

There are many fine word processors. My choice is *WordStar*®, but *WordPerfect*™ is the most popular of these programs.

WordStar®, MicroPro® International Corporation
WordPerfect™, Satellite Software International
MS Word™, Microsoft® Corporation
PC-Write, Buttonware, P.O. Box 5786, Bellevue, WA 98006 (shareware)
Galaxy, OmniVerse, P.O. Box 2974, Renton, WA 98056 (shareware)

Desktop Publishing Programs

Probably the leading desktop publishing programs are *Ventura* and *Page-Maker*®, but there are many others.

The Newsroom Pro™, Springboard Software, Inc.
ClickArt Personal Publisher™, Software Publishing Corporation

Fontasy™, ProSoft®
FormWorx™, Analytx International, Inc.
Page Maker®, Aldus Corporation
Harvard™ *Presentation Graphics*, Software Publishing Corporation
Ventura, Xerox Corporation

Idea/Outline Processors

I do not use outlining programs, sometimes called "idea processors," but there are those who are quite fond of them and find them useful.

Ready™, Living Videotext, Inc.
PC-Outline, Softwork Development, 750 Stierlin Road, Suite 142, Mountain View, CA 94043 (shareware)

Readability Measurement

Readability—how easy or difficult it is for the average reader to read and understand the text presented—is a matter that should concern writers of proposals at least as much as it concerns anyone else.

Maxi-Read, RWS & Associates, 132 Alpine Terrace, San Francisco, CA 94117 (shareware)

PC-Read, Joey Robichaux, Wash 'n' Ware Software Products, P.O. Box 91016, Baton Rouge, LA 70821 (shareware)

Read: A Program to Calculate Flesch Readability Scores, Glenn Spiegel, 4821 Morgan Drive, Chevy Chase, MD 20815 (shareware)

Fog Finder, Joey Robichaux, 1036 Brookhollow Drive, Baton Rouge, LA 70810 (shareware)

Mailing List Manager

Mass Appeal, Steve Hughes, 1422 Applegate Drive, Alabaster, AL 35007 (shareware)

Communications

Telix, PTel, 276 Guildwood Parkway, Toronto, Ontario M1E 1P9 (shareware)

Procomm, PIL Software Systems, P.O. Box 1471, Columbia, MO 65205 (shareware)

Qmodem, The Forbin Project, c/o John Friel III, 715 Walnut Street, Cedar Falls, IA 50613 (shareware)

Miscellaneous

Office Collection, The, Info-Source, 530 Lawrence Expressway, Suite 500, Sunnyvale, CA 94086. This collection of shareware programs comes on eight disks (in the 5.25-inch version) and includes a word processor, a database manager, a collection of business forms, and an assortment of useful utilities, all with a nice, easy-to-read manual.

A FEW BULLETIN BOARD SYSTEMS

This is a small sampling of the many electronic bulletin boards. Call a few, and you will soon find listings of many, many others. (Extensive listings appear each month in *Computer Shopper* magazine also.)

Some U.S. Government BBS

ARMY COE/Planners	703 355-2098
Census Bureau	301 763-4576
Department of Commerce (DOC) Economic News	202 377-3870
Department of Commerce (DOC)Planning & Budget	202 377-1423
Department of Defense (DOD)/ADA Info DB	703 694-0215
Department of Defense (DOD) Export License II	202 697-3632
Department of Energy (DOE) Radioactive Waste Mgmt	202 586-9359
Department of Education	202 626-9853

Department of Transportation (DOT)/FHWA	202 426-2961
Export–Import Bank	202 566-4602
Federal Commerce Commission (FCC)	202 725-1072
Federal Deposit Insurance Corporation (FDIC)	202 737-7264
General Accounting Office (GAO) End User (S. Gee)	202 275-1050
MSG-RBBS David Taylor #2	301 227-1042
MSG-RBBS David Taylor	301 227-3428
National Aeronautics and Space Administration Info Tech Center	202 646-6197
National Aeronautics and Space Administration Space Science Data Center	301 286-9000
NAVDAC (Naval Data Automation Command)	202 433-2118
NAVWESA (Naval Weapons Engineering Support Administration)	202 433-6639
NAVY ADV GEN	703 325-0748
NAVY AVIATION NEWS	202 475-1973
NIST/NCSL (National Institute of Science and Technology/National Computer Systems Laboratory)	301 948-5717
NOAA (National Oceanic and Atmospheric Administration)	301 770-0069
SRS (Science Research Studies)— National Science Foundation	202 634-1764
STATE/AID (Agency for International Development)	703 875-1465
Veterans Administration	301 376-2184
World Bank	202 676-0920

A Small, Miscellaneous Assortment of Private BBS

Chevy Chase	301 522-0540
Tax Assistance	301 237-8430
NEC (Nippon Electric Corporation)	617 635-4461
Computer Confabulation	205 344-7606

The Rock BBS	501 864-0699
The French Connection	415 581-0449
Willi-Board BBS	203 456-1933
Ace-Hi BBS	808 261-2184
The Nighthawk BBS	319 338-2961
Macropoedia BBS	312 295-6926
Soft Stone BBS	502 241-4109
The Gemini BBS	316 722-0182

Public Databases for which subscription fees and use fees are charged (the following is a brief listing):

Home Office Newsletter, Genie	1 800 638-8369
BBS/Bibliographic Retrieval Services and	
BBS After Dark	518 783-1161
	1 800 833-4707
Data Resources, Inc.	202 862-3700
Dialog Information Services, Inc.	415 858-3785
	1 800 227-1927
NewsNet	215 527-8030
	1 800 345-1301

These have been only partial listings of the thousands of electronic bulletin boards, public databases, and various information services. These exist in a dynamic environment, with many changes taking place. However, the more you use these, the more you will come to appreciate their value for gathering information efficiently.

INDEX

INDEX